The Empress of One

Also by Faith Sullivan

Repent, Lanny Merkel

Watchdog

Mrs. Demming and the Mythical Beast

The Cape Ann

The Empress of One

Faith Sullivan

MILKWEED
EDITIONS

Published 1996 by Milkweed Editions
Printed in the United States of America
Cover design by Adrian Morgan, Red Letter Design
Cover painting by Edward Hopper. Detail from "Cape Cod Morning," oil on canvas, 1950. Used by permission of National Museum of American Art, Smithsonian Institution. Gift of the Sara Roby Foundation.
Interior design by Will Powers.
The text of this book is set in Cochin.
96 97 98 99 00 5 4 3 2 1
First Edition

Milkweed Editions is a not-for-profit publisher. We gratefully acknowledge support from the Bush Foundation; Target Stores, Dayton's, and Mervyn's by the Dayton Hudson Foundation; Ecolab Foundation; General Mills Foundation; Honeywell Foundation; Jerome Foundation; The McKnight Foundation; Andrew W. Mellon Foundation; Kathy Stevens Dougherty and Michael E. Dougherty Fund of the Minneapolis Foundation; Minnesota State Arts Board through an appropriation by the Minnesota State Legislature; Challenge and Literature Programs of the National Endowment for the Arts; the Lawrence and Elizabeth Ann O'Shaughnessy Charitable Income Trust in honor of Lawrence M. O'Shaughnessy; Piper Jaffray Companies, Inc.; Ritz Foundation on behalf of Mr. and Mrs. E.J. Phelps Jr.; John and Beverly Rollwagen Fund of the Minneapolis Foundation; The St. Paul Companies, Inc.; Star Tribune/Cowles Media Foundation; Surdna Foundation; James R. Thorpe Foundation; Lila Wallace-Reader's Digest Literary Publishers Marketing Development Program, funded through a grant to the Council of Literary Magazines and Presses; and generous individuals.

Library of Congress Cataloging-in-Publication Data

Sullivan, Faith.
    The Empress of One / Faith Sullivan.
      p.   cm.
    ISBN 1-57131-011-8
    I. Title.
  PS3569.U3469E48   1996
  813'.54—dc20   96-21666
                                CIP

This book is printed on acid-free paper.

For two brightly shining stars in my little universe:
Jeanne Sorel and Bill Eknes.

And for four whose passing left so many of us bereft
of their grace and encouragement:
Pat Hilton, Coral Browne, Vincent Price, and Greg Lamont.

My gratitude to Dr. William Erickson, Medical Director, St. Peter Regional Treatment Center, who graciously shared his time and his historical knowledge of the state hospital. Thanks also to Barb Krohn, R.N., at the Treatment Center, for helping provide answers to my many questions.

I am not resigned:
I am not sure life is long enough
to learn that lesson.

George Eliot, *The Mill on the Floss*

The Empress of One

June 1935

Stella brushed sand from Sally's pink seersucker romper, adjusted the matching sunbonnet, and cooed, "There, there, don't cry. It's all right. Mommy's here."

Three-year-old Lark patted her friend's dimpled elbow, echoing, "It's all right. Mommy's here."

Through elm boughs high above, sunlight winked and flirted over skin and hair and pastel seersucker. Stella set Sally back in the sandbox from which she'd tumbled. With an old tablespoon she dipped sand, ladling it into a tin pail, then placed the spoon in Sally's plump fingers. "All better?"

"All better," the child laughed, reaching for a tin teapot, pouring sand from it into an enameled tin teacup, and handing it to Lark. "Tea," she pronounced with importance and care.

Stella turned and wandered back to the park bench where Arlene Erhardt stretched bare arms high and reached wide, catching the fickle warmth of the early June sun.

How perfect, Stella thought, to be idling away an afternoon in the park with Arlene, watching the little girls play in the sand. How perfect.

"I get crazy the first few days of summer," Arlene said.

Stella smiled, smoothed the back of her skirt, and sat down.

"No, I mean it. I get . . . crazy. I can't sit still. I'm happy when I don't have anything to be happy about, and I feel . . . fluttery inside, like when I've had too much coffee.

I'm kind of drunk and dangerous and not in control of myself."

Stella laughed. "It sounds awful."

"Don't you ever feel like that?" Arlene asked, lifting the hair at the back of her neck to let the breeze find the exposed skin.

The long, thin fingers of Stella's hands were intertwined. As she considered Arlene's question, she rubbed the heels of her hands slowly back and forth against each other.

"I think I used to be crazy when I was a girl. In my teens." She stared off to the left at the rear of the high school across the street, as if that were where she had been crazy, which it wasn't, since she'd gone to school in Mankato, not Harvester. "Yes, I'm sure I was. At summer camp, especially. Camp Lakota," she added, eyes narrowed with recollection. "But, I got over it. It went away."

When she was young, she'd dreamed of being a nurse and setting up a kind of Hull House for the sick and poor—a quixotic dream about climbing to the highest pinnacle of herself where the air was clear and bracing and she trembled with purpose.

"I get crazy every time the seasons change," Arlene went on, "and I look forward to it. Sometimes I get crazy in between, but I can count on it when the seasons change. Then I want to have my hair hennaed, change my name, and kick over the traces. I'm so restless at night, I can barely lie still in bed, and when the night freight train goes through, I cry. I don't know why, you know, I just cry. I say to myself, 'It's got your name written on it, Arlene. That one's got your name written on it.'" She lifted her feet out in front of her and shook them as if they, too, made her crazy, as if she couldn't sit still.

"But you're going to build a house," Stella said. "That's exciting."

Arlene crossed her arms, resting them on top of her head, and stared off into the Land of Mulish Women, which is where Willie said she came from. Yes, she was by God going to build a house and move them out of the big rent-free room in the depot that the railroad let them use because Willie was the depot clerk.

The depot agent and his wife lived in an apartment, a real apartment, on the second floor, but the railroad had allowed her and Willie to use the empty room on the first floor. That was three years ago, when Lark was a baby. A temporary arrangement until they could save money to build their own place.

But she didn't like the way Willie was getting used to it. He didn't talk any more about building a house. And *he'd* been the one shocked when she'd originally suggested living in the empty room. People would think they were trash, he'd said. They had to use the toilet off the depot waiting room and haul slop pails from their "kitchen" across the tracks to empty them. Arlene didn't care what people thought as long as she and Willie were saving money for a house. She wasn't trash, and she knew it.

"I've got a million plans for that house," she said. "When I think about that house, I get crazy. Crazy is different from insane. If I don't get that house, I'm going to be insane. You will see an insane person then."

Stella laughed. "What's the difference between crazy and insane?"

"Insane is when they haul you off to the state hospital in St. Peter. And you eat a lot of Jell-O and rice pudding and mashed potatoes, I think. Crazy is when you are so excited, you can hardly stand to be around yourself."

Stella smiled, reached into the small brown paper bag of gumdrops on the bench between her and Arlene, extracted a green one that resembled a tiny mountain, and held the bag out to her friend.

She and Arlene were very different. She was quiet; Arlene was ebullient. She was shy; Arlene was self-confident. Beside Arlene, she felt colorless, yet she keenly looked forward to being with her. Being with Arlene was like sitting in bright sunlight on a day like this, which was cool in the shadows. You soaked up the heat, storing it against the evening chill.

The morning was overcast and warm, muggy and pregnant with rain that would not fall. Stella led Sally by the hand up the wide walk to the central doors of the school.

"Mommy," Sally complained, pulling free, "you're holding too tight."

"I'm sorry. I didn't realize."

Sally wiped her palm on the skirt of her pink and green plaid cotton dress with its many rows of smocking across the chest. Stella bent to blot the child's damp brow with a limp, wadded handkerchief. A strange, oppressive morning, she thought, wiping her own brow.

Straightening, she took Sally's hand again. "Now, remember, I'll be here to meet you when Miss Babcock dismisses kindergarten, so don't worry."

"I know," Sally said, her patience tried by Stella's many reassurances.

Although she would miss Mommy and might even cry when Stella left her with Miss Babcock, Sally looked forward to kindergarten. She wanted to learn to read and write. She was tired of having to rely on adults for stories. But before the school would teach her to read and write, Daddy had explained, kindergarten was required. Very well, she would do kindergarten. Besides, Lark was going to be in morning kindergarten. They would do kindergarten together.

The big double doors clanged behind them, and Stella led Sally up several wooden steps to a wide hall, so wide in fact, it was nearly square. Kindergarten and the first three grades opened onto this hall, one in each of the four corners. Sally had been in this part of the school before, in August, when Mommy and Mrs. Erhardt had brought Sally and Lark to familiarize them with what awaited in September.

The janitors had been waxing the wooden floors that day. The smell of paste wax still hung in the air now, along with a memory of varnish and decades of pail lunches. Would she have a lunch pail when she was in first grade? she had asked Daddy. They lived only a block from school, he had pointed out, so she would probably come home for lunch, most days. He had included the "most days" knowing that she longed for a lunch pail.

Other mothers and a great number of children mingled in the hall. Many of the children were older: first, second, and third graders as well as fourth, fifth, and sixth graders who were headed for the stairs leading to the second-floor rooms.

These older children were so knowing, so familiar with everything. Their faces bore no trace of apprehension or wonder. They were jaded and very sophisticated, some even naughty, snapping rubber bands at one another, pulling braids and teasing until a teacher grabbed them by the shoulder, steering them on their way.

Stella tugged Sally's hand, drawing her to a halt. Kneeling in front of the child, she pulled up Sally's anklets, smoothing their cuffs, tightened the bows on her braids, and again blotted the brow where tiny black curls coiled against pale skin. Why wasn't the day dry and golden as September days were meant to be? Why on Sally's first day of school must it be breathless and, yes, vaguely ominous?

Stella studied Sally's face, the cheeks a deep pink, as if rouged. It was their normal color, but weren't the eyes too bright? Wasn't the child perhaps feverish? She placed a hand against the generous forehead, but could not be certain.

"Mommmmy," Sally whined, intolerant of the concern. "Do you feel all right?"

What was it about smocking on a child's dress? As if a five-year-old didn't look vulnerable enough, the tiny puckers of fabric lent a further impression of brave and innocent helplessness.

Mrs. Albers led Katherine into the kindergarten room, both of them looking as tranquil and cool as if they'd been kept overnight in the refrigerator, like cut flowers. Mrs. Erhardt and Lark were climbing the several steps from the double doors, Mrs. Erhardt breezy and glamorous in a tan sharkskin shirt with brass buttons and white military braid and tan trousers to match, all of which she'd run up on the sewing machine, as she did nearly everything she wore.

Mrs. Erhardt was the only woman in Harvester, Minnesota, who wore trousers. Sally knew her mommy admired Mrs. Erhardt's style, although Stella herself did not wear trousers. Sally wanted to look like Mrs. Erhardt when she grew up, a little different from the other ladies in town.

Lark was wearing a red dress with many pleats. Lark had told Sally that she liked pleats because she wanted to learn to tap dance, and when you spun around tap dancing, the pleats flew out around you, as if you were one of the whirling rides in the street carnival that set up on Main Street for Harvester Days.

Sally waved to Lark.

"Stella," Mrs. Erhardt called, "I'm glad we're not the last. Lark wanted me to curl her hair around my finger, but the humidity played hell with it, so she's got these little weeny pigtails. Makes her look like Judy Garland in *Pigskin Parade*."

Mrs. Erhardt was fond of movies. Sally's parents went only rarely, and Sally never, except to the penny movies shown in the park during the summer. This past summer Mommy had let her go for the first time, and she'd seen *The Broadway Melody* with Bessie Love. Mrs. Erhardt had said that the movie was old and the sound squawky, but Sally had thought it thrilling.

Mommy had promised that when Sally was seven, she could see a movie at the Majestic Theater. Sally hoped that she did not die before her seventh birthday.

When she was four, Sally had often thought that she might die of polio or spinal meningitis. She had heard those illnesses mentioned when Grandpa and Grandma Elway visited. Grandpa Elway was a doctor in Mankato, and he sometimes talked about people who had come down with diseases there, people Mommy knew from growing up in Mankato. The reason that Sally had thought she would die of one of those things was because she could not imagine being five, and if you couldn't imagine something, it probably wouldn't happen.

However, Mrs. Erhardt and Lark were good at imagining. They played imagining games, and they had taught Sally to imagine. No longer did she believe that things wouldn't happen if you couldn't imagine them, because she could.

"Ready?" Arlene Erhardt asked Stella, giving Lark a nudge in the direction of the kindergarten room.

Stella hesitated, biting the corner of her lower lip, raking her eyes over the hall as if an excuse to say no might lollop past.

"Yes, well, I suppose it's time." She glanced at her wrist, but she'd come away without her Bulova.

Lark took Sally's hand, and together they stood beside the kindergarten door recalling with difficulty the rare delights they'd been told awaited. Lark's face had clouded; her chin quivered. Sally held tight to her friend's hand and stared at the first-grade door, diagonally across the hall. She wished that was where she was going.

None of the children going in there was crying, and none was accompanied by a mother hanging on too tightly. The children seemed especially attractive, haloed in the golden light of *Reading*.

Moments later, Sally was standing in front of the kinder- garten teacher's desk, Lark beside her, Mommy and Mrs. Erhardt behind them, introducing themselves and their children to Miss Babcock, who smiled and checked their names against a list on her desk.

Behind the little group, some children were sitting on the five-year-old-sized wooden chairs pulled up to low wooden tables, four to a table. Others were saying brave and soundless farewells to their mothers, and two or three, like Angela Bussey, were clinging to their mothers' skirts, bleating, "No, Mommy, please," over and over, tears streaming down their faces, wetting pretty new dresses or starched shirts.

At one of the tables, Neddy Barnstable in sharply creased gray blue trousers, white shirt, and navy blue bow tie, tilted his head back slightly to lift his gaze out into the trees beyond the windows, seeming to study them intently, and only now and then blinking quite casually, as if a dust mote had gotten in his eye.

The blue eyes were solemn; the very rim of the nostrils of the small, perfect nose were pink tinged, and the full lips were folded inward and held firm. A Barnstable boy, even on the first day of kindergarten, would not cry in public, Grandmother had admonished.

Mommy's hands on Sally's shoulders began to pinch. Sally squirmed beneath the delicate but painful vise of her mother's slender fingers. Against her back, Sally felt a trembling. Her mother's legs. She tried to ignore this and concentrate on what Miss Babcock was telling Mommy and Mrs. Erhardt about dismissal time, which would be at eleven-thirty today, half an hour earlier than usual, since it was the children's first day of school.

The trembling at her back and the pinching of her shoulders were alarming Sally now, and she wrenched away. "Mommmmy."

Her mother sobbed, looked aghast, and ran out of the room. Sally started to follow, but Mrs. Erhardt put a hand on her cheek and said, "Mommy will be all right. The first day of school is . . . hard on everybody. She'll be all right. I'll find her, and we'll go for coffee at the Loon Cafe."

This sounded sensible, but Sally wasn't sure. ". . . but . . ."

"Your mommy would want you to stay here so you can tell her about kindergarten when we come to pick you up at eleven-thirty."

At length, the moment came when Miss Babcock led Sally and Lark to one of the low tables, showing them the two chairs (facing one another across a wide expanse of pale oak) that would be theirs.

Several children were murmuring to each other and looking at Sally, whose mother had burst into tears and bolted from the room. What did it mean, a mother running out that way? Their mothers would never do that. Would they?

Sally felt their glance, knew the murmuring was about her mother. She pressed her Mary Janes together until her ankle bones hurt, wove her hands together prayerfully on the table, and stared unseeing at the blackboard behind the teacher's desk.

She thought she might have to sit in just that way for a day or two, because her imagining had failed her, and she couldn't imagine getting up and facing the other children.

Across from her, Lark was wiping her face with a clean little white handkerchief that Mrs. Erhardt had tucked into the pocket of her dress. Mommy hadn't remembered to put a handkerchief in Sally's pocket, but Sally realized that she herself was not crying. Inside, though, her stomach was clenched up in a tight fist as if she were.

At his table on the other side of the room, Neddy Barnstable admired the way Sally didn't cry. Did her throat ache like his? Did she have a stomachache? If they had not been told to remain in their assigned seats until Miss Babcock was finished processing pupils, he would have wandered over to Sally's table and asked whether she knew her ABC's. Or he might have asked if she had a big tricycle like the red one he'd gotten for his birthday.

Slowing for the stop sign, Arlene Erhardt shifted the pickup into second and ground away from the final intersection at the edge of town, spraying gravel and trailing a feather boa of dust that obscured the elms, box elders, church spires, and the gray water tower, which rose from the lawn in front of the Water and Power Company on Main Street.

Clattering and slewing down the washboard country road, the pickup turned left at the first mile intersection and shimmy-danced beneath overarching cottonwoods.

"You don't mind if we don't go to the Loon Cafe, do you?" Arlene asked.

She wiped the steering wheel with her handkerchief.

"Strange weather, isn't it? Feels like Missouri," she observed. "Lark and I took the train to southern Missouri a couple of years ago. Mama's cousin Nettie had lost her little farm in the Crash, and she was too old to work any more. She was, well, she was starving when we got there. Staying with people who couldn't feed *themselves.* Sounds like something in the movies, doesn't it? Anyway, Lark and I went down and brought her back north.

"Six months later she was telling everybody how she wished she was back in southern Missouri , made it sound like Shangri-la." She laughed. "That was her little revenge for the humiliation of being rescued. Nobody likes being rescued, even when it's necessary."

From the corner of her eye she saw that Stella Wheeler was staring straight ahead, not sobbing or trembling, but weeping silently, relentlessly.

"If it were May instead of September, I'd say this was tornado weather," Arlene resumed, aware that she was babbling, nevertheless anxious to maintain a connection with Stella, however silly or tenuous it might be. "Of course, you can have tornadoes in September." Were she to fall silent, Stella might drift out of reach.

The Giraffe reading group sat in a semicircle of small chairs at the front of Miss Hagen's first-grade room, reading from a book about Dick and Jane, Spot, Puff, and Baby Sally.

At their desks, the Tiger and Kangaroo reading groups practiced printing on sheets of cheap, freckled paper with blue lines and waited their turns to be called to the front to read aloud.

In the Giraffe group, Neddy Barnstable sat next to Lark Erhardt and directly across from Sally Wheeler. Each time Miss Hagen asked him to read from a page on which the word *Sally* appeared, Neddy's stomach performed strange, not unpleasant, flip-flops, and he wiped the palms of his hands on the knees of his brown corduroy knickers.

Sally Wheeler resembled the woman in the painting in the upstairs hallway of his Grandmother Barnstable's house. No one they knew, his mother had told him when he'd asked. The woman of the painting was merely an unknown model some artist had chosen to paint.

Pale shoulders rose from a deep red gown and curved upward into a slender neck adorned only by a narrow black ribbon. The woman's dusky hair was piled high on her head in a loose arrangement from which several tendrils had escaped to droop against her cheeks. Although a smile lay on the rosy lips of the painting, thinly disguised sadness gazed out from behind the dark eyes.

Neddy had not of course analyzed the woman's expression, but he found her glance endlessly fascinating, even hypnotic. And very much like Sally Wheeler's.

"'Oh, Puff,' said Baby Sally. "'Funny, funny Puff,'" Neddy read, curling his toes inside his brown oxfords.

Across the semicircle, Sally Wheeler's hands trembled with anticipation as she waited to perform. She knew all the words, even the ones toward the back of the book. Daddy had bought her flash cards, and, on the weekends, he helped her learn words that weren't even in her first-grade reader. Next Saturday he was going to take her to the public library so that she could get her first library card. And then she would read books and books and books! What could be more important than reading? It was the key to *everything!*

Like a movie actress pretending to be someone she wasn't, Sally pretended to be the people in books. Just now, she was Jane, and she had a brother named Dick. Jane and Dick lived in a house much like her own, and they had a baby sister named Sally, a dog named Spot, and a cat named Puff. Their mommy took them places and laughed when they did silly things.

Jane and Dick's daddy drove a car not so different from her daddy's blue Dodge. But their daddy came home from work every day instead of being out on the road all week for Fidelity Office Supply of St. Paul like Sally's.

Miss Hagen pointed to Sally who read, "See Jane run. Run, Jane, run."

She was flying! Up over the school, the trees, and the water tower, across the fields and the lakes to that place where she was Jane. It was magic. *Sally* was magic. She could read.

June 1939

The stylish and meticulous Miss Alice Penny, ready-to-wear salesclerk in Lundeen's Dry Goods, inclined her head and upper torso across a table piled with bathing dresses and boys' swim trunks, causing a pair of navy blue wool swim trunks with a white webbing belt to slip to the polished wooden floor.

"Mrs. Wheeler, are you all right?"

Stella Wheeler, who stood opposite, clutching a red bathing dress, child's size seven, stared through voluptuous tears, out the big front window of the store.

"Mrs. Wheeler?"

Great pendulous drops clung to Mrs. Wheeler's chin, then fell to the bathing dress, leaving small dark stains. Sally Wheeler, who stood waiting to have the garment held up and measured against her tall-for-almost-seven-years' body, backed away, hunching her shoulders and bending her knees slightly, shrinking perceptibly.

Inching behind the adjacent table stacked with short pants and polo shirts, she watched and listened with mortified fascination as her mother broke off gazing out the window and glanced at Miss Penny.

"It's so sad . . . the babies. The Chinese babies. Killed by Japanese soldiers," Stella Wheeler murmured haltingly. At the Majestic Theater across from Lundeen's Dry Goods, she had seen a newsreel depicting the horrors of the Japanese warfare in China.

Like startled birds, sudden explanations of her frequent tears fluttered from Stella's lips. On one occasion she had deplored ". . . boys throwing stones at Hilly Stillman. Down by the Sinclair gasoline station." Hilly Stillman, a shell-shocked veteran of the Great War, was frequently the target of naughty boys.

The first time, so far as anyone knew, that Stella had publicly burst into tears had been the day less than two years ago when Sally Wheeler had started kindergarten. That might have been dismissed as a mother's natural sadness at seeing her only child, her beautiful little girl, heading out into the world. Women had such feelings. But it had so resembled subsequent weeping occasions that it now appeared to have been the beginning of what some in town called "Stella Wheeler's crying sickness."

In Lundeen's Dry Goods on that sunny Tuesday afternoon in June 1939, Stella gripped the red bathing dress so tightly that her bony fingers blanched until they looked like bleached chicken bones. "They're shooting *babies*. And *bayoneting* them."

At this moment Mr. Johnson, manager of the store, opened the screen door from Main Street. He was returning from his afternoon Coca-Cola at Eggers' Drug Store. Catching sight of Stella clutching a red bathing dress, her face wet with tears, he glanced quickly about to note whether other customers were in the store.

"Mrs. Wheeler, may we help you? You're looking a bit peaked. What if I go upstairs and telephone Don?"

Don Wheeler was on the road and wouldn't be home until Friday night. Mr. Johnson knew this but, frankly, was stumped as to what he should say to a woman "having a spell" in his store. Damned lucky thing it wasn't Saturday. The store would have been full of customers.

For long moments Stella Wheeler stood riveted with embarrassment, unable even to lay the red bathing dress aside. She had done it again. She'd wept unexpectedly and inexplicably, right out in public.

"Did you wish to purchase the swim dress?" Miss Penny inquired, hoping to grease the skids under Mrs. Wheeler's departure. An important customer — Lawyer Shane's wife or Dr. White's missus — might stroll through the door any minute.

At long last, Stella Wheeler lay the bathing dress on the table. "I'll have to think about it," she whispered and glanced about abstractly, shifting the white purse on her arm, straightening her shoulders, smiling a bright and empty smile. "I'll think about the bathing dress," she said and started out of the store, forgetting that she'd brought Sally with her.

When the screen door closed behind Mrs. Wheeler, Miss Penny and Mr. Johnson exchanged a look of pity and relief. Miss Penny raised a prettily manicured index finger, tapping it against her temple. Mr. Johnson nodded thoughtfully and turned, heading toward his office, which was up a flight of stairs, on a balcony overlooking the sales floor.

Miss Penny bent to retrieve the navy blue swim trunks. While she folded them and returned them to the proper pile, Sally, who had made herself inconspicuous behind the table of shorts and shirts, slipped out the door.

By the most wonderful coincidence, the kind of coincidence Sally had come to associate with Lark Erhardt's mother, Mrs. Erhardt telephoned that very evening. Could Mrs. Wheeler and Sally accompany Mrs. Erhardt, Lark, and Beverly Ridza to Sioux Woman Lake for a picnic the next afternoon? Lark was recovering from tonsillitis, but Sally and Beverly might like to go swimming.

Stella Wheeler explained that Sally didn't have a bathing dress that fit her, as she'd shot up like a weed over the winter, and, unfortunately, she herself was going to be tied up, doing bookkeeping for Mr. Wheeler. This last was her all-purpose excuse when she couldn't bear going out in public. Don Wheeler had never asked her to keep his books, and she wouldn't have known how if he had.

Mrs. Erhardt, who often invited Stella Wheeler to go places with her, said she was sorry that Stella couldn't get away, but if it was all right with Mrs. Wheeler, Mrs. Erhardt would take Sally down to Lundeen's Dry Goods the next morning and see that she was fitted out with a bathing dress so that she could make the trip. Stella was so muddled by gratitude and a hot, rankling jealousy of Arlene Erhardt that she began weeping on the telephone and had to ring off.

The next morning, Sally stood beside the table of bathing dresses, clutching the $1.37 that her mother had sent with her for the purchase and hearing Mrs. Erhardt opine confidently that the red wool garment she was holding up to Sally would fit her nicely.

"We'll take it," she told Miss Penny crisply, handing her the bathing dress and leading the way to the counter where Miss Penny wrote up the sale. Miss Penny took Sally's money, stuffed both money and sales slip into a metal cup, and hooked the cup onto a wire above her head.

Grasping a thick cord depending from the wire, Miss Penny gave it a firm pull, sending the cup, with money and receipt in it, flying along the wire, up to the office where the bookkeeper, Mrs. Henry, reached up from her desk, removed the cup, tipped out the money and receipt, checked for error, tucked the carbon of the receipt back into the cup, and sent it careening back down to them.

Swinging the red bathing dress, wrapped in brown paper and tied with string, Sally followed Mrs. Erhardt and Lark from the store, passing the elegant and courtly Mr. Lundeen, who raised his panama and held the door for them.

Mrs. Erhardt had an air of confidence and strong opinions. She did not wring her hands or dither or weep. Every click of her high heels rang with purpose and plans, and Sally felt safe and lighthearted, swanning along in her wake.

On the drive out to Sioux Woman Lake, Mrs. Erhardt let Lark and Beverly and Sally sit in the back of the pickup truck that Mr. Erhardt used in the mornings for delivering freight.

"If you promise to sit right behind the cab and hold on tight," she admonished.

The hot sun beat down on their heads, and dust rose up from the back tires, leaving a cloud of Importance behind them. The girls held onto each other's hands and giggled, imagining that people were thinking, when they saw them, "Aren't those children lucky, to be riding out to the lake in the back of a pickup truck?"

For two or three miles of country roads, they jounced along between fields planted with corn, which, if weather cooperated, would be "knee-high by the Fourth." Interspersed with cornfields were cottonwood-dotted meadows where holsteins or, occasionally, guernseys lay about like indolent and slightly retarded absolute monarchs.

Sioux Woman Park, a mowed half-acre of land lying along the east side of the lake, was furnished with picnic tables, fire pits, and a tidy little bathhouse painted white with dark green trim, and set off prettily by gravel paths lined with white-painted rocks.

Ignoring the tables, Mrs. Erhardt and the girls carried the picnic gear to a grassy knob overlooking the dock. Lark, Beverly, and Sally spread the faded blanket on the grass, smoothing it and securing the corners with a rock, a thermos, and two pairs of girl's sandals.

Beverly had come barefoot. The Ridzas were poor, so poor it made Stella Wheeler weep. Mr. Ridza had decamped, Sally had heard Mrs. Erhardt tell her mother, leaving Rose Ridza, who was no brighter than she ought to be, with Beverly, her little brother Charlie, and Baby Delores.

Times were hard, and harder still for a woman with three little ones to look after. People donated things to the Ridzas: produce from the garden and fish from Sioux Woman Lake;

clothes their own children had outgrown; and ladies' dresses past their prime and out of style.

But this summer, charity had not provided Beverly with a pair of sandals—only a cast-off brown swim dress whose hem drooped to her knees and whose shoulder straps kept slipping down to reveal her bony pigeon breast.

Emerging from the bathhouse and handing over their street clothes to Mrs. Erhardt, Sally and Beverly listened to her admonitions about water safety. The park had no lifeguard. A row boat, beached near the dock, was the only provision for the rescue of distressed bathers. So, they were told, be careful.

Both Lark and Beverly could swim, although Beverly had a stronger, surer stroke. Sally could dog-paddle a little. But, compared with Lark and, especially, with Beverly, she was still a beginner and wasn't allowed to swim to the diving raft.

Shrieking and splashing each other, Sally and Beverly waded into the lake while Lark stood by, watching. Beverly spied a glittery white stone lying where the water nudged up against the beach, and they tossed it again and again into the shallows, racing after it, ducking under the tiny waves to retrieve it, pretending they were treasure hunters.

When this palled, Beverly lit out to join half a dozen roistering children playing tag around the raft. Lark and Sally sat on the edge of the dock, dangling toes in the lapping water, teeheeing when minnows tickled them, and discussing Miss Bailey who would be their second-grade teacher in the fall.

Miss Bailey wasn't pretty, just the opposite, towering and broad-shouldered, with a florid, lantern-jawed face and plain brown hair pulled into an untidy arrangement at the back of her head, as if by the time her toilette had proceeded as far as coiffure, she were sick and tired of the whole business.

But Miss Bailey had a laugh that, if you were standing nearby, made you feel a part of something enviable. Her entire face became a kind of O and from it rang a high-pitched "hoo hoo hoo hoo hoo," which grasped you in its hug.

Lark and Sally knew, from peeping into the second-grade classroom and talking with soon-to-be third graders, that Miss Bailey's pupils at the beginning of each school year built a post office in one corner of the room, using orange crates and shoe boxes. Each child had a shoe box/mail box with his or her name on it. All the corrected spelling papers, arithmetic exercises, and so forth were sorted into the appropriate shoe boxes by that day's pupil/post office worker, and at specified times during the day, children could collect their mail from their box or drop a letter in the post basket, to be delivered into another child's shoe box.

Sally would have a box with her name on it, and probably Lark would write letters that Sally would collect when stopping for her mail! It made her giddy to imagine it.

Sally hoped that Miss Bailey would like her and think that she was pretty and good and smart. Maybe sometimes Miss Bailey would put an arm around her as Sally had seen her do to other children when they'd fallen playing tag or lost their milk money.

Her mother didn't hug Sally nowadays, although Sally could recall when she had hugged her often. When Mommy drew back from her, Sally thought that it was because she imagined the weeping might be contagious.

"Are you girls ready for watermelon?" Mrs. Erhardt called, strolling down to the sand. "Lark, yell out to Beverly and ask if she's hungry."

While Lark wandered down to the point of the beach closest to the raft, Sally trailed Mrs. Erhardt up to the picnic blanket.

"I hear they're showing *Animal Crackers* at the penny movie this week," Mrs. Erhardt noted, pouring a glass of lemonade and handing it to Sally.

In the summer when the Majestic Theater was closed on account of the heat, old movies were shown in the town park. People paid a penny and sat on benches and blankets to watch Janet Gaynor or Wallace Beery or John Barrymore.

"I hope it's not sad," Sally said, recalling past movies from which her mother had abruptly departed in tears.

"Oh, no, I saw it when it first came out. It's a comedy with the Marx Brothers." She sat down, folding her legs gracefully beside her. Sally arranged hers similarly. They could have been mother and daughter in a magazine article about sports togs, Sally thought, Sally in her red bathing dress with an embroidered navy blue anchor in the center of the bodice, Mrs. Erhardt in red shorts with navy blue piping around the legs and across the pockets and, above these, a red middy shirt piped in navy, with a white tie knotted loosely at the vee of the sailor collar.

Mrs. Erhardt wasn't as pretty as Sally's mother, but she was zippier, and she took care with her hair and makeup, something that Sally's mother no longer did. When Sally was with Mrs. Erhardt, she knew that things were going to go according to plan.

"*Grand Hotel* was sad toward the end," Mrs. Erhardt observed, referring to the previous Saturday night's penny movie, from which Sally and her mother and father had exited early.

Sally nodded, her face hot with embarrassment for her mother.

"I was sure glad I'd brought a hankie," continued Mrs. Erhardt. "You should have seen me dabbing my eyes and sniffling."

"Really?"

Mrs. Erhardt nodded sincerely, but Sally saw through her kindness and knew that there was a great difference between Mrs. Erhardt's sniffling and her own mother's tears.

Sally's Grandma Elway had explained her daughter's tears by saying that Stella was going through her "change." When Sally asked what that meant, Grandma Elway had become discomposed and played agitatedly with the covered buttons on the front of her navy blue crepe dress.

"When women get to a certain age . . . 'middle age' . . . their bodies change inside. And some women get weepy or . . . or angry." Then, not unkindly, she had dismissed Sally, saying, "Run along. You ask too many questions."

So something had changed inside her mother's body, Sally had reflected. Where? In her head, surely. But why did it happen only to *some* women? Why couldn't it happen to all middle-aged women, so that her mother wouldn't stand out? Sally tried to picture how her mother's head might have changed, but she didn't know what a head looked like inside *before* it changed.

Mrs. Erhardt handed Sally a thick slice of melon on a plate and lay two other slices on plates for Lark and Beverly, who were slogging up from the beach.

"Yippeee! Watermelon!" Beverly whooped, dancing around the blanket like an Indian. "Dyja buy it from that Texas guy?"

Mrs. Erhardt nodded.

Later, wiping melon juice from her chin with the back of her forearm, Beverly sprang up from the blanket, demanding, "We gotta have a seed-spitting contest!" So saying, she puckered her mouth and blew a seed over the heads of Sally and Lark who ducked as if it were a bullet.

"If you're going to spit seeds, go over there," Mrs. Erhardt ordered, pointing to a spot on another knob some distance away.

Off the three traipsed with their plates of melon.

"How come you went home before the movie was done?" Beverly wanted to know, folding her legs beneath her, Indian style.

Sally stiffened and swallowed a mouthful of melon, seeds and all. Why did people like Beverly want to know everything?

"None of your business," Lark told Beverly.

"Godsakes," retorted Beverly, exploring between her toes for leeches, "Whatsa matter?" Finding nothing untoward, she picked up her slice of melon and prepared to begin the seed-spitting contest. "I 'spose her ma cried, and they hadda leave. What's so bad about that?" With a nod in Sally's direction, she pointed out, "She's got a white fur muff 'n hat," as if this fact alone ought to mitigate Sally's unhappiness.

"Wouldn't *you* be sad if your mama was sad?" Lark insisted.

Beverly considered, then wondered, "What's she so sad about?"

Sally lifted her shoulders up around her ears and looked off toward the bathhouse.

"You don't know?" Beverly persisted.

Sally shook her head slowly from side to side.

"Does yer pa hit her?"

The slow head movement continued.

"Does he get drunk?"

Long black plaits at either side of Sally's head slid to and fro across her bare back. Sally's daddy did not beat her mommy or get drunk.

Beverly took a practice spit, hitting the rough trunk of a cottonwood. "Then she must be crazy," she concluded matter-of-factly and without a trace of scorn. Beverly knew about crazy. Before he lit out for parts unknown, her pa had burned little Charlie with a Camel cigarette, on purpose. He'd been crazy drunk.

"Shut up," Lark told her.

Knees drawn up against her chest, Sally stared unblinkingly at the bathhouse. I won't cry, she thought. I won't ever cry. Not as long as I live.

July 23, 1939

Saturday evening, Donald Wheeler appeared at dinner freshly shaved and wearing a clean shirt. His aftershave lotion called to Sally's mind alfalfa and clover and other perfumes of the countryside.

Once handsome, his features had grown mild and soft at the edges. Two years ago he had cultivated a thin, precisely drawn mustache, as if in this way he might gain some measure of control over his face. Like an ebbing tide, his formerly thick, straight blond hair was receding from a broad brow. Still, he was a pleasant looking man whose tall frame had not thickened with the years, nor had his eyes lost the other-worldly green-blue color of ocean waves flung up against strong light.

Pulling out a chair at the breakfast-nook table, he told Stella, "I wish you'd come with us."

She set a bowl of beans and a plate of frankfurters in front of him. "I'd rather stay home," she said without rancor, trying not to sound weary or self-pitying. Tears oozing into her eyes, she turned away. Beans and franks and sauerkraut from a jar was the only sort of meal she was capable of putting on the table these days.

"Why?" Sally asked, spooning canned baked beans from a Pyrex bowl.

"What was it?" Stella cleared her throat. "What did you ask

me?" She ran water in the sink to cover the huskiness in her voice.

"Why would you rather stay home?"

Why would she rather stay home? "I'm not fond of Katharine Hepburn." That much was true.

"That's not a good enough reason."

"Sally," her father cautioned, shaking his head very slightly. He stood and raised first the shade and then the sash of the window beside his chair. Lately Stella was in the habit of keeping everything sealed up like a tomb.

A warm breeze drifted in from the backyard, carrying the smell of grass. For a moment he felt sanguine. Nothing could be too wrong when a man sat in his own kitchen with his wife and child and drank in the scent of newly cut grass. "Come, sit down now, Stella."

With a flush of pride, he watched her slip into her chair. Even in the loose-fitting, unattractive brown housedress, she was a beautiful woman. Too thin, maybe, but the best-looking woman in Harvester.

Her large eyes were a blue so dark that at first glance they appeared brown, and her hair, like Sally's, was thick and black — well, showing a little gray, but still thick, and falling in waves to her shoulders.

Right now, right here, with the frankfurters on his plate growing cold in the juice of unheated sauerkraut, he would like to hold Stella, tell her that she was beautiful and loved and that she needn't be afraid, because he would look after her.

But she did not much care anymore for being held. Something to do with "the change," he supposed. However, he would catch her at odd moments, looking at him with tenderness, even love, then stiffening, looking away, fearful that he would touch her, caress her.

Stella, for her part, knew without glancing up that her husband was studying her with that devouring, bewildered expression that drove her into a corner of herself. He wanted responses and explanations that she didn't have. When he looked at her in that way, she became sick with guilt.

"Please come with us," Sally pleaded.

"No, thank you," Stella said rather sharply. Then, in a more lenient tone, "I'm tired. But you two go. I insist."

As they left the house, setting out for the park, Donald took Sally's hand. It lay limp in his.

"Maybe she'll come next week," he said.

Like a night disturbance in a musical zoo, the squeaking, honking, piping sounds of the band warming up leapt out into the quiet streets. Letting go of Donald's hand, Sally skipped ahead, then raced back, begging, "Hurry, Daddy. They're starting!"

On summer Saturday nights, it seemed to the child, Harvester woke from a long, gray dream of worry and work to the true world where Main Street swelled with farm families come to town after supper for shopping and jawing and, later, a penny movie; a band played popular songs, however off-key; and women in flowered housedresses and men in clean overalls watched women in sequined gowns and men in patent leather shoes flicker across a fluttering screen, kicking up their heels and calling each other "darling." Summer Saturday nights were the real world.

The summer band, composed of high school students, a gaggle of grads home from college, and a sprinkling of grown-ups who kept a hand in, was playing "Swannee" as Sally led her father to a spot near the music where they spread their blanket. How could her mother bear to miss all this? Sally wondered.

"Popcorn?" Donald inquired as twilight deepened and the projectionist began setting up.

Old "Grandpa" Hapgood pulled his popcorn wagon into the park on movie nights and sold a heaped-up bagful for five cents.

Plumping down suddenly on the blanket beside Sally, Lark Erhardt announced, "Mama says you can sleep on our

davenport tonight if it's okay with your mama. Is she here?"
She looked about for Mrs. Wheeler.

"Daddy brought me," Sally told her.

"Will he let you go home with us?"

"He might. I could ask. He's getting popcorn. Do you have
popcorn?"

Lark opened her fist to reveal a nickel. "I'll be right back.
Would your papa care if I sit with you? Mama's sitting with
Bernice McGivern and her sister, Maxine."

As it turned out, *Morning Glory*, with Katharine Hepburn,
wasn't showing. *After the Thin Man*, with William Powell and
Myrna Loy, had been sent by mistake.

As the title rolled onto the screen, Lark cried, "Yippeee!"
William Powell and Myrna Loy being her favorite stars.
Indeed, she'd named her best doll after Myrna Loy.

"Would *you* like to be a movie star?" Sally asked her friend
later as they climbed into the Erhardts' pickup.

"I'd like to be Myrna Loy," Lark told her.

"No, I mean, would you like to be Lark Erhardt *and* a movie
star?"

Lark considered. "My teeth are too big, and Mama says my
hair's straight as a stick." She grabbed a hank of her hair and
held it out. "If they could make me beautiful, I guess I'd like to
be a movie star."

"You're prettier than Beverly," Sally assured her.

"Would *you* . . . like to be a movie star?" Lark wanted to know.
"You're so beautiful, I bet you could be a movie star easy."

"I'd like to be somebody else. That's what movie stars do.
They get to be somebody else and ride on a train to San
Francisco and catch murderers," Sally rhapsodized, recalling
events of the movie they'd just seen.

"Movie stars don't really do all those things," Lark pointed
out. "They just pretend. If somebody gets a baby in a movie,
that doesn't mean they get one in real life."

"They *kind* of do the things," Sally differed. "If you pretend really hard, it's practically the same as doing the thing. At least, I bet it is. That's what I'd like best about being a movie star . . . pretending to be somebody else."

Mr. Erhardt wasn't around when they opened the door to Lark's depot apartment. His absence aggravated Mrs. Erhardt. "Christ," she swore under her breath, slamming the door and tossing her purse on the kitchen table.

Brightening again, she told Lark, "Get one of your nighties for Sally. Are you girls hungry?"

When they had shrugged into plissé nighties, Sally and Lark pulled kitchen chairs close to the table and ate Mallomar cookies, breaking open the thin, crisp chocolate domes and scooping out the marshmallow filling with prehensile tongues. Mrs. Erhardt poured each of them a cup of milk, adding a splash of coffee, since that was the only way Lark would drink it.

Filling her own cup with reheated coffee from supper, Lark's mother sat down with the girls, now and then glancing at the purring electric clock on the wall above the table. Mrs. Erhardt's old Royal typewriter, which could often be found on the kitchen table, was not in evidence.

Sally was impressed by Lark's mother owning a typewriter, even an old one that the railroad had been throwing out, and impressed by the typing chart tacked on the wall by the clock. Mrs. Erhardt was teaching herself to type. That was *something*. Sally could not imagine her own mother teaching herself to type.

Mrs. Erhardt was a crackerjack, Sally recalled someone saying. Sally wished that *she* were a crackerjack, but it required a fearlessness she did not possess.

Mrs. Erhardt was learning to type so that she could get a job. That was something else Sally could not imagine her own mother doing. Few married ladies in Harvester had jobs. Times were hard, and whatever jobs developed went to men. But here was Mrs. Erhardt, determined to find something. "Secretarial," she'd said, "or something in Civil Service." Whatever that was.

Probably Mrs. Erhardt felt she had to earn some money, Sally reasoned. Beverly had said that Mr. Erhardt was a gambling fool. Beverly had overheard this while hanging around the Sinclair gas station, looking needy and hoping for a customer to buy her an Orange Crush from the pop cooler.

After tucking Lark in for the night, Mrs. Erhardt made up a bed for Sally on the sofa, and when Sally was settled under a flannel sheet, Mrs. Erhardt bent to kiss her cheek. Sally reached up and hugged her, blurting, "I love you."

Mrs. Erhardt didn't answer at once. She seemed to consider, but at length she said, "I love you, too, Sally."

The moment Sally had spoken, she regretted it. She *did* love Mrs. Erhardt, who was her idol and everything that Sally hoped to be, but surely saying it was disloyal to her own mother.

"It's never wrong to love somebody," Mrs. Erhardt told her, as if she'd read Sally's mind.

If Mrs. Erhardt said it, it was true. Sally was relieved. More than relieved, she was happy. It was never wrong to love somebody.

"Good night," Mrs. Erhardt said.

"Sleep tight," Lark called from the bedroom.

"Don't let the bedbugs bite," Sally giggled and curled up beneath the flannel sheet.

Miss Bailey's second grade was, indeed, all the good things that Sally had hoped. On the very first day, Miss Bailey exhorted her pupils to round up orange crates and shoe boxes for the post office, before the week's end! And when seat assignments were made, Sally discovered herself catty-corner from Lark, so close they could reach out and touch hands.

The second week, Sally was appointed cloakroom monitor for the month of September. A cloakroom monitor saw to it that wraps were hung on the proper hooks and that pupils took coats, sweaters, caps, scarves, and lunch pails home with them at the end of the day. Imbued with an enduring odor of peanut butter, apples, damp wool, and radiator paint, the cloakroom, with its single tall window overlooking Main Street, was a comforting place.

Since Lark was eraser-clapper for the same month, the two girls shared one another's chores and lingered together in Miss Bailey's company.

"What's the second grade going to do for the Christmas Program?" Lark wondered one afternoon.

Miss Bailey hoo hoo hooed. Slipping several big, imitation tortoise-shell hairpins from the disorderly bun at the back of her head, she pulled the long hank of no-color hair over her shoulder and looked at it with amused disappointment.

"The Christmas Program! You're six pages ahead of me," she exclaimed, though she was not displeased.

For the Elementary Grades Christmas Show, each class, kindergarten through sixth, was given fifteen minutes to fill. The resulting program was presented to parents and community in the school auditorium/gymnasium on the last evening before Christmas vacation.

The Christmas Program was a great preoccupation during the fall, with each grade trying to come up with something new and different to fill up fifteen minutes. Brain-wracking notwithstanding, crèches and carols and recitations from Luke and "The Night Before Christmas" were still standard fare, although the past few years had seen talent acts creep in among the traditional presentations. Last year's entertainment had included baton twirling by sixth-grader Marilyn Donaldson dressed as a Christmas fairy and tap dancing by fifth-grader Myrna Samuels, who took lessons at Martha Beaverton's Tap and Toe.

Winding her hair up again into a confusion that strove vainly for order and then shoving the huge pins back into the mess, Miss Bailey confessed, "I haven't a notion what we'll do for the Christmas Program. I surely hope one of you will come up with an idea," she added, wafting a substantial arm to indicate her twenty charges. When Miss Bailey threw herself on your mercy that way, you wanted to work like a demon to help her out of the pickle.

"Could we do a play?" Lark ventured.

Last year Sally had seen her first and only play when the Senior Class Thespians had given three performances of *Charley's Aunt*, one of them for the elementary grades. Although some of the players had giggled out of turn or forgotten their lines, Sally had thrilled, sitting in the darkness of the gymnasium/auditorium, watching boys and girls create a hilarious imbroglio, which, after all, turned out happily.

"A humdinger of an idea," Miss Bailey enthused, and Sally regretted that the idea of a play had not been *hers*.

"Where can we get a play?" Sally wondered.

"Why, you'll have to write it, you and the others. We'll talk about that tomorrow during Language," the teacher said, scooping up an armload of books and grabbing a gray cardigan from the back of her chair. "Lark, put my handbag over my arm, please," she requested, nodding toward the enormous and shapeless black bag lying beside the desk. "Now, turn out the lights." Then, "Sally, the keys are on top of the desk. Lock the door with the longest one."

Out they swept, Sally locking the door after them, then dropping the ring of keys into the black handbag.

"I'll see you girls tomorrow," Miss Bailey called over her shoulder. "Don't forget to read tonight. Books are proof of God's mercy." And off she tramped on her long legs, whistling "Beer Barrel Polka."

The second grade did write a play. Lark thought of the story, but everyone contributed ideas. The narrative went like this:

At the edge of a village called Barley Field, in a great mansion, lived six-year-old Boris (a name agreed upon because no one in the class knew a Boris), son of the snobbish Mr. and Mrs. Mandarin (a name suggested by Miss Bailey and admired by all, because it had a distinctive and foreign sound).

Thoroughly spoiled, young Boris was denied nothing by his doting parents, nor was he taught generosity and compassion.

One very still and hot summer day, a tornado rose up on the horizon and swept down upon the lands of the Mandarins, exploding buildings as if they were eggshells. A Mandarin cow was tossed over the moon. The family escaped by hiding in a root cellar. Then, gathering their few remaining belongings, they moved into the cellar to live.

At first, the villagers and the poor farmers of the area spoke with relish of the Mandarins' loss. "No more than they deserve" was the general feeling.

The Mandarins had money in the village bank, but all of it was required to buy livestock and rebuild the barn and other farm buildings. When the stable was rebuilt, the family lived there with the horses. They ate porridge and the few roots that remained in the cellar.

In the village, one early December day, a sister and brother, Anastasia and Bartholomew, were playing in the yard, making angels in the snow.

"I feel sorry for Boris," Anastasia told her brother. "The Mandarins don't have enough money for Christmas."

"Mama and Papa barely have enough for *ours*," replied Bartholomew.

"But we'll get *some* toy. Last year we got a sled, remember. And I have my rag doll and my hoop. You have your wagon that Papa made you and your spinning top. Boris has nothing."

"Do you remember how he laughed when we asked if we could ride in his pony cart?" Bartholomew reminded her, but he was at heart a kind lad. "What can we do?" he asked.

"You are so clever with your hands, Bartholomew, maybe you could carve him a little wooden bird like the one you made for me, the one whose beak opens and closes. And I could sew him a little rag dog from the scraps in Mama's sewing basket."

When their friends learned what Anastasia and Bartholomew were doing, they thought that it sounded like fun, and they joined in.

Word soon spread in the village that the children were making Christmas gifts for Boris, and the grown-ups felt ashamed that they'd been hard-hearted.

On Christmas Eve the entire village showed up at the Mandarins' stable, bearing clothing; good things to eat; and household items, which they had made or could spare.

Mr. Mandarin stood at the door of the stable and told them, "We have not deserved your kindness, but we thank you for it and hope in the future to repay it. A stable is not the worst place to learn about kindness."

In the years that followed, the Mandarins regained much of

their wealth and rebuilt their home. But their riches were used to bring happiness and good health to others.

After much debate of the options, it was decided that a narrator would read the story while pupils dressed as the characters performed in dumb show, illustrating the events.

Language period was lively with the shared writing of the story. Hands waved impatiently in the air, and spontaneous chatter and giggling bubbled as boys and girls poured their ideas into an invisible kettle of imagining.

Miss Bailey, writing frenziedly on the blackboard, hoo hoo hooed and sighed with delight and was heard to say to no one in particular, "This is 'The Kingdom of Making Sense.'"

Halloween came and went, and the time arrived when Miss Bailey must choose a cast. The day before Thanksgiving vacation, she drew Sally aside.

"I'd like you to be the narrator," she said. "Think about it over Thanksgiving and tell me your answer on Monday."

Outside the school, the sky was low and heavy, portending yet another snowfall. But the heat wave of sudden stardom warmed Sally all the way home.

Throwing open the front door, Grandma Elway trilled, "Happy Thanksgiving! We're here! Stella!"

Stella did not answer. Although it was nine-thirty in the morning and the turkey ought to be in the oven, she was still upstairs.

Carrying large pieces of monogrammed luggage, Herb Elway followed his wife. He set the suitcases beside the door, then returned to the car for the Elway contribution to Thanksgiving dinner: sweet potatoes, white potatoes, and pearl onions, which Edna would prepare in Stella's kitchen, and three pies baked in Mankato.

When they had unloaded the food in the kitchen and the luggage in the upstairs spare bedroom, leaving the smaller, downstairs room for the Wheeler grandparents, Edna and Herb hugged Sally and drew her into the kitchen.

"You and Grandad sit there," Grandma Elway told her, nodding toward the breakfast nook by the window. Rummaging through drawers until she had found an apron, she pulled it on, tying it in front with a flourish of capability.

"Where's your daddy?" she asked Sally.

"In the garage, changing a flat tire."

"Have you had breakfast?"

"Wheaties."

Grandma Elway shook her head and set to work. Soon the

turkey was stuffed and in the oven, while a platter of pancakes and bacon appeared in the middle of the breakfast-nook table, along with a pitcher of milk and a pot of coffee.

By now, Stella had slipped into the kitchen, wearing a soiled housedress, her hair unkempt. She hung back, leaning against the refrigerator.

"Sit down, Stella," her mother told her, "and have some breakfast. Didn't Sally set the table nicely? Herb, make room for Stella there, and get another chair for Don." Little lines deepened between her brows as she poured coffee, glancing at her daughter, at the dark circles around the eyes, the ragged-looking, uncared-for hands.

"When are your folks arriving?" she asked Donald, who was at the sink washing his hands.

"Noon, I think," he said over his shoulder. "That right, Sally?"

Sally nodded, pouring syrup onto her second stack of pancakes. She had not had pancakes since the last time her grandparents visited.

Edna Elway stood at the stove, sipping coffee and turning cakes on the griddle, all with a bustling, not to say, impatient skill. She was a woman who could accomplish several tasks more or less at once without seeming harried or burdened, but with an air of wonder that everyone was not able to do the same.

Her silver hair was arranged in an intricate and graceful chignon, her makeup applied subtly and flatteringly, her hands neatly manicured, the nails lacquered a soft rose color. Beneath the large apron, she wore a gray blue dress of light wool, which did not call attention to itself but, when noted, was seen to drape well and set off the silver hair and blue eyes.

Edna was of average height and delicate frame, her features small and doll-like. Not from her but from Herb Elway did Stella and Sally inherit their elegant height and longish features.

Stella turned the handle of her cup this way and that, now and then smiling vacantly at someone, bending great effort toward normality or what she thought she could remember of normality. Normality was a foreign country whose language she'd once spoken. Now that language was retrieved in bits only, and those through exhausting concentration.

Breakfast dishes washed, Edna Elway turned to Sally. "Get out the Hoover and run it around the living room before your Grandma and Grandpa Wheeler get here." Stella she led upstairs, closing her daughter's bedroom door behind them.

When the two women descended, Stella was bathed, and her long hair shampooed and arranged in a French knot. She wore a gray wool skirt, a blue sweater, a single strand of pearls, and at her ears, pearl earrings with which she fussed.

She looked just like *anybody's* mother, Sally thought, like a mother who baked pies for the St. Boniface Fall Bazaar or sang silly songs while washing dishes.

In the living room, Don and Herb Elway talked about the war in Europe and the likelihood that the U. S. would be drawn into it.

"Hell," Herb noted, "there're Americans in it already. Son of a friend of mine's gone off to fly for the R.A.F. Damned fool. He's not alone, though. And you know Roosevelt's going to get us into it, one way or the other."

Sally wished they would talk about football. She didn't like war talk, but she loved listening to masculine palaver. Her father and grandfather jawed at each other over politics sometimes — Daddy was a Democrat; Grandpa Elway, a Republican. But they never cried. No matter what topic they discussed or how thoroughly they disagreed, neither of them shed a tear.

"Herb, for heaven's sake, I wish you wouldn't swear like that in front of Sally," Grandma Elway told him, not with real heat but with a fond impatience. There'd be cussing enough in the house when Harry Wheeler arrived, she thought. That man thought he'd invented Hell and Damn.

Stella was sitting at the breakfast-nook table, hands folded in front of her like a child who has been told not to muss her clean clothes. Grandma Elway pulled another apron from the drawer where she'd found her own. "Put this on, Stella. I want you to peel the pearl onions. You can sit right there, if you like. Sally, let's set the dining-room table now so it's ready. Get out the good china."

Wasn't this pleasant? Sally thought. Daddy and Grandpa Elway were tuning the radio to a football game, and the women were preparing dinner. Even at Katherine Albers' house, where life appeared to be lived as if it were one of those movies periodically shown at school, about proper behavior at a birthday party or how to make a new pupil feel welcome, Thanksgiving could not be progressing in a more normal and correct fashion than it was here in Sally's house.

Soon the doorbell rang and Grandpa and Grandma Wheeler arrived, stomping snow from their boots in the vestibule and calling out greetings to everyone. Grandpa handed over a basket containing homemade dinner rolls, a bowl of mixed peas and carrots, and a bottle of Schenley's whiskey to Donald, while Grandma Wheeler gave Sally another Bobbsey Twins book, then folded the child to her bed-pillow breast.

"Bub!" Grandma Wheeler cried now, turning to her son and hugging him around his still slim middle. "You're getting thin, Bubby."

In the kitchen doorway, Edna Elway winced at the name "Bub" and bristled at the implication that Donald was suffering in Stella's care, although she knew that he was, and this made Irmgard's comment the more thoughtless and painful.

In the midst of the men sitting around the radio drinking bourbon and water, Sally settled down with her new book, feeling cosseted and safe.

Before dessert, Grandma Wheeler suggested, "Why don't you men walk Sally down to the skating rink? We women will do dishes, and by the time Sally's cold, everyone will be ready for pie."

The rink was less than a block away, halfway between Sally's house and the school. Most years the rink wouldn't be ready for use yet, not till around Christmas, but because of early snows and continuing cold, the town council had voted to flood it early.

Skipping along between the two grandfathers, galoshes shlump-shlumping, Sally savored the heavy aroma of Grandpa Elway's cigar, its pudding-thick redolence calling up, as it always did, holidays and treats and a feeling of safety.

Skates hissed and clicked, and warm breath hung in the air like a mist of gaiety. Grabbing her skates from her father, Sally dashed ahead to the warming house and began yanking off galoshes and shoes, tugging on heavy woolen socks, so that she was ready to have the skate laces tightened when he joined her.

Too impatient to linger while her father pulled on his own skates, Sally thunked across the battered wooden floor of the warming house and out the heavy door, skimming across the ice, darting in and out between bigger and older skaters. Like a swallow, strong and swift and eloquent, she flew—until Delmore Preuss pushed her from behind.

Delmore pushed her precisely because she was strong, superior to any seven-year-old skater he knew, including himself, and because her cheeks were rosy from the cold, her red knit cap sat at a cockeyed angle, and her blue-black braids lay like sable against the soft gray of her coat.

Even at seven, Delmore was half-choked with conflict: whether to push her down or snatch up her red-mittened hand and skate with her for a moment before anyone saw him. He opted for the cachet of notoriety and did not understand the shame he felt, however briefly.

Across the rink, Neddy Barnstable stood with his mittened

hands clapped under his arms, debating whether to head back to the warming house. His toes were numb.

Sally Wheeler skimmed past, her new shoe skates flying like a pair of white doves. And there went Delmore Preuss, arms pumping furiously, trying to catch up. And now he was almost even. And now—he was giving her a great whomp on the back, sending her sprawling across the ice.

Neddy started forward, then stopped, turned away, and pretended not to have seen. He knew that Sally would rather no one had seen. She picked herself up, brushing snow from her coat and leggings. She wasn't crying, though she'd gone down hard. Her red knit cap sat lower over her right eye, and Neddy thought it looked fine, just the way every girl's cap ought to sit.

Later Sally skated with her father, arms crossed in front of them in an old-fashioned duet of movement, 'round and 'round the rink, past her grandfathers, stamping their feet and waving. Then Beverly Ridza, who was always horning in on other people's fathers since she had none, asked Donald if he would skate with her. Beverly, too, was a strong skater and loved nothing better than to show off her speed and daring, slowed only by the clamp-on skates she wore.

Sally's white leather figure skates, which hugged her legs in a firm and supple grip, had been a recent reward from Grandma Wheeler for Sally's winning a St. Christopher medal and several other tinny little medals at summer catechism. The skates were an extravagance for Grandma Wheeler and evidence of the importance she placed on Sally's Catholic upbringing. Stella, being a convert and being Stella, might not possess the proper focus and fervor required to ensure the success of her little catechumen, so Grandma oversaw discreetly.

When at length Sally headed into the warming house and began unlacing her skates, Beverly dogged her to the bench on which she sat, plunking down and pressing, "C'n I come home with you?"

What could Sally say? Despite her reservations, she had no

legitimate excuse to refuse her. She couldn't say, "I don't want to share my grandmas and grandpas with you." And Sally was convinced that one way or another you got paid back tit for tat for misdeeds and unkindnesses.

This very afternoon Delmore Preuss had knocked her down and, not long after, had been mercilessly teased by sixth-grade boys for crying after a pileup with several careless skaters.

Unlike her friend Lark, Sally rarely thought about purgatory or hell or even the mortal sins that blackened her soul. Lark worried constantly about her soul. Sally thought it was because Mr. Erhardt, her daddy, worried so constantly about it.

Nearly every Friday afternoon after school, Lark and Beverly and Sally studied the *Baltimore Catechism* together at Lark's or Sally's house in preparation for Saturday morning catechism classes with Sisters Mary Clair and Mary Frances, classes which were themselves in preparation for First Confession and Communion in the spring.

The Sisters had suggested that in preparing for first confessions, children should keep track of their sins in a little notebook. Lark's stenographic pad, she'd confided to Sally, contained pages and pages of sins. If she died before her First Confession, she would go straight to hell and stay there even after the end of the world.

Sally had acquired a little notebook and for several days had duly listed her offenses. But before a week was out, the project lost its urgency and the notebook disappeared into the back of her closet. She supposed that when spring came and First Confession drew near, she would have to dig amongst the armless dolls and colored-up coloring books in the nether regions of the closet to unearth the notebook.

For now, she had more pressing worries than her soul.

Sally was not *entirely* irreligious. Much about St. Boniface and what went on there pleased her, even made her feel lifted up and transported to a mysterious plane of existence, a place like Oz or Italy or somewhere.

She told her father, "Beverly's coming over," and he nodded, grasping the heel of his left skate and tugging.

"She can have pie with us," he said. "What do you like, Beverly, pumpkin or cherry?"

The two girls tore ahead of the men, Sally throwing open the backdoor, Beverly at her heels.

Beside the kitchen table, the cords in her neck standing out rigid, Grandma Elway stood rooted, her body bent forward, thrust toward Grandma Wheeler across the room.

"I say she's going to be all right!" she screeched and scrabbled in her apron pocket for a handkerchief as she rushed from the room.

"Please stay," Sally begged as the quiet farewells began, but Grandma Wheeler shook her head and looked with meaning into Sally's eyes. The meaning was "Don't fuss, child. It's all so embarrassing, and least said, soonest mended." Grandpa Wheeler took one of Donald's hands in both of his.

"I'll write to Edna," Grandma Wheeler told her son. "It will be all right." She patted his arm, eyes bewildered, then suddenly hugged him violently, her battered black hat with the fluffy purple feather sluing sideways. Clutching at it, she hurried from the house and down the four steps to the sidewalk, Harry Wheeler close behind.

"We gonna have pie?" demanded Beverly who had observed with mesmerized and uncharacteristic silence the subdued, polite leave-taking, so unlike anything that might have occurred at her house had there been a row between grandmothers. Of course, she had only one grandmother and that one piss-poor and living in Minot, North Dakota. Also, Beverly lived in a tar-paper shack south of the lumberyard where the Ford would have gotten stuck in the snow, since the street was just about nonexistent, and everybody would have had to go out and push.

"Yes," Mr. Wheeler told her, smiling, "and what did you say you preferred, pumpkin or cherry?"

"Pumpkin," she told him, following him to the kitchen. "With whipped cream, if you got it, but also I like cherry, 'specially if it's à la mode, but I'll take what you got." She sat down at the breakfast-nook table, resting her chin on her palms as she watched Sally's father slice wedges of pie and lay them on small, gold-edged plates.

Mr. Wheeler was nearly as exotic to Beverly as a movie star. His refinement, his gentle weariness, and his slightly worn-away good looks enchanted her. If she didn't think that getting married was a stupid idea in the first place, she decided that she might marry him when she grew up. Mrs. Wheeler's presence in the world was so flickering, it didn't occur to Beverly that she might stand in the way.

"If you'll excuse me?" Mr. Wheeler said when he'd set the plates in front of Sally and Beverly. "There's more pie if you want it." At the kitchen door, he recalled, "When you're ready to leave, Beverly, I'll drive you home. It's getting dark."

Sally wished that Beverly would leave immediately, well, at least after wolfing her fill of pie. No one would be able to prize her out with a crowbar before then. Sally wanted to discover, if possible, what had caused the Thanksgiving holiday to end suddenly.

Instead of women laughing and discussing the reheating of leftovers in a warmly lit kitchen, silence and deepening shadows filled all but the breakfast nook where the scraping of forks against dessert plates was the only sound until Beverly asked, "How come your grandma was jawing?"

Sally lifted her shoulders.

"Something to do with your ma, I bet," Beverly went on cannily.

Sally did not respond.

"What d'ya think?"

"Let's not talk," Sally said.

Beverly fetched herself another piece of pumpkin pie. "That's okay with me." Licking whipped cream from her fingers, she added unreasonably, "You'd prob'ly talk about dumb stuff anyway."

After wordlessly stuffing herself with two slices of pumpkin and one of cherry, Beverly conceded, "I'd better go home now." And while Sally called her father down from upstairs, Beverly poured a tall glass of milk and gulped it down. She was wiping the mustache on the back of her arm when Mr. Wheeler came into the kitchen, dressed in overcoat, leather gloves, and a snap-brim gray felt hat.

"Pie sure makes me thirsty," she told him.

"Me too." Digging in his pocket for car keys, he told Beverly, "Wait in here while I start the car. I'll honk when it's warm."

Moments later, Sally and Beverly heard the engine moan and eventually clutter to life. A thick cloud of exhaust roiled from the open garage door as Beverly began pulling on her old brown plaid wool jacket, frayed down the placket and around the collar and cuffs.

Thrusting bare hands into the pockets, she observed suddenly, "My pa usta beat up my ma and he burned Charlie with a cigarette when Charlie wouldn't stop cryin'. I hope he never comes back. I would shoot him if he came back." She paused, staring out the breakfast-nook window at the garage where the Wheeler car was being warmed for her. With suspect nonchalance, she said, "It ain't so bad havin' only one parent." Rocking philosophically on her heels, she concluded, "I'm used to it. You get used to it."

What had that been about? Sally pondered while pulling on her nightgown and brushing her teeth. "It ain't so bad havin' only one parent. . . . You get used to it."

Tucking Sally in, her father sat down on the edge of the bed and reached for *Fairy Tales from Near and Far.* Riffling through the pages, he stopped at "The Empress of One Hundred," a favorite of his, and began reading about the young empress who ruled a small country on the far side of the world.

To the east of her realm lay a great forest inhabited by an ogre who destroyed or eluded every army sent against him.

Early in the empress's rule the ogre snatched away a shepherd whose flock had wandered too near the woods. The empress was overcome with grief and self-blame. She no longer smiled, nor did she allow herself the pleasure of jesters or minstrels or circuses. Eventually no jesters or minstrels or circuses performed in her land, not because she was cruel, but because such things were frivolous. And she did not believe that she deserved frivolity. A shepherd was dead. Life was serious. An empress must protect her people.

To the west of this country lay a realm where the old queen had long ago declared that one day of each fortnight would be a holiday. On that day, acrobats and musicians and clowns entertained in every village square. The citizens came out and picnicked and played on the green with their babies.

One by one, two by two, and three by three, the young empress's subjects stole away to the west, across the border into the land of fortnightly holidays, to settle and work. And the empress worried even more. Who would till the fields and make the boots and clothes and bread? Who would keep watch against the ogre? When only one hundred citizens remained in the empire, a retired lord chamberlain, much loved and respected, came to court, asking for an audience.

"Your Highness," he said, "ogres will come and go. They will snatch shepherds. Your unhappiness cannot prevent it. My advice is this: Laugh. Sing. Learn to play the lute. Hire clowns and order sweetmeats sold each Saturday."

The empress frowned at this advice. So frivolous. So risky. So self-indulgent. Learn to play the lute, indeed. But what was she to do when she had only one hundred subjects left?

At length she gave way and sent for singers and dancers and players of lutes. She ordered the baker to lay up a supply of sweetmeats and proclaimed a holiday every fortnight. Although the empress's subjects did not forget about the ogre now that their lives were jollier, they did not mind so much standing watch against him.

Weeks went by, then months, and one by one, two by two, and three by three, the people returned to their old homes and their work. From across the sea others came, swelling the ranks and protecting the borders.

Each Midsummer's Eve, the empress joined the entertainment in the great park beyond the castle gates, playing her lute with only passable skill but with much delight. And there in the park she ordered the statue of a jester erected with a plaque at his feet that read "The world will have ogres, do what we may. So we must have music, sweetmeats, and play."

Though Sally was not nearly so fond of this story as *The Wind in the Willows*, she listened because she knew that her father enjoyed it. When he had kissed her good night, however, she fetched *The Wind in the Willows* from the bookcase and found her favorite chapter.

Mole and Rat had finally found the door to Badger's house after a terrifying and freezing wander-about in the Wild Wood. ". . . they gathered around the glowing embers of the great wood fire, and thought how jolly it was to be sitting up *so* late, and *so* independent, and *so* full; . . ."

Edna Elway, coming out of the bathroom, saw Sally's light and inquired, "Still reading?"

Crossing to the bed, she said, "The little argument between your Grandmother Wheeler and me this afternoon had nothing to do with you. You mustn't be upset." She took Sally's hand and patted it.

"What *did* it have to do with?" Sally pressed.

Edna sighed and studied the closet door. She had hoped to avoid this.

"It was about Mommy," Sally ventured.

Edna wouldn't tell Sally anything she herself could not accept. And she could not accept that Stella wouldn't be her old self when she was done with "the change."

"Don't worry," she said, rising. "Grandma Wheeler and I'll make it up again. When you're a child, every quarrel seems like the end. When you're old, you know they're just . . . unhappy chapters in a long book and happy chapters are coming."

After Grandma Elway had gone, Sally sat staring at her book for some time, mulling over what her grandmother had said and, more significantly, what she hadn't.

That Mommy was crazy Sally no longer doubted. And she wished her grandmother had discussed it with her. But maybe the craziness made Grandma Elway sad. If that were the case, Sally would pretend that her mother's behavior was not strange.

She thought so hard working this out, her head buzzed like an electric clock. Setting the book aside, she climbed from bed and padded to the window overlooking Second Street. Pressing her warm brow against the cold glass, she watched snowflakes as large as fairy handkerchiefs flutter to the street below the lamp at the corner.

At length she climbed back into bed and, taking up *The Wind in the Willows* once more, turned the pages, studying the illustrations until she grew sleepy. Extinguishing the light and sailing the gulf between awake and asleep, she spied Beverly on the approaching shore, looking a little like Ratty and assuring her, "It ain't so bad havin' only one parent. You get used to it."

In the morning, before the final bell, Miss Bailey stood beside the open door of the second-grade room, greeting pupils as they straggled in and keeping an eye out for shenanigans in the hall.

On the Monday following Thanksgiving, as Sally approached, she hadn't decided whether to narrate the Christmas play. Every time she thought about it, she got hot and sick to her stomach.

But as Miss Bailey lifted an eyebrow of inquiry, Sally made up her mind all at once. Something about the eyebrow and the unpatronizing speculation in Miss Bailey's ruddy face decided her.

Mouth dry, voice quavering, Sally said, "I'll be the narrator, Miss Bailey."

The gymnasium/auditorium smelled of basketball games and unwashed gym rompers, vaulting horses and wrestling mats, as well as lunches brought from home. At noon, at folding tables set up for those who did not go home to eat, children sorted through cheese or liverwurst or brown-sugar sandwiches. The folding chairs on which they sprawled were the same ones on which their parents would perch, craning to see and hear the Christmas Program.

On this first day of stage rehearsal for the Christmas Program, Miss Bailey ushered the second graders down a dim, unfamiliar corridor to the backstage area of the gymnasium/auditorium.

Shushing them, she gathered the troupe into a squirming, murmuring clot in the shadowy stage wings where props and scenery, ropes and pulleys, sandbags and teaser curtains, heavy electrical cords and a forbidding-looking light panel all threatened to trip, trap, and electrocute them.

"Godsakes," swore Beverly, "ain't it a mess?"

"Quiet," Miss Bailey ordered.

Out on the stage, the first grade was concluding, "Up on the Housetop." Mr. Hansen, the bandmaster, was at the piano, drowning out, purposely perhaps, the thin, tuneless voices.

When at last the second grade took the stage, Sally stood downstage right at a microphone adjusted to its lowest height. Miss Bailey advised her, "Take several deep breaths before you begin."

But Sally's hands shook so violently, the words danced on the page and she stammered to a halt. Behind her, Delmore Preuss, Ronald Oster, and Leroy Mosely sniggered, falling entirely out of their roles as the priggish Mr. Mandarin; his spoiled-rotten son, Boris; and kindly Bartholomew, a poor boy of the village.

From backstage, Miss Bailey emerged, bearing aloft a music stand on which to lay the text. However, this necessitated further fussing: rearranging of the microphone and adjusting of the music stand. Acutely aware of the second-grade eyes fixed on her and conscious of the jealousy prickling behind many of the eyes because of the consideration being given her, Sally could hear in her mind, ". . . thinks she's so smart. I don't think she's so smart. Nor pretty, neither. And her mother's crazy."

The odor of sweat and liverwurst moiled Sally's innards until the basketball pattern painted on the gym floor, the metal gridwork shielding the gymnasium lights, and the rows of benches filling the balconies along either side of the room floated and heaved like her stomach.

Again Sally launched into the narration, knees knocking.

The twenty-minute rehearsal swelled and extended like a grotesque living thing to which there seemed no end.

As the days of rehearsal wore on, several times Sally nearly asked Miss Bailey if she could exchange roles with Lark, who was playing Mrs. Mandarin. Lark was nearly as good a reader as Sally. However, on each occasion, she lost her nerve when she saw the look of trust and confidence in Miss Bailey's eyes.

The first week of December, the *Standard Ledger* announced the Christmas Program and what each grade was presenting. "Warm Hearth, Warm Heart," an original play by Miss Bailey's second-grade class, was listed with Sally Wheeler named as narrator. Now it was too late to drop out. Sally's only hope was to get sick.

Morning after morning she set off for school without her red woolen cap or scarf or mittens, but was nonetheless unable to catch a cold. Colds jumped out of the path when they saw her coming.

Once the notice had appeared in the *Standard Ledger*, people began remarking on it to Sally. When she ran an errand to Truska's Grocery Store for a loaf of bread, Mrs. Truska observed while wrapping the purchase, "Yer in the doings at school, I see by the paper." Handing Sally the bread, she added, "The mister and me'll be there, so see you do good."

Though these words were accompanied by Mrs. Truska's coarse, well-meaning laugh, they struck Sally a blow. "See you do good." If she didn't, what then? Would people bring it up in public later? Would Mrs. Truska point out, "A shame you didn't do good."

Mrs. Bensinger next door hailed Sally from her back stoop as Sally trudged up from the alley one afternoon after school. "I see we're an important person these days."

What did you answer to such a statement? Surely not "yes."

"I said, 'I see we're an important person these days.'"

Mrs. Bensinger's son, Lester, had *had to* marry Evangeline Steuben a number of years ago. Sally knew this from Lark who'd overheard it at her mother's bridge club. Sally had asked her friend to find out *why* someone would *have* to marry someone else. It was frightening, wasn't it, to think you might *have* to marry, say, Delmore Preuss? But Lark's mother, when queried on the matter, had passed it off with "I'm sure I don't know." Lark had not been convinced and had made her mother promise that she and Mr. Erhardt would never make *her* marry someone.

In any case, Mrs. Bensinger, for whatever reason, was a woman who laughed a good deal, a laughter filled with little needles.

"I'm the narrator," Sally admitted. "But I'm not very important," she fibbed, hoping that Mrs. Bensinger would lose interest.

"How did they come to choose you?" the neighbor asked with a laugh, as if she and Sally shared the hilarious knowledge that Sally was all wrong for the narrator.

"The teacher asked me." Sally was on her own back stoop now, and she reached for the knob of the storm door.

"Well, good luck!" Mrs. Bensinger sang out in a voice larded with sympathy and girlish affinity. "I'm sure glad *I* don't have to be narrator."

On the other hand, Helen Stillman was genuinely tickled to learn that Sally was narrator. The day after the encounter with Mrs. Bensinger, Lark suggested that they pay a call on Mrs. Stillman after school. Not infrequently they visited her in the little apartment above Rabel's Meat Market that she shared with her son, Hillyard, a shell-shocked veteran of the Great War.

Lark and her mother had long been friends with Mrs. Stillman and Hilly. It was chiefly through Mrs. Erhardt that Sally and Stella had come to know them.

Many years ago, when Hilly was a baby, Helen Stillman's husband had died. In order to support herself and baby

Hillyard, Mrs. Stillman attended Mankato Normal School, training to be an elementary schoolteacher. Teaching school in a small town was an uneasy life for someone of her temperament, for she had been raised a *true* Christian, as Mrs. Erhardt observed, not given to paddling about in the shallows where the peccadillos swam, but sailing in the deep waters of love and charity.

Before Hilly was old enough to go to school, a cousin of Mrs. Stillman's, Elvira, a country girl who hungered for the glamour of town, asked if she could come live with the Stillmans and help out with the little boy while Helen Stillman taught third grade. It seemed a sensible and serendipitous arrangement, but the girl got into trouble with an unknown married man and had to leave town.

On account of Elvira's pregnancy, Hilly's mother nearly lost her teaching position. And when, years later, Hillyard came home from the war without all his wits, the Stillmans were doubly stigmatized. Now the two lived a life of unembittered, genteel poverty in a sort of Indian Summer of Hope.

Sally and Lark and sometimes Beverly dropped in on the Stillmans from time to time. Beverly had at first to overcome that reluctance one déclassé may feel at associating with another, fear of being additionally tainted, but Mrs. Stillman's generosity with cookies and her blind eye to Beverly's low-class ways broke down the child's defenses.

Invariably, Mrs. Stillman welcomed callers with grateful and delighted amazement, as though she and Hillyard dwelt at the summit of a forbidding peak where visitors were a luxury not realistically to be anticipated.

So on that December afternoon, when Lark proposed a call on Mrs. Stillman, Sally agreed at once. And when they climbed the open wooden stairs outside Rabel's Meat Market and knocked on the Stillman's door, Helen Stillman answered almost immediately, beaming and exclaiming, "Hillyard saw you coming from his bedroom window and wondered if you were going to stop. I can hardly believe our good luck!" White and soft as the under-feathers of an angel's wing, Mrs. Stillman's bobbed hair fluttered in the breeze of her delight.

She stepped back. "Come in out of the cold, and I'll make tea. You can put your coats on my bed. If your mittens are wet, lay them on the oil heater for a few minutes."

Sally and Lark pulled off their galoshes, standing them neatly side by side on the newspaper next to the door, then proceeded to Mrs. Stillman's bedroom, where they shucked off their coats.

Sally was fond of this room where soft, faded pieced quilts covered the bed and the scent of Lady Esther talcum commingled with lavendar oil-embued furniture cream. On a crocheted scarf, covering the top of the dresser, sat a lady, regal and insouciant, with china head and shoulders above a wide pincushion skirt. Her features reminded Sally of Grandma Elway.

A hand mirror and brush with mottled green celluloid backs lay beside her, along with a brass comb edged along its back by the same green celluloid. Sally thought the dresser set sophisticated and refined and wondered who had given it to Mrs. Stillman. It was the sort of small luxury that Hilly's mother would deny herself in favor of cheap, store-bought cookies and weak tea with which to ply her guests.

When the two girls turned to leave the bedroom, they saw Hilly standing inside the open door of his room, across the tiny hall, watching them with an expression benign and pleased, yet removed, like someone watching a wedding from the last pew.

"Hilly," Lark asked, "are you going to have tea and cookies?"

He nodded solemnly and followed them into the living room, easing down onto the old wicker rocker.

Hilly had changed appreciably since last spring. He was saner and sadder, quieter and more fearful. Something strange and terrible had happened to him last spring and, in some sense, to Stella too. Sally wasn't sure *what*, but her mother had been upset for weeks afterward and had never completely put it behind her. The event surfaced again and again, but only in shrouded allusions, as if it could not, should not be spoken of candidly. The mysterious event made Sally shiver, but filled her with a morbid and compelling curiosity as well.

"Well, here we are," piped Mrs. Stillman, bearing a tray of tea and cookies from the kitchen. When they were all dunking pale, frangible vanilla wafers in the weak brew, she reported, "I see by the *Standard Ledger*, Sally, that you're narrating the second-grade Christmas play." Turning to Lark she inquired, "And what part are you playing? Something major, I'm sure."

"I'm Mrs. Mandarin," Lark told her, spooning a mushy gobbet of cookie from the bottom of her cup. "She's mean and stuck-up at the beginning, but she gets to be nice at the end."

"Well, I should hope so," exclaimed Mrs. Stillman. "You're one of the nicest people I know."

"Lark thought of the story on her own hook," Sally told Mrs. Stillman, knowing that Lark herself was unlikely to reveal this.

"I'm not surprised to hear it," Mrs. Stillman observed. "Lark has a wonderful imagination."

She passed the plate of cookies once more. "Isn't it exciting, Hillyard, how our girls are going to be stars in the Christmas Program? I'm so proud of them."

Hilly, whose mind had drifted away, looked blankly at his mother, waiting for something more.

"I was saying how proud I am that our girls are going to be stars in the Christmas Program at school."

Slowly he traced the path back to them, a hint of pleasure lighting his eyes and tweaking the corners of his mouth. "Stars," he repeated, his glance bending toward Lark. "Who will be the moon?" he wondered, gratified to make a rational contribution to the conversation.

Mrs. Stillman and the two girls were careful not to guffaw but only to giggle so as not to alarm or embarrass Hilly. But they turned such beaming faces on him that he grew flushed with pride and returned their smiles.

"There isn't any moon, Hilly," Lark told him. "Only stars."

"No moon?" He considered this. With scrupulous reflection and weighing every syllable, he advised, "Then you will have to shine brightly."

"You put me in mind of Miss Merle Oberon, the actress," Mrs. Stillman breathed with unselfconscious admiration for the movie star. "I saw her in *Wuthering Heights.*" She tucked a cookie into each girl's hand, then held the door for them, a youthful, abstracted expression on her face.

Merle Oberon? Sally shuddered with happiness.

Laying a speller and an arithmetic workbook on the kitchen table, she went in search of Stella. "Mommy, Mommy, Hilly thought Lark and I were going to be *stars* in the Christmas Program! He asked us who was the moon!"

Racing up the stairs, she called, "Mommy! Where are you?" At her mother's door she knocked, then turned the knob. "Mommy?" In the densely shadowed room, Stella sat at the window, staring down at the sidewalk where now and again a bundled-up skater, like an inkblot against the banked snow, trudged home from the rink in the urgency of the late afternoon, table-setting hour.

"Mommy, Lark and I visited Mrs. Stillman after school. We had tea and cookies."

Stella wrenched her gaze from the window, fixing it on a point somewhat to the right of Sally. "That's nice," she said, as though she'd not actually heard what Sally had said.

"Hilly had tea with us, and he said something funny. Do you want to hear?"

"Yes . . . that would be nice." A trace of warmth crept into Stella's voice. Because of events the previous spring, news of Hilly could rouse Stella from her lethargy.

The Friday before Memorial Day, Stella had driven into the country to plant a flat of petunias and another of geraniums on the graves of Wheeler cousins in the Catholic cemetery. When she was done setting out the flowers, she'd pumped water from the well to water them.

Driving out of the cemetery, she stopped the car in order to close the gate and noticed another car approaching from town. Someone was running ahead of the car. From a distance, Stella had imagined it to be a high school boy training for a race, though of course, the school year was nearly over.

As the car drew near, Stella realized that the young men in the front seat were honking the horn to frighten the runner and that they were yelling threats at him (threats that caused her to tremble even in the recollection), warnings of heinous things they would do to him.

She saw, too, that it was Hilly they were tormenting, Hilly, who could run only haltingly because of the loss of several toes during the Great War. Frightened half to death, he was about to collapse when Stella ran to the end of the cemetery drive, screaming and waving her arms at the men who, noticing her at last, sped away, leaving Hilly to tumble naked into the grassy ditch beside the road, crying like a child.

Much of this Stella had poured out to Sally and Lark that afternoon after school while they studied catechism at the Wheeler kitchen table. She had been distraught, unaware of what she was saying, and when realization overtook her, she grew apologetic, then silent. In the ensuing months, there were vague, tearful references to "the abuse of innocents," but nothing more.

Sitting down on the edge of her mother's unmade bed, Sally explained, "Mrs. Stillman said that Lark and I would be stars in the Christmas play, and Hilly asked 'Who will be the moon?' Wasn't that funny?"

Stella didn't answer at once, but seemed to consider the implications of what Sally had told her. Sally noted that her mother's hair was uncombed and that she was wearing an old maroon wool skirt whose hem had come undone. Above this, she had on an equally disreputable brown cardigan covered with lint and missing a button. Had her mother gone out to the stores looking like this? Sally wondered.

The bedroom had the same faded, frowzy look as Stella. Though the furnishings were unchanged—white lace curtains, pale blue walls; bird's-eye maple suite, a tenth anniversary gift from Grandma and Grandpa Elway; and underfoot, a pale blue carpet strewn with soft pink peonies—the furniture went undusted, the bed unmade, the curtains unwashed unless Sally or the grandmas took a hand.

Sally retrieved a gray housedress from a chair and slipped it onto a hanger. Clothes lay where Stella had abandoned them on the closet floor. This extreme untidiness had begun only in recent months. Previously Stella had been, if anything, overly concerned with keeping the house up, flying upstairs and down on rampages of cleaning. None of that seemed to matter to her now.

At length Stella asked, "You didn't make fun of Hilly, did you, when he asked about the moon?"

Why must her mother find sorrow everywhere, even in this small joke that Sally'd brought home to please her?

The following afternoon, when school let out for the weekend, Sally and Lark and Beverly dawdled down Main Street, admiring the colored lights and evergreen boughs hung on the lamp posts and the Christmas displays in Lundeen's Dry Goods and Eggers' Drug Store. The drugstore window was especially beautiful and thrilling, featuring an extensive array of Coty products and elegant vanity sets like the one Mrs. Stillman had on her bureau. The hand mirrors and brushes and combs lay in satin-lined boxes with niches built right into them for each lovely piece to fit snugly. Nail buffers and files and even fancy pumice stones found their way into the more costly sets.

Mrs. Eggers, who did not work in the drugstore but had dropped in for a Coca-Cola, was coming out the door, looking very stylish in a beaver coat, matching hat, and brown suede gloves.

"Don't put your fingers on the windows, girls," she said, hurrying past them toward the Eggers' white Buick.

Immediately Beverly began blowing on the window, steaming it up, then drawing an ugly face and beaver hat in the condensation. "Godsakes," she swore, "them Eggerses think their farts don't smell."

Sally broke away from the others and dallied along, past Rabel's Meat Market and across the street, waiting there for her friends to catch up. When they reached Truska's Grocery Store, they turned west and crossed the street, passing Johnson's Chevrolet and Oldsmobile, where a shiny new Oldsmobile filled the display window, an enormous red ribbon tied to the hood. "That's like your pa's," Beverly observed.

Mr. Erhardt had bought a new Oldsmobile earlier in the year, vexing Mrs. Erhardt, who was saving up to build their house. Beverly had ridden in the car once or twice, bragging of it afterward to her several enemies.

The Erhardt Oldsmobile was parked in the postage stamp-size graveled lot beside the depot. A brick platform ran from the parking area, alongside the tracks, all the way to the opposite end of the station. And down there, Mr. Erhardt could be seen, pushing the freight wagon back into its accustomed spot in front of the freight-room door.

The girls waved to him as they stepped across the platform to the entrance of the Erhardt's living quarters. Mrs. Erhardt had heard them coming and opened the door before Lark reached for the knob.

"You girls took your time getting here," she said without serious reproach. "I've been keeping cocoa and cinnamon toast warm for more than half an hour." Beverly began jumping up and down.

The warm cups felt good in their hands as they lolled on kitchen chairs, growing half sleepy with repletion and content.

"You'd better start the catechism," Mrs. Erhardt admonished, "or you won't know the answers tomorrow morning, and what will the Sisters think of me then, letting you lollygag the afternoon away?"

So for half an hour, they questioned each other from the *Baltimore Catechism*. Just as this pious activity was transmuting inexplicably into talk of Christmas and what one hoped to receive, the telephone rang in the living room, and Mrs. Erhardt answered, settling in for a gossip with her close friend Bernice McGivern. Hushed references to Mrs. Erhardt's sister, Betty, drifted now and then into the kitchen, but the girls were more interested in Christmas than in aunts who'd last summer lost babies and seemingly their husbands named Stanley as well.

Beverly longed for new shoes and a gun.

"What about toys?" Sally wanted to know. "Don't you want Santa to bring you toys?"

"Santa?" Beverly hooted. "Godsakes, you still believe in *him?*"

A moment of pure, buzzing confusion filled Sally's brain. She stared blankly at Beverly. "Whhhhat . . . ?"

"Seven years old and you believe in *Santy* Claus," Beverly sneered. She did not have much of an edge over anybody in this world, but she had *this.*

Beverly's words knocked the wind out of Sally and Lark. They sat leaning against the kitchen table, trying to breathe.

Sally heard herself crying, "Santa doesn't come to your house, Beverly, because you're so naughty. Santa only comes to good children." Even as the words left her lips, she knew they were empty and faintly embarrassing in their falseness. Yet she had to strike out. "You don't know the answers when Sister calls on you, and you're going to hell!"

She rose from the table, trembling and stumbling through the doorway to the Erhardt bedroom. Because no real walls separated the rooms, only partitions built of compoboard, Sally could not close a door behind her, so she stood with her back to the kitchen, promising herself, "I won't cry I won't cry I won't cry."

Santa was a lie, a conspiracy of grown-ups, like the lie that her mother wasn't crazy.

December 22, 1939

"I won't cry I won't cry I won't cry," Sally chanted in her head
as she stood, eyes closed, leaning against the cool, smooth plaster wall of the grimly lit hallway. It was Friday evening,
December 22, 1939, night of the dreaded Christmas Program.

Beyond this thick wall and beyond the athletic equipment
rooms that lay behind it, the auditorium/gymnasium was alive
with the running-water sound of murmuring townspeople edg-
ing down rows of folding chairs. Rubbers and galoshes
squidged on the highly varnished floor.

High up, on either side of the gymnasium, the balconies were
filling, according to Miss Borgen the fourth-grade teacher who
had sneaked out on the stage; peeped through the curtain; and
returned to the long, linoleumed hallway where kindergarten
through sixth grade huddled in shapeless little individual
masses. Chewing fingernails and pigtail ends, scratching scabs
and picking noses, they waited. A couple of kindergarteners
had begun to cry and wanted to go home.

The teachers, in their Sunday best, smiled and whispered encouragement or frowned gimlet-eyed and shook their heads.
Except for Miss Bailey (who was in every circumstance the
same imperturbable enthusiast), the elementary schoolteachers
were prancy on their best high heels, like skitterish horses at
the starting post. They wore cologne and a bit of makeup,
brooches and, one or two, a bracelet.

The children thrilled to see their teachers dolled up and feverish, to glimpse the woman that teacher might be when she wasn't teacher, when she took the train to the Black Hills on vacation or had her female chums over to her little apartment above Lundeen's Dry Goods for an evening of bridge.

It was incredible, heady, and slightly disturbing to pupils to think that teacher had a life she enjoyed beyond the classroom. Oughtn't *they* to be enough?

Sally, wearing her rose velveteen dress, long white stockings, and Mary Janes, did not chew the ends of her braids, which Grandma Elway had tied with thick, luxurious rose satin ribbons brought from Mankato. Rather, she stood cold and still as a funerary angel, wishing that she could fly away to heaven.

The kindergarten was led away, through the door at the end of the hall and up the short flight of steps leading to the stage. Sally's eyes sprang open. Only the first grade remained to perform before she would be led down the same path to the brilliantly lighted stage where humilation waited.

Her lips stuck to her teeth. Her fingers, holding the script, were icy and paralyzed, and she doubted she'd be able to open them when the time came to lay the pages on the music stand.

Her mother was in the audience. Grandma Elway, who'd arrived by train from Mankato that day, had insisted. "Our Sally is a narrator!" she'd exclaimed.

Donald had dropped Sally at school soon after dinner, so she had not heard all the cajoling, scolding, inveigling, and begging that had resulted in Stella's presence at the program, clean, made-up, and wearing a burgundy wool dress with a soft flounce collar.

Stella could prevail with Donald but not with her mother who, although she loved Stella with a daunting passion, did not believe that giving in to Stella's megrims was the way to see her through the Change.

Edna did believe that if one forced oneself to get out of bed in the morning, as she occasionally had to force herself; if one bathed and dressed in clean clothing from the inside out; then ate a proper breakfast and picked up the house before sitting down with a second cup of coffee to draw up a grocery list, well, one soon cleared the vapors from one's head. Work, organization, proper nutrition, and cleanliness. Marching down that path, you'd soon be right again.

Edna Elway occupied a center aisle seat about midway back in the rows of folding chairs. To her left sat Stella, fastening and unfastening the clasp of her handbag, and beyond Stella, in the third seat, Donald.

Edna held her head up and studied the motley assemblage with satisfaction. Her tiny tribe compared well, and soon Sally, her Christmas angel, would appear, a child sweeter and lovelier than any other in this school. A true beauty.

Sally, like Stella, had inherited the tall, pale-skinned, dark-haired beauty of Herb's side of the family, Edna was quick to admit. Her own people were attractive, but they were squat. Well, what did one expect? Until emigrating, they'd been Alsatian miners for as far back as anyone knew.

But they'd been the sort who took hold, took advantage, and made something of themselves. Backbone and wits. That was what she'd come from. Was there something wrong with that? Ambition it was called. God knew, its importance had been borne in upon her. Hard work, respectability, ambition.

Edna had always had a tender and unquestioning regard for her parents. They had been strict but generous. She had tried never to disappoint them, and their assurances that this filial regard and obedience would bring her happiness had not been wrong.

She had married the "catch" of her girlhood, Herbert Elway, whom she adored. And she had raised a pretty, sweet-natured daughter. A good and loving daughter.

Edna poked daintily at her coiffure. A hairpin was stabbing someplace just there where she seemed unable to reach it. She closed her eyelids until the tears behind them were dispelled.

Across the aisle and near the last row of chairs, Harry and Irmgard Wheeler settled themselves, Harry with his hat on his knee. The Wheelers had almost been late. Something had come up at the last moment down at the registrar of deeds office, and it was nearly six by the time Harry had got home from work. A quick bowl of tomato soup, the twenty-five mile drive, and here they were, slightly out of breath, but none the worse for wear.

Irmgard Wheeler observed Edna Elway poking at her beauty parlor hairdo, but immediately reminded herself that her hair, too, had been styled by a beauty operator, Vera Swenson, at Clarice's Beauty Parlor in Worthington.

Poor Bub, Irmgard thought, craning a bit to catch sight of her son. He looks almost as old as his dad. Stella's Change was going to put him into an early grave. Out on the road all week, then back to look after things at home on the weekends. It was too much.

Irmgard eased her right foot out of the plain, squared-off black pump. Her bunion was tender. More snow, no doubt about it.

Was Sally someplace back there behind the blue curtain, waiting to perform her turn? Tied up in knots, she probably was, poor little thing. If only there'd been time beforehand to tell her that everything would be just fine.

Behind the blue velvet curtain, back in the grim hallway leading to the stage, Sally breathed shallow flutters of air, little bird breaths, her knees rigid as clothesline posts.

Miss Bailey placed a firm hand on each shoulder and delved into Sally's eyes, 'way back where she knew the fear monster sat. "Take a deep breath."

Sally tried. Her expelled breath came out in a shudder.

"Again. Fill your lungs all the way down."

Sally sucked in air with a ragged gasp.

"Now, out. Get rid of it all."

Thus they stood for two or three minutes, Miss Bailey coaching Sally's breathing.

"Now, I want to tell you something about your job as narrator," Miss Bailey said. "Three hundred or more people are in the auditorium."

Sally's eyes widened, her lips compressed in a thin grimace.

"They want to hear a story. People love stories. Don't *you?* Didn't you say that your daddy was reading you *The Wind in the Willows?*"

Sally nodded, unsure where this was heading.

"And you really get caught up, don't you, when you hear about those nasty stoats moving into Toad Hall?"

Again Sally nodded. Miss Bailey straightened, glaring at Ronald Oster, who kept untying Sue Ann Meyer's sash. Ronald thrust his hands into his pockets and stared at his shoes.

"Well," Miss Bailey resumed, "when people come to a play, that's what they want . . . somebody to tell them a story, help them understand what's going on, and make it exciting." Her large hands on Sally's shoulders gave them an affectionate squeeze. "Our play isn't about how scared Sally Wheeler is or how bad a reader she thinks she is."

She smiled and Sally smiled back. "Tell yourself, 'I'm giving everybody a Christmas present tonight. For fifteen minutes, I'm going to make them forget that the car wouldn't start this morning, and the dog died last Saturday, and all we had to eat this week was beans and bread.'" She held Sally's chin in one of her big hands and said, "I chose you for narrator because I knew that you could do that."

They heard the first grade concluding "Up on the Housetop." "All right, class," Miss Bailey said softly, "it's time."

Just before the blue curtain parted, she reminded Sally, "Don't rush. You are the hostess."

And when the audience was revealed to her, programs rattling as they looked down to mind who this little girl in the rose velveteen dress might be, unhurriedly she carried the music stand to the apron of the stage, placed it beside the microphone, then calmly lay the text before her.

Smiling, she said, "Hello." This "hello" was not part of the script. Sally wasn't even aware that she'd said it, but Miss Bailey's words had filled her with a tender generosity and sense of responsibility toward the audience.

And when she greeted them, they responded, smiling back, some mouthing the word *hello.* She saw that they had indeed come to hear a story, and she began slowly and clearly to tell them one, coloring the words, when appropriate, with disdain, sadness, or delight so that the dead battery and the dead dog and the memory of beans all week would slip away, under the folding chairs, for fifteen minutes.

Stella sat on the edge of the bed and arranged the blankets around Sally's shoulders. She did not want to cry. She wanted to be serene and maternal.

"The second-grade play was the best part of the Christmas Program," she told Sally. "And to think that the class wrote it!"

"It was Lark's idea."

"Was it?"

"But we all helped."

Stella nodded. "I was sitting there on a cold, hard folding chair, thinking, 'It's going to get too hot in here with all these people, and the radiators knocking and hissing.' And the next thing I knew, this little girl, as calm and poised as a head nurse, began telling me a story, and then I didn't even notice how hot it was and how the man sitting behind me kept sucking on his tooth."

When she had left, Sally thought, "So it's true, what Miss Bailey said. You can make people forget their troubles if you tell them a story."

Christmas of 1939 was nearly perfect. While Stella was quiet and occasionally withdrawn, she was more *present* than at any time in the past two years.

"I knew it," Sally heard Grandma Elway tell Grandma Wheeler. "She's coming out of it."

Because of Stella, everyone felt permission to be gay. Christmas day was a Monday, so the grandparents were on hand until early Tuesday, playing bridge and arguing politics.

Even a bit of good news from the European war conspired to create an air of hopefulness: the German ship *Graf Spee* had been sunk in Montevideo harbor.

Edna Elway, successfully concluding a little slam in spades, gathered up the deck to shuffle, observing philosophically, "I don't suppose *Gone With the Wind* will show up here for a year."

"In Harvester?" Stella asked.

"Anywhere in this neck of the woods."

"It's playing in Sioux Falls, I believe," Irmgard Wheeler noted. "We'll wait for it to come to Worthington. Harry won't drive all the way over to Sioux Falls for a movie."

"Is Merle Oberon in it?" Sally asked.

"I don't believe so," Grandma Wheeler told her, scooping up cards in her plump hands. "Vivien Leigh and Clark Gable." She rolled her eyes in mock ecstasy. "I loved him in *It Happened One Night* with Claudette Colbert."

Edna Elway, in a charitable mood, suppressed the impulse to point out that there was no end of movie actors whom Irmgard loved—Robert Taylor, Jimmy Stewart, Cary Grant—the list went on and on. Irmgard was the only person of her acquaintance who actually bought film magazines at the drug store.

Edna picked up the cards dealt by Harry Wheeler, her partner. Seventeen points. The cards were running good. She hummed "Falling in Love with Love" and waited her turn to bid.

And so the hours passed, with the adults taking time from bridge and from eating to play Monopoly and Parcheesi, the Royal Game of India, with Sally. They took her skating and to Bacal's hill behind the football field where children brought their Flexible Flyers.

In the end, Sally hadn't told the family what she'd learned about Santa Claus. The grandparents spoke of him as of a much

71

loved uncle, producing details of his life and affairs until he seemed more real than Sally's distant cousins.

Flicking ash from an expensive cigar into a heavy glass ashtray, Grandpa Elway explained, "He has those red suits tailor-made by a fellow in downtown St. Paul. Bert Broder. Seventh Street. Wonderful with the tape measure, Broder. Came out from Philadelphia in '21." Grandpa Elway had taken his medical training at the University of Minnesota in Minneapolis, and he prided himself on his familiarity with the Cities. St. Paul tailors; Minneapolis restaurants.

"I wouldn't know about that," Grandma Wheeler said, pulling her upper lip tight to prevent a smile, "but Mrs. Claus . . . Clara . . . is a shirttail relation of some Telfords over in Marshalltown, Iowa. That I do know." She folded her hand of cards on the table and picked through the dish of mixed nuts searching for a pecan. "The Marshalltown Telfords are all real active in the American Legion. Isn't that so, Harry?"

"Hell, yes," said the wiry little terrier of a man. "Real active. Heard 'em mention Claus more than once. Likes a glass of beer now and again, they told me."

Although all this recounting and characterizing was pleasant, Sally did not feel easy about misleading everyone. Neither was she prepared to disappoint them however. Clearly, Santa meant a great deal to the grown-ups.

On Christmas morning, she made a point to rise early; pull on her pink chenille robe and her pink satin slippers with shearling cuffs, which Grandma Elway had brought from Mankato; and steal downstairs. When she caught sight of the bride doll and play stove and aluminum cooking set (with utensils and bowls and pie tins and cake pans and rolling pin) and child-sized cupboard filled with tiny pretend boxes and cans of food, she let out a squeal, as planned, and rushed to the tree, pulling the bride doll from its box and the pretend food from the cupboard, scattering her pelf, like a child who believed in Santa.

Snatching up her stocking, she emptied the candy and fruit on the rug, then glanced up with rehearsed surprise and joy to note the family gathering at the foot of the stairs.

"Come see what Santa brought!"

Mrs. Navarin, behind the big checkout desk, was date-stamping books for Mrs. Stillman.

"I've been hoping to see you," Mrs. Stillman exclaimed as Sally came in, pulling off her cap and mittens. "I was so proud of your narration in the Christmas Program."

Sally set her galoshes on the rubber mat near the radiator. Her cheeks burned pleasantly from the compliment and the warmth of the room.

"I told Hillyard," Mrs. Stillman continued, "'Sally has a future on the stage or the silver screen.' I wish he could have seen you. Would you bring your script and come visit us while school's out?"

"This afternoon?"

"We'll be home all afternoon."

Sally hung her coat on a hook and wandered through the big double doorway into the children's room. The public library had once been the private residence of Mrs. Juliet Lundeen of the Lundeen's Dry Goods Lundeens. When she grew old, Grandma Lundeen, as she was called, gave her house to the town for a public library and built a Queen Anne style cottage for herself.

Sally drifted around the children's room, searching for something a mother might find engrossing. She slipped several likely looking books from the shelves, among them *A Little Princess* by Frances Hodgson Burnett and *Little House on the Prairie* by Laura Ingalls Wilder.

Mrs. Navarin strolled into the children's room. "Can I help you find something?" she asked, sitting down on the low table, next to the books Sally had pulled from the shelves. Her long legs stretched out in front of her, ankles crossed.

With her black-olive eyes, sooty hair coiled at the nape of her neck, and skin the color of tea-dipped linen, Desiree Navarin looked like Romany royalty. And indeed she was of Hungarian, if not Romany, extraction.

Although not an insignificant number of Harvester residents bore eastern European names, Desiree Navarin was from Biwabik in Iron Range country. This fact, coupled with her exotic features, explained perhaps why many in town considered her, well, foreign. The Iron Range was, who could deny it, different from southern Minnesota.

"I was looking for books about people getting well."

Mrs. Navarin looked sideways at Sally from large, hooded eyes, opaque and mysterious, the lids like heavy drapery, guarding, perhaps, knowledge or opinions alien to Harvester.

"Well," Mrs. Navarin said, glancing at the books Sally had pulled, "Mr. Carrisford in *A Little Princess* has trouble getting over brain fever, because he's very sad."

"But does he get well?"

"At the end, because of Sara, the Little Princess." She picked up the book in question, sighted along the top of it, and blew, as if blowing away dust, though none rose up. "But, if I tell you how the books end, will you want to read them?" Mrs. Navarin asked, returning *A Little Princess* to the stack on the table.

Ignoring the question, Sally asked, "Is there a book where somebody gets well because somebody else reads to them?"

Mrs. Navarin leaned back, placing her hands on the table behind her, propping herself in a casual, triangular attitude. "Do you have a friend who's sick?" she inquired lightly, as if merely in passing.

A friend who was sick. Of course. A friend who was sick. Sally nodded.

"Offhand, I don't know of a book where reading makes someone well. But let me think about it. In the meantime, there are children's books with sick people in them. *Heidi* comes to mind and *The Secret Garden*," she said and rose to pull them from the shelves.

Laying them beside the pile of books on the table, she told Sally, "See what you think of those," and returned to the tall desk where the Wheelers' neighbor, Mrs. Bensinger, waited to check out *Back Street* by Fanny Hurst.

Sally opened *The Secret Garden,* which she and her father had checked out of the library last year. It started right off with terrible illness, cholera. *Perfect.*

At ten past three, Mrs. Stillman carried Sally's wraps to the bedroom, assuring her, "Hillyard will be so pleased."

It was difficult, at first, to tell if Hilly was pleased. Still wearing his pajamas and his robe, he sat in the green rocker, hands tucked between his knees, and listened or, at any rate, stared without speaking at a spot just above Sally's head. When Sally reached the place in the Mandarins' story where the tornado swept down on their farm, crushing and twisting and uprooting it, Hilly frowned and pulled his head down into his hunched shoulders as if expecting debris to fly at him.

Should she stop? Sally wondered. Instead, she hurried past the tornado, and Hilly soon discovered that none of the characters had been killed or badly injured. Still, he seemed to hold his breath as she described the grim hardships the Mandarins suffered, and the indifference most villagers felt toward them. Reaching the winter day when Anastasia and Bartholomew decided to make presents for Boris, Sally noticed that Hilly had relaxed only a little, his shoulders were still hunched, and his eyes, as dark as unlighted windows, were fixed elsewhere, as if Sally and the story had powers that he feared. And although she was sorry to distress him, Sally was struck anew by the effect she could have.

The Christmas Eve celebration in the Mandarins' stable, with food and presents and warm feelings all around, loosened Hilly's shoulders and even raised a little smile. When Sally read, "A warm hearth, a warm heart, and a merry, merry, merry Christmas," directing them at Hilly, he repeated, "Warm heart" and "Merry, merry."

If Hilly had a car and it wouldn't start, Sally believed that she could have made him forget.

It was nearly dark when Helen Stillman held the storm door for Sally. "Should I call your mother to let her know you're on the way?"

"No. She won't worry."

Until recent months Stella *had* worried. She'd worried about everything. And once she'd got hold of a worry, she'd worry it to tatters. But lately she had stopped worrying. The burden of worry had grown so great, she had let it fall from her back, and she could not raise it up again.

The house was dark. Sally found the switch inside the kitchen door. Cold, indifferent light bore down from the ceiling fixture.

Yanking off her galoshes, she crossed to the breakfast nook and pulled the tiny chain on the wall lamp with its red and white shade trimmed with red pompom fringe. A glow fell across the table. Next, she flicked on the hooded light on the electric stove and, finally, climbing onto a chair, the frosted fixture above the sink. Extinguishing the overhead globe, she stood by the backdoor and looked at the kitchen. This was the cozy way it had once looked, before Stella had changed.

Upstairs, the hall light fell across the unmade bed where Stella lay catty-cornered, wearing the sweater and skirt Sally had chosen for her that morning.

"Mommy?"

Stella turned her head away from the light.

"Should I make cheese sandwiches?" Sally asked.

Her mother murmured something indistinguishable.

"It's after six. The whistle blew."

Stella started to speak, muttered something about sleep, and drew a forearm across her eyes. "I'm tired."

"Do you want your nightgown?"

Beneath the forearm, Stella shook her head side to side, back and forth, back and forth, as if the movement were satisfying.

At length, she dragged herself to a sitting position, thrusting a hand through thick, salt-and-pepper hair that had not been brushed. Normally springy and ribbed with waves, tonight it lay limp on her shoulders.

Sally fetched the hairbrush on the bureau, climbed onto the rumpled bed beside her mother, and cautiously began to pull the brush through the long hanks of coarse, heavy hair. "Does that hurt?"

"No." Stella tipped her head back, allowing Sally to reach to the hairline in front and pull in long, continuous, hatcheling strokes. "It's . . . restful."

Stella's hair gave off a stale smell of scalp oil.

When she had brushed every strand, Sally found a piece of claret colored ribbon in the top drawer of the bureau. The ribbon had not been laundered or pressed in many wearings, but she lay it on the bureau, pressing out wrinkles with the palms of her hands. Gathering Stella's hair at the nape of her neck, Sally tied it with the ribbon.

When they had eaten cheese sandwiches and a can of apricots by the yellowy light of the red and white lamp, Sally cleared the table. She scraped their leavings into the garbage can under the sink, emptied that can into the larger one by the garage, and washed up the few dishes.

"Would you like a bubble bath with the Miss Twinkle bath set that Grandma gave me?" she asked, grasping her mother's hand and pulling her up. "It makes so many bubbles, it's like a movie-star bath. What movie star do you want to be? I pretend I'm Merle Oberon when I use it."

Bubbles, whispering, hissing, rose in a thick batt of pink froth, nearly to the rim of the tub when Stella stepped into the perfumed water.

"Should I scrub your back?"

"That would be nice."

Sally soaped her mother's back with a bar of Lux and a cloth, then untied the claret colored ribbon and worked Miss Twinkle apple blossom shampoo into Stella's scalp, scooping up hand-fuls of water to create lather until a swirling turban of hair en-circled Stella's head.

"That looks like one of Grandma Elway's hats," Sally giggled.

Stella wanted to soak for a while, she said, and Sally advised, "Keep the water warm so you don't catch cold." Closing the door on the steamy bathroom, she went to find *A Little Princess* and practice reading chapter 1.

Stella lay back against the tub and closed her eyes. Tears, vile and poisonous, burned behind her eyes and oozed from their corners. Almost daily she examined her life, searching for the tragedy or deprivation out of which the inexhaustible pain arose.

Her mother had always been finical and bourgeois, but she'd been affectionate and loyal too. Dad? Bluff and inarticulate, but supportive and generous.

Gustavus Adolphus College in St. Peter, Minnesota, less than twenty miles from home, had been what she'd expected: Protestant, traditional, vaguely familiar, a place of wide lawns and matronly buildings.

She had drifted through an English major, which, like the college itself, had seemed familiar, wonted, neither surprising nor disjunctive.

In her sophomore year, she had met Donald, a history major with plans for graduate degrees. He had a job as a night janitor at the school. The first member of his family to attend college, he had reminded her of a crusader riding eastward, the banner of a PhD. borne before him. Excelsior.

Then, in early January of their senior year, right after the holiday break, Donald's mother had called. His seventeen-year-old sister, Florence, was hospitalized with pneumonia. She was asking for Donald.

He left immediately, hitchhiking, which was the only way he could get there before the middle of the next day, and he'd been lucky. A streetcar conductor from Minneapolis, himself hightailing it home to Omaha for a family emergency, had picked him up outside Mankato and left him in front of the hospital in Worthington.

But Flossie's temperature had soared to a hundred and six, and she'd been dead an hour when Donald sprinted across the waiting room to the information desk.

Stella had drawn closer to Donald after his sister's death, trying to talk him out of abandoning plans for graduate school. Not going on to school was, so far as she knew, the only neurotic and self-destructive thing he'd ever done. Would she and Donald have married if Flossie had lived?

Apart from that death, their lives had been notably free of tragedy and upheaval, very ordinary. "We're the Great *Washed* of the world," she'd once remarked laughingly. Now, scratching daily amongst the detritus of personal history, she came away without answers for her immense sadness.

When she had dried off, Stella slipped an arm into the sleeve of her robe. Trembling and feeling for the toilet behind her, she let herself down onto the icy lid, pulling the pitilessly cold satin robe close.

"Have you noticed how the mothers all seem to die?" Stella asked as Sally read the first few pages of *Heidi.* *"A Little Princess, The Secret Garden,* and now *Heidi."* She stared at the bedroom windows, eyes moist.

"The fathers die too," Sally quickly pointed out, then lay the book discreetly aside as if recalling something she wanted to discuss. Scrambling to come up with a topic, she asked, "Are we going to deliver May baskets?"

"May baskets?"

"Next Wednesday's May Day. Lark and everybody are delivering May baskets. Even Beverly, because Mrs. Erhardt's going to help her. Should I ask Mrs. Erhardt if she'll help me?"

"No. No. But I . . . How will we deliver them? Daddy won't be home till Friday."

After running over the Rabel's dog, Stella had refused to drive again, and they had long ago sold her old Mercury.

"Mrs. Erhardt's going to drive Lark and Beverly in the back of Mr. Erhardt's pickup. She'll let me ride, too, if I ask."

Stella's tears which had only threatened, now began to fall, and she threw her arms in the air and waved them wildly for Sally to leave. As the door closed, she snatched her hair in great hanks, tossing her head on the pillow in a paroxysm of envy. *Arlene Erhardt.*

When the frenzy subsided, Stella rocked her head slowly side to side. Rarely did she react with such violence. She'd imagined herself beyond violent feelings. And mostly she was, only infrequently rising to the surface of her watery world to snap at the air before sinking down again into the half-light.

The liquid sadness in which she swam flowed, she imagined, out of her female parts, springing from the same source as the blood.

The blood.

When she was thirty-eight and Sally not quite five, her body had lost control of its own blood. A week might pass between periods or two days or a month. When she bled, it was as if from a spigot. She grew weak, faint. In the middle of the night, she woke to find herself lying in a pool of blood, and panic squeezed her until she could not breathe.

Hot flashes surprised her day and night. Sweat, like blood, poured from her until she could not stand up. Her hands shook; her knees crumpled.

She had tried to deal with it without making a spectacle of herself. Eventually she'd approached first her mother and then Donald's, looking for reassurance, advice. But each swore that her own "change" had been a brief annoyance, nothing more: six months of hot flashes, irregular periods for a year.

"You mustn't coddle yourself," her mother had warned. "Ignore it, and it'll pass."

After a year of menopause, Stella had made an appointment with Dr. White, who assured her that the symptoms and duration were a nuisance but not unusual or fatal and suggested calf's liver once a week and an iron pill once a day.

What she had not described to the doctor was the sadness that, like the blood, flowed out of control from deep inside her.

Another year passed with little change. Her body was coming apart, she felt, breaking down, turning on her, emptying itself of blood and water, as if she were to be preserved in a bizarre state of desiccation.

She could no longer look at calf's liver, and she stopped taking the iron because it constipated her, and the enemas it necessitated were finally unendurable. What cooking she did, she now did in an iron skillet, a measure she'd heard Arlene Erhardt name as a way to prevent anemia.

Donald was aware of her physical symptoms but misunderstood the sadness, interpreting it as a failure on his part. He advised Stella to talk to her father about the "change." After all, Herb was a doctor.

Stella recoiled. Talk to her father about her body? Worse, about her mind? It was unthinkable. He could do no more for her than Dr. White, yet, being her father, he would feel a deep responsibility.

She began seeing a doctor in St. Bridget, but when her complaints persisted beyond what he considered reasonable boundaries of time and custom, he suggested in an avuncular manner that she was perhaps dramatizing? Playing for sympathy? Even, possibly, avoiding her husband's attentions? Sometimes menopause did rather drag on, but if a woman got involved in church work or some other worthy pastime, she would soon find her way through it.

Stella went to pieces in the consulting room. "If *you* don't believe me . . . ," she cried, tears filling her eyes.

"Now, now," the doctor muttered gruffly, embarrassed by her emotion, patting her shoulder, "get hold of yourself, girl, get hold of yourself," and he pulled a clean handkerchief from his pocket and handed it to her.

Donald was waiting for her in the car. She slid in, closed the door and pulled her winter coat around her, feeling entirely alone, cut off from everyone, especially from the person she'd once been.

She wept for her dead self, for her child, for her husband.

For the war in Europe and the war in China. For the starving children in India and the men who couldn't find jobs. She wept for stray cats and dead dogs.

One thing she knew. She would not go to another doctor.

At the end of the hall, behind a closed door, Sally arranged her biggest doll, a nearly life-size Raggedy Ann, on the chair, then climbed into bed, mussing the covers around her.

She smiled at the doll and reached to pat its arm.

"Thank you for reading that story, Sally," she said. "All the little girls in the books you read are wonderful, but none of them is as wonderful as my own little girl."

Pause.

"No, it's true." Flicking back the covers, she announced, "I'm feeling so good, I'm going to get up and make pancakes and cocoa for supper."

April 26, 1940

After school the next day, Sally stopped at Mather's Five and Dime and bought little paper cups, pale green crepe paper, pipe cleaners, and pink and green paper ribbon.

"May baskets?" Mr. Mather inquired as he rang up the purchases on the huge brass-trimmed cash register.

Sally nodded.

"They gonna have a maypole up at the school?" A faint, not unpleasant odor of whiskey and mints insinuated itself between Mr. Mather and Sally.

"Yes, sir." On the south lawn of the school the senior girls were already practicing their maypole dance. Miss Bailey's class was making crepe-paper flower coronets to wear on their heads in the May procession.

"Mrs. Mather," he said, jerking his head toward the back room of the store where his wife was perhaps unpacking stock, "says we shouldn't have May Day celebrations any more. She says May Day is a Ruskie day now, and we shouldn't look like we're celebrating their revolution.

"But I say there were May Day celebrations before there were Ruskies or Communist revolutions, and I don't think we oughta let 'em ruin our good time. What d' *you* say?" All this he opined while counting Sally's change into her hand.

"Yes, sir." Sally nodded, pocketed her change, and left, trying not to look as if she were hurrying. Mr. Mather could keep you visiting for half an hour if you weren't careful, especially when whiskey and mints were in the air.

At Anderson's Candy and Ice Cream next to the Majestic Theater, Sally spent ten minutes selecting jelly beans, gumdrops, and Spanish peanuts to fill the May baskets.

Katherine Albers and her mother came in while Mrs. Anderson was filling Sally's order. Katherine was the queen of second grade, and her mother the queen of Harvester, according to Beverly who disliked perfect people on principle. Mrs. Albers always looked as fresh as newly ironed clothes, and she smiled without showing her teeth, a habit Sally considered extremely genteel. Katherine's big hair bow remained crisp and unsullied all day and sat on top of her head like a reward for being good.

Neither Katherine nor Mrs. Albers ever lost her temper in public, and Mrs. Erhardt said that Mrs. Albers' slip strap never broke — she was that kind of woman. This had not been said in a mean way, but wonderingly, as if it were a phenomenon Mrs. Erhardt appreciated without comprehending.

Sally was torn between jealousy and pity where Katherine was concerned. The calm flawlessness of Katherine and of her family life was enviable. Her father was a lawyer who did not have to be on the road Monday through Friday, and her mother was president of the Methodist Ladies Aide.

Katherine's perfect blonde finger curls grazed her shoulders, and her second teeth had come in looking as if they'd always been there. Her cream-colored skin was unfreckled, her blue eyes extravagantly fringed, their gaze so impassive as to be remote.

And yet, while Sally envied the Albers' utter respectability (she could not imagine Mrs. Albers hanging around the house in a dirty dress, crying about Heidi's mother), she appreciated that perfection was a full-time job, not undertaken lightly. You had to be powerfully impelled.

"Is the candy for May baskets?" Mrs. Albers asked Sally.

"Yes."

"Those look like good choices," she said and smiled her closemouthed smile. "I'm sure everyone will want to receive one of your May baskets."

"Thank you."

"Say hello to your mother. Tell her we miss her at P.T.A." A sudden fear that she'd said something awkward or hurtful marred her buttery glance. "She's always been such an addition to the meetings."

Well, it was obvious the whole town knew about Stella. Sally paid and plucked up her several small bags from the counter. "Good-bye." She hoped that it was not rude to dash away, but in Mrs. Albers' presence she was always nervous lest some failure on her part should mar the occasion.

"How about *The Railway Children*?" Mrs. Navarin asked, pulling that book from the library shelf.

"The mother doesn't die?" Sally asked.

Mrs. Navarin shook her head and handed the book to Sally. "She gets sick, but she doesn't die." Mr. Navarin had just come into the library, wearing his green work uniform and sweeping the Sinclair cap from his head. Mrs. Navarin went to meet him.

Mr. Navarin owned the Sinclair gas station by the depot where Lark Erhardt lived. He was a tall, big-shouldered man whose belly was beginning to hang over his belt a bit, and whose blond hair was thinning back from his forehead in two deep vees.

People liked Mr. Navarin. Although he was not college-educated like his wife, he was respected in town. Sally's father had once spoken of him as "shrewd and fair."

He leaned a muscular forearm on the high desk and spoke to Mrs. Navarin. A word here and there reached Sally, and she gathered that Mr. Navarin and some of his friends were going to play cards out at the Navarin's cottage on Sioux Woman Lake that night. Mrs. Navarin nodded, spoke a few words, and smiled. Her husband chucked her affectionately under the chin, thrust his cap toward her in a gallant little flourish, and left.

Sally gathered up her May Day purchases as well as *The Railway Children.*

Mrs. Navarin removed the card from the pocket inside the book and pressed the dater down on the appropriate line. *Kachung.* Sliding *The Railway Children* across the desk, she looked long at Sally.

"Your sick friend will enjoy this book."

Late April and May — 1940

That evening, Sally pulled the slipper chair close to the bed and had read several pages of *The Railway Children* before her mother inquired vaguely and without curiosity, *"Heidi?"*

"I can't find *Heidi*," Sally told her. "I lost it."

It seemed all one to Stella.

But, to Sally, *The Railway Children* was perfect. The mother didn't die, and she was an inspiration. Although the father was wrongly sent to prison, the mother kept her spirits up, worked hard, and guided the family through their misfortunes. Would Stella see that a person could pull up her socks and be a normal person if she just tried hard enough?

The next day, which was Saturday, Sally ran the Hoover, dusted, and picked up. Donald rose early, gathered the laundry, and sent it down the chute.

Helping her father hang the clothes on the line, Sally shook each item out and handed it to him along with the necessary clothespins from the bag swinging ahead of them on the strong steel wire.

"Can you help me with my May baskets?" Despite her mother's assurance yesterday that she would help, Sally would not rely on her.

"When?"

"This afternoon?"

"You'll have to show me what to do, and remember, I'm kind of clumsy with frilly stuff."

Mrs. Bensinger next door came out her backdoor to shake a throw rug. "Want to wear my apron?" she teased Donald and laughed a laugh meant to sound good-natured and chummy, but which succeeded only in sounding shrill and spiteful.

Donald jammed a clothespin on the line with such force it flew apart. Sally handed him another and picked up the pieces of the first from the grass. They finished hanging the clothes in silence.

The May basket materials lay spread out on the dining-room table. Donald sat on one side, Sally opposite, instructing him how to cut the circles of pale green crepe paper. Sally herself punched holes on either side of the paper cups. One end of a pipe cleaner was inserted into one of the holes, bent on the inside so that it wouldn't slip out again, and the other end of the pipe cleaner was inserted into the other hole, thus forming a handle, like the handle of a pail.

"How will you deliver all these?" Donald asked when he saw that there were to be twenty-five baskets.

"Mrs. Erhardt's taking me and Lark and Beverly in the back of the pickup."

He nodded. "Do you give to everyone in your class?"

"Yes. And also Miss Bailey and Mrs. Navarin and Father Delias and Mrs. Stillman and Hilly."

"And your classmates deliver baskets to you?"

"Yes."

"But what if you're not here? What if you're out delivering when they come?"

"They leave them on the front steps and ring the doorbell and run. And if I'm not here, then I don't get to run after them and catch them and give them a kiss." She looked up from her work to see if Donald understood. "But not everybody delivers theirs at the same time so usually I get to catch quite a few people."

"If you catch a boy, do you kiss him?"

"Daddy."

"Well, do you? What's so bad about that?"

She took a long minute fixing a pink bow on the cup in her hands. "Welllll, it depends on who the boy is," she said at last.

"Not every boy gets a kiss?"

"Especially not Delmore Preuss."

"Why not Delmore Preuss?"

"Because he hits me and says mean things to me."

"Then he must like you," Donald told her, setting a cup on a circle of crepe paper to measure it.

"If he liked me, he'd be nice to me."

"Some boys are afraid to be nice to a girl for fear the other boys will tease them, so instead, they do mean things."

"That's not the kind of boy I like."

"What kind of boy do you like?"

"I like boys who tell me I run really fast, because I *do*."

"Do you know any boys like that?"

"Hmmm. Maybe. But I'm not going to say their names."

Donald laughed, and Sally did too.

Stella, in her robe and slippers, was descending the stairs. Through the archway between living and dining rooms she saw Sally and Donald, heads bent together, laughing. Pausing to watch, to listen to the chatter, she clutched at her middle, a look of hunger pinching her face. Silently, she turned and climbed the stairs again.

The first of May dawned gray as doomsday. The children complained and stamped their feet, disappointed. Several kindergarteners cried. If it rained, the school May Day celebration would be cancelled. The janitors had risen early to erect the maypole, and the senior girls were already decorating it when the younger children came to school. The celebration was scheduled to begin at two.

"If it rains," Miss Bailey told her second graders, "we'll have a party in our room and wear our coronets and play games and drink up every drop of the Kool-Aid."

At every opportunity, pupils wandered to the windows to check the sky, then slunk back to their seats when its threat was confirmed. Not enough blue to make a pair of Dutchman's britches, as Miss Baily was wont to say.

The only good thing about the celebration being cancelled, if it was, was that Stella couldn't possibly show up, not that Sally really expected her to, but there was always the slim chance. Stella's weeping over a child's loss in one of the competitions or over the beauty of the senior girls dancing around the maypole would ruin the day. Even so, Sally didn't quite want the event cancelled. Which was just as well, because a breeze sprang up a little before one o'clock, pushing the clouds away to the east.

At a quarter to two, the classes began lining up one after the other in the hallways, kindergarteners first, their coronets already slewing this way and that. The kindergarten led the procession, down the steps and out the big double doors, held open by two senior girls, Estelle Preuss and Martha Everson, barefoot and looking virginally pagan. Each wore a white twin-bed sheet draped gracefully from her shoulders and tied around the waist with gold satin rope.

Along the wide walk they came, class after class, singing "Beautiful Dreamer," grade-school girls in pretty summery dresses, boys in short pants and white shirts, all wearing paper-flower coronets. Behind them marched the upper classes, dressed similarly, except for the seniors who came last, girls in gowns like Estelle Preuss and Martha Everson's, boys in white tunics, which, like the gowns, appeared to have been contrived from bed sheets but were folded in a clever way that made them shorter and more masculine.

Halfway to the street, the classes began peeling off, left and right, halting at last when they were assembled in a crescent-shaped choir before which Mr. Hansen, the music director, stood with his pitch pipe at the ready.

Between the street and the choir, townspeople, mostly women and toddlers since it was a workday, lolled around on the grass to listen as the school children launched into "Believe Me If All Those Endearing Young Charms," followed by "I'll Take You Home Again, Kathleen" and other songs from Mr. Hansen's repertoire.

Babies stood on unsure legs swaying to the music until at length they toppled onto their diapered behinds. Mothers hummed along to familiar tunes, and grannies sat on folding camp chairs, the heels of their sensible black shoes keeping time to the simple rhythms.

Across the way, at the library, Mrs. Navarin opened the windows, while in the street, cars slowed and some pulled to the curb. Mr. Hardesty from the *Standard Ledger* slipped amongst the young people, snapping pictures for next week's paper. And almost none of the singers forgot the words to the songs.

When the choir concluded, the senior girls in single file, bare feet gliding through the grass like pale fish through green water, proceeded to the maypole, singing thinly but sweetly "Tip Toe Thru the Tulips with Me."

The first eight girls to reach the maypole each took up one of the pastel satin streamers adorned with tiny paper flowers and began a slow, dipping and rising, hesitating and swooping dance around the pole while the remaining girls sang "Greensleeves." When the song had been sung through once, the dancers, one by one, handed the ribbons to the next eight, and the song continued until everyone had danced. As the last notes died away and the senior girls curtsied, the crowd gathered on the lawn clapped and called out, "Wonderful!" and "Hooray for Sarah!" or Nancy or Estelle.

The younger children jumped up and down and Yippeeed because it was time for the games and races and other competitions to begin and time also to sell Kool-Aid and cookies and popcorn with sale proceeds going to benefit European orphans.

Each child could enter three competitions. Sally entered a

relay race with Lark and Beverly, as well as the gunnysack race and the archery competition. Never mind that she knew nothing about archery; the arrows had rubber suction tips and the bows were no longer than your arm.

Although all her arrows fell short of the target and she came in fifth in the gunnysack race, behind three sixth-grade boys and a fifth-grade girl, Sally, along with Lark and Beverly, won their relay race, and each received a blue ribbon with a gold star glued to it.

When their competitions were done, the girls waited in line to dance around the maypole. The satin streamers were grimed, and the tiny flowers had long since been plucked, but it was still a maypole and tomorrow it would be gone.

Before they'd got their fill of maypole dancing, Mrs. Erhardt came for them with the pickup. Lark and Beverly's May baskets were already in the back of the truck, so Mrs. Erhardt swung by Sally's house to pick up hers, which were lined up in two large cake pans.

Starting at the north end of town, they wove their way back and forth across Harvester, each leaving a basket beside the door of a child or favored adult, ringing the bell or knocking, then dashing back to the truck before they could be caught and kissed.

When they reached the big Barnstable house, Brenda's yellow wagon was in the drive. The girls crept up the long gravel drive, peering about to see if Neddy were hiding behind a tree or bush ready to jump out and kiss them when they left the baskets on the front porch.

That would not be Hoyle, Neddy had decided, and so he'd waited in the foyer, pulling aside the lace curtain now and then to peek out one of the tall windows bracketing the front door. From the endless chatter and giggling at school, he'd learned that Mrs. Erhardt was chauffering Lark and Beverly and Sally on their deliveries.

Mr. Erhardt's pickup truck turned the corner onto Catalpa.

Neddy let go the curtain. The truck pulled to the curb in front of his house, and Lark, Beverly, and Sally climbed down from the back, each with a basket in her hand. He could just make them out through the lace. Sally was wearing a pale green dress.

Carefully, silently, he turned the knob so that the door was unlatched. Surely that small advantage wouldn't be unfair. The girls were on the porch. He pulled back from the window. "Brnnnng" pealed the bell in the kitchen as Lark pushed the button beside the door.

Throwing the door wide, Neddy ran, faster than he'd ever run, his eyes trained on the green dress. Down the steps and down the front walk. He was gaining. Sally had a hand on the gate of the truck. And then he caught her by the waist. Planting a kiss on her cheek, he backed away, gasping "You're a fast runner."

Once a week, the Majestic Theater had a Bank Nite drawing after the movie and gave away prizes such as a set of drinking glasses or a cash prize of five dollars. The big final drawing each year was held the first week in June before the theater closed for the warm summer months.

The day after Mrs. Erhardt won the two-hundred-and-fifty-dollar grand prize for 1940, she marched downtown and bought a secondhand white Ford coupe for a hundred dollars, then took out an ad in the *Standard Ledger* for her new business, Erhardt's Typing Service.

And the day after she bought the car, she drove by the Wheeler house to take Stella and Sally for a spin. Stella in her nightgown was in the basement sifting through a footlocker full of keepsakes and souvenirs from her girlhood.

When Sally came running down the stairs to tell her that Mrs. Erhardt wanted to take them for a ride, Stella said, "I'm in the middle of this."

"In the middle of what?"

"Well, I can't explain. It's difficult to explain."

On the floor around her was spread the fading history of herself: report cards and prizes for penmanship; autograph books; dance cards and pressed corsages. A snapshot, brittle and ghostly, revealed a calm and confident little girl, holding a beach ball and kneeling in the sand in front of several other girls who seemed to be at a summer camp, judging by the cabin behind them. In another photo, Stella was a tall, stunning and stunned looking adolescent in a tulle and taffeta dance gown, standing before the fireplace in the Elway living room. On the back was scrawled in Edna Elway's hand "Job's Daughters' Dance."

When she had driven past her friend Bernice McGivern's house tooting the horn and down Main Street, waving to people, Mrs. Erhardt turned the car toward the highway and headed south. With the windows rolled down and air streaming through, blowing the words back toward town, she sang in a strong but tuneless voice, "Put on your Old Gray Bonnet with the blue ribbon on it, While I hitch old Dobbin to the shay."

Lark and Sally joined in, "Through the fields of clover, we'll drive up to Dover," as a meadowlark swung down across their path and up to a telephone wire where he watched them roll along down the road to Bussey's Corner.

"On our Golden Wedding Day!" the three sang out, and Mrs. Erhardt turned the little white Ford into the drive of the old filling station where a pop cooler stood beside the screen door, filled with bottles of soda pop and blocks of ice. Driving past the pumps, Mrs. Erhardt pulled the car under a stand of cottonwoods and flicked off the engine with a flourish.

"Everybody out!"

The lower portion of the screen door bellied out where Brownie, Mr. Bussey's big mongrel dog, lay against it. You always had to step over Brownie to get to the counter to pay. Since Brownie was fond of chasing customers' cars, but not smart enough to find his way back, he must in consequence be kept inside.

In the summer, he lay by the door watching cars wheel past. His ears pricked and his nose twitched. His tail straightened meaningfully, and the muscles along his tired old flank hardened. As a car disappeared into the highway's lonely vanishing point, he sighed and shuddered and lay his head back on his paws.

When Mrs. Erhardt had paid the fifteen cents for three Orange Crushes and they had all petted Brownie, she led the girls to the picnic table under the cottonwoods, provided by Mr. Bussey for travelers.

Sally and Lark had each drunk half their pop when a pale yellow station wagon with wood trim drove up and parked beside the Ford, dwarfing it.

"Neddy," Lark said and turned to see if indeed Neddy Barnstable was with his mother. The yellow wagon was the only one of its kind in Harvester and belonged to Brenda Barnstable, wife of the local veterinarian.

From the driver's side, Brenda emerged wearing a tan twill skirt and tan and white polo shirt. Neddy, who followed, wore tan twill shorts and a shirt like his mother's. Behind him came another boy, Neddy's size but with dark brown hair and brown eyes.

Brenda lifted an index finger in recognition of Arlene as she headed toward the pop cooler, her smooth blonde pageboy stirring as a breeze caught at it. Neddy slid onto the picnic bench opposite Sally, the other boy beside him.

"This is my Cousin Cole," Neddy told the others.

"What kind of pop?" Brenda called.

"Root beer."

"Cole?"

He shrugged.

"Where you been?" Lark asked Neddy.

"St. Bridget."

"What'd you do?"

"Watched ladies play golf," he said without enthusiasm.

"Your mama?"

He nodded and stared at his folded hands. "And Cole's mama."

"Wasn't it any fun?"

"Not very much."

"Couldn't you stay home with your Grandma Barnstable?"

Brenda was approaching and Neddy didn't answer.

"Did you just watch and that's all?"

"He found my lost balls," Brenda told her, handing each of the boys a root beer.

A slender twig on one of the lesser branches of a Minneapolis milling family, Brenda had met Edward Barnstable through a sorority friend. A romantic short story in *Red Book* about a veterinarian and a beautiful blonde young woman must have influenced her, she decided later, because she married Ed and came to live with him in Harvester.

The couple lived in Ed's grandparents' house, sharing it with his widowed mother, an eventuality not thoroughly anticipated by Brenda before her marriage.

Ed's grandfather had been one of two Barnstable brothers, Edward and Philip, who had moved to southern Minnesota from Pennsylvania after the Civil War. Philip, the older by two years, had settled in the town of St. Bridget and launched Barnstable General Goods, which became Barnstable's Department Store. In addition to dry goods, he had invested in the local bank, grain elevator, and lumberyard.

His son, Pierce, added to the family holdings the bank in Red Berry and a privately held telephone company in St. Bridget. Pierce's son, Hal, currently oversaw the family fortune, which his boy, Coleman, sitting beside Neddy, would come into.

Edward, on the other hand, had settled in Harvester and "gone into land," investing in acreages as far south as St. Louis and as far west as Denver. For a number of years, both brothers prospered, each building, in his chosen town, an impressive home with broad porches and deep lawns.

But Edward eventually lost nearly everything in one of the many and inevitable land slumps, and his son, Edward Junior, was forced to make do with a land business of very little consequence.

Raised with an inordinate sense of what it meant to be a Barnstable, Edward Junior drove himself to drink and death at forty-two in a successful effort to hold onto the house and business.

The wife of Edward Senior and, later, the wife of Edward Junior loyally adhered to the Barnstable men's views regarding what it meant to be a Barnstable. They did not ask whence came these notions nor how solidly they might be grounded, but accepted the idea that Barnstables did not weep, fart, or beg.

Keeping up appearances was next to godliness, and though you might patch your petticoat until it looked like a crazy quilt, you did not dismiss the cleaning woman. Privately doing without while publicly maintaining face, the family struggled on until Young Edward, Edward Junior's son, came of age.

He sold the business to Dave Kolacky, who'd been running it since Edward Junior's untimely death, and enrolled in the University of Minnesota to become a veterinarian. His mother, who doted on him, was appalled and said it was a blessing that his grandmother had gone to her reward and couldn't see what had become of Barnstable Land Company. Think, she said to him, what his grandmother and she, his mother, had endured out of family loyalty and wifely duty.

Now that Ed, as he was called by all but his mother, supported her, Mabel Barnstable lived in greater ease of mind and body than she had in all the years since she'd married. Still, the old, known pain is hard to relinquish for the new, unfamiliar comfort. Pride and sacrifice and not letting the side down had been the air that she breathed for too many years to countenance change. They were what she was. And so while she agreed to a Hoover, she kept the carpet beater and each spring saw to it that the carpets were hauled out to the clothesline and flogged. She acquiesced to a Maytag but kept the washboard for her "personals." She disdained her daughter-in-law

Brenda's prodigality, which she deemed the result of never having "endured."

"Golf!" she sniffed.

In the eyes of Mabel, acquiring Brenda and selling Barnstable Land Company were Young Edward's only two sins. In the eyes of Harvester, Ed had committed only one sin.

"Brenda," Arlene Erhardt asked, "how's golf?" Arlene had neither the time nor the money for golf, but she did not entirely disdain it. It looked pleasant enough, though at times it had the appearance of a wall thrown up between the small handful of the comfortably off and the rest of Harvester, and she did not regret that those who played had to travel to St. Bridget to do it.

"Well, I'm no Patty Berg," Brenda told her, "but I finally broke a hundred." She sipped her Coca-Cola triumphantly.

"Neddy," Lark said, "would you and . . . Cole? like to come with Sally and me over by the fence and pick clover? You can take your grandma a bouquet."

Neddy rose and his cousin trailed behind, kicking imaginary rocks and huffing with displeasure.

"Cole's mom and dad are going to . . . where are they going?" Neddy turned back toward his cousin.

"British Columbia," the boy grumbled.

"British Columbia. So Cole's gonna stay with us for a week. He stays with us a lot."

Reaching the fence, the girls and Neddy began gathering clover. Standing some distance away, Cole thrust his fists deep into the pockets of his shorts and scowled across the fields.

With the children out of sight, Brenda asked, "Is that the little Wheeler girl?"

"Yes."

"How's her mother?"

"How *is* she?"

"The last time I saw her, about a year ago I guess, she'd run over the Rabel's dog, and she came lugging the damned thing

101

up to our front door for Ed to save. Of course it was dead as a doornail, but she was weeping and carrying on. 'Can't you do something? Please? Can't you *do* something?' she kept saying. I felt sorry for her, but she was out of her mind." Brenda arched a brow significantly. "Out of her mind. I just hope they don't have to take her to St. Peter. That would be a shame, especially with a child."

"I don't think you have to worry," Arlene lied. "I see her regularly, and she's not in any danger of St. Peter."

July 1940

In the mid-July heat and stillness, the lake smelled brackish and fishy. Not unpleasant. Organic. The sun burned the surface, sending the bullheads and catfish and pickerel to the cool, shadowy bottom to wait out the hot spell.

Donald spread the faded Indian blanket under a box-elder tree. When the girls had changed into swimsuits, they flopped down on it, dividing up its space and playing idly with the inoffensive box-elder bugs, creatures without sting or bite who took wing when child's play grew tiresome.

"Delmore Preuss says on his grandma's farm you can hear the corn grow," Sally told Donald, smoothing the blanket. "Is that true?"

"At night, when it's quiet, if the weather's hot like this, and there's been enough rain, you can hear it," Donald told her. "I used to work on my Uncle Ray's farm, down by LeMars, Iowa, when I was a kid in high school. I heard it."

"Godsakes," Beverly breathed.

He nodded.

"What's it sound like?" Lark wanted to know.

"Kind of a soft crackling."

"Godsakes," Beverly repeated. Mr. Wheeler knew everything.

When the girls wandered off to use the outdoor toilet, Donald peeled off his undershirt and leaned back on his elbows, surveying the beach.

Dozens of families had driven to the lake, looking for a

breeze. They'd be disappointed today. It was a day for paper fans and few words. The water was cool, though, and those with swimsuits would be in and out of it all afternoon.

Stella should have come along and sat in the shade waiting for a breeze, he thought. She hadn't even let him set up the oscillating fan. "It makes me nervous," she'd said when he'd suggested placing it on the bureau.

She hadn't looked at him. She rarely looked at him any more. If you looked at a person, you felt constrained to explain yourself, constrained to say, "I'm sorry I'm this way. I don't know when it will end. Will it end?"

The grandparents had come for the Fourth of July. "Something's got to be done," his mother had said several times, pulling him aside. "She ought to see a, what d'ya call them, a psychiatrist. Why don't her parents do something? He's a doctor, for crying-out-loud. What about Sally? And you, Bub?" Tearful anger seized her, and she fled to the bathroom.

Stella's mother knew, and so did Stella, what was being said. But the diminutive Edna drew herself up tall and taut, and set her mouth tight. Her daughter was not crazy. Stella was . . . frail and . . . melancholic. There was no history of anything more severe than that in her family. Nor, really, in Herb's either. His Aunt Constance had been *delicate* and hadn't gone out much, he said. That was all.

But Stella was not eating properly, and Edna thought that she ought to come and stay in Harvester for a while and look after things. Stella had gone to pieces at this suggestion. "I'll be all right!" she'd screamed.

Donald squinted across the bright lake.

From the outhouse the girls came flying, Beverly calling, "Race you to the raft."

"You always win," Lark complained.

"Sally almost beat me last time," Beverly rejoined, sprinting away on thin, strong, animal legs, Sally and Lark behind her, hand in hand.

"May I sit here?" Arlene Erhardt stood in the dusty grass beside the blanket. "I decided it was too hot to type after all. I'll do it tonight, if it cools off."

Donald shoved the girls' clothing to one side, and Mrs. Erhardt sat down, fanning herself with a hanky.

"I'm glad you changed your mind," he told her.

"Too bad Stella couldn't come. I know she sometimes gets awful headaches in the hot weather." She waved to the girls on the raft, then fished a tiny mirror from her purse and looked into it. "Oh, I'm a mess," she said and laughed, patting her hair down with her hand, "like something the cat dragged in."

Still wearing the cotton housedress she'd had on when Donald stopped to pick up Lark, Arlene looked as if she'd left the depot in a hurry. When she raised her hand to pat her hair, the short sleeve of her dress rode up, revealing bruises on her upper arm where someone's fingers had grabbed her. Donald looked away, sickened.

"It's not much cooler here than at home," she observed, "but at least there's, well, room. If a breeze came up, it'd know where to find you."

When he glanced at her again, he noticed that the rims of her nostrils were tinged pink, as if she'd been crying, and a tiny patch of excess face powder dusted one cheekbone, like frost. He would have liked to touch her cheek there, brush away the powder, but of course he wouldn't. It would be indelicate. It was only that she seemed so brave.

The realization that Arlene Erhardt had recently been manhandled, maybe this afternoon, drove all conversation from Donald's head. But she plugged the gaps.

"Half a block east of the Catholic church there's a big vacant lot that I want to build our house on. It's got plenty of shade trees. I don't know if you've noticed, but there's not a single tree around the depot. I think that's sad, don't you?"

"Yes."

"No one ought to live without a tree. Trees . . . even young

105

ones . . . are like old folks who give you comfort without advice.
When we build, we'll have a big backyard because the lot
is a deep one." She smoothed her skirt assiduously, as if self-
conscious at having come away in a wrinkled housedress.
"A house is going to make a big difference in our lives. It can
do that."

She knew she was rattling on like a fool. What must Donald
Wheeler think? She could not shut herself up. Her head felt hot
and light and empty inside, the way it always did when Willie
pushed her around, as if everything sensible and substantial in
it had flown out and was perched on a branch somewhere waiting for the storm to blow over.

Erhardt's Typing Service, her own car, and saving for a down
payment on a house—it all made Willie crazy. It was
unwomanly, he said, and a reflection on him.

"Sounds like your business has taken off," Donald told her.

"It's catching on. Mind you, I don't think I've got Rockefeller
worried yet."

He laughed a reassuring little laugh. He didn't seem to think
that she was trying to wear the pants in her family. It was a pity
that Stella was the way she was, unhappy. Donald Wheeler was
a kind man, intelligent, even attractive in a quiet, bookish sort
of way. She'd bet that he read novels, maybe even Hemingway
and Fitzgerald and writers like that.

Arlene had not been to college, but she kept track of what
was considered good reading, and Desiree Navarin put her
name on the list for the "good" books when they came into the
library. Steinbeck and John O'Hara and Willa Cather. Had
Donald Wheeler read *O! Pioneers* or *My Antonia*? Or *Tender Is the
Night*? She didn't think she could talk to him about *Tender Is the
Night*, but she would like to ask him what he thought of *To Have
and Have Not* by Ernest Hemingway.

She wouldn't ask however. To talk about novels seemed an
intimate thing, like touching. When people talked about fiction,
they revealed themselves unsuspectingly, gave away their

secrets innocently. And she did not want to lead Donald Wheeler to betray himself.

When it was time to pack up and drive back to town, Lark went with Arlene in the white coupe. Shouted urgings flew back and forth as the two parties climbed into separate cars.

"Don't forget to listen to *Fred Allen* tonight" and "I'll see you at catechism tomorrow" and "Remember about playing paper dolls Wednesday. Bring your Dorothy Lamour paper dolls."

Opening the backdoor, Donald called, "Stella, we're home."

She did not answer, so Sally ran upstairs. Her mother often closed the bedroom door when she lay down. Sally checked the guest room where Stella had slept the previous night, then Stella and Donald's room.

"She's not up here, Daddy."

Though he didn't expect to find her there, Donald descended the stairs to the basement. An old roll-away cot had been un-folded, and Stella lay on the bare, musty mattress. Around her on the cement floor was scattered the memorabilia from the footlocker.

Stella did not stir, and for the briefest moment it seemed that she was dead. When he went close of course, he saw that she was asleep.

Awakened, she was groggy and disoriented. "Is it morning?" She looked around, not recognizing her surroundings.

"It's nearly five. Time we started thinking about supper," he told her.

"Supper?"

"Well, we usually eat about this time on Sunday."

"Do we?" She thought about it for a moment.

"Would you like me to see what there is?"

She sighed and glanced around the basement, her face a blank. "I think I'll go upstairs. Upstairs. To bed."

Sally, who was standing on the bottom step, stared as though at strangers engaged in an obscene act.

In her room, Sally closed the door and lay across the bed, listening without wanting to hear, as her mother came up to the guest room, her father close behind, insisting that the oscillating fan be set up on the bureau.

"It's ninety-five in here, Stella. You'll make yourself sick."

Beyond Sally's wall the bedsprings complained as Stella lay down. "It makes me crazy. Back and forth. Back and forth."

"Then I'll switch it to stationary and train it on the bed."

Now he was raising the windows. "Let's get some ventilation in here. That's better."

"But I *like* to be closed in, Donald. I don't like everything open."

"For Christ's sake, Stella, be reasonable!" he exploded.

Sally recoiled. She had not known that her father's patience had a limit. She wished that she did not know it now. Who was this person who shouted at her mother? Might he shout at *her?*

"I'm sorry, Donald," her mother cried. "I'm so sorry."

"Don't be sorry, for God's sake," he groaned. "Be *different.*"

Third grade with its endless Palmer Method penmanship exercises was a letdown after Miss Bailey's second grade. And multiplication tables, instead of merely being dull and murky as ditch water, were a nightmare, at least for Delmore Preuss and several others.

Mrs. Shank, the teacher, kept a bell on her desk, like those on hotel desks in the movies, the kind you hit to bring the desk clerk running. And when she called out Delmore's name or Louis Flegel's and held up, say, the "3 x 6" card in her right hand, she silently beat the seconds on her desk with her left hand. If the correct answer was not forthcoming in five seconds, she dinged the bell and called someone else's name in a drill-instructor's voice. Angela Bussey often cried.

Despite Mrs. Shank, they all learned their tables well enough to be passed from third grade, and the summer between third and fourth grades was especially sweet.

The last week before Labor Day and the start of fourth grade, the scheduled penny movie was *The Private Life of Don Juan* with Douglas Fairbanks and Merle Oberon.

"Merle Oberon," Sally sighed, walking home afterward with Lark and Beverly.

She had cleaned house nearly all day, preparing for the girls to sleep over. Donald had lugged the mattress from the rollaway cot out into the yard to air it in the sunlight, then carried the frame and mattress up to Sally's room.

Late in the afternoon, he'd picked up a quart of vanilla ice cream at Anderson's Candy and Ice Cream and Hires root beer at Truska's. When the girls arrived home from the movie, he got the ice cream and root beer out to make floats, thinking that this might be the sort of thing Arlene Erhardt would do. In his effort to fill the space in Sally's life that Stella had once occupied, he looked to Mrs. Erhardt for a model.

"Mommy's asleep, so don't talk too loud," Sally admonished the other girls as they climbed the stairs with their root-beer floats. "I'll sleep on the roll-away because I'm the hostess. We pushed it against my bed so it's like one giant bed, except the roll-away's a little lower."

Both Lark and Beverly thought Sally's room very grand. It had a double bed, bureau, bookcase, and bedside table with a lamp. On the wall above the bed were framed pictures of flowers. Its luxury enhanced the game of movie stars in which Lark was of course Myrna Loy, and Sally was Merle Oberon. "Who do you want to be?" they asked Beverly.

"I'll be Judy Garland."

With a worn-down lipstick, which Grandma Elway had thrown out last Christmas, they colored their lips and rouged their cheeks. Then, from a cardboard box in the back of the closet, Sally dragged out a couple of panels of tattered lace curtains and several cast-off dresses of her mother's.

"We're going to a party at the Stork Club. That's a fancy place I heard about on Walter Winchell, I think," Lark said.

"And we live in mansions," Beverly insisted.

"And we ride in taxicabs and send telegrams to people and drink champagne," Lark demanded.

"And we're so beautiful, people can't hardly stand it," Beverly laughed.

Lark bobby-pinned one of the lace curtains to her hair. "Have you got any high heels we can wear?"

Standing in front of the bureau mirror, fastening her braids on top of her head, Sally nodded toward the closet. With a piece of toilet paper, she blotted her lips as she had seen women do, then wet the tip of her little finger and ran it along her eyebrow, smoothing the line. Poring over her features, she concluded that her eyes were not as slanted as Merle Oberon's, but her lashes were thicker. Maybe she *was* beautiful, but what good was that? She'd rather be somebody whose mother wasn't crazy.

They dressed and dressed again and chattered endlessly, making dates for tennis and golf, which seemed to figure prominently in sophisticated movies about rich people, along with shopping and dancing in nightclubs.

With all this planning, they did not get around to playing out the scenes before Donald, who had been reading downstairs, came up and told them it was bedtime.

"Scrub your faces."

Long after he was in bed, the girls lay giggling and whispering, amending and refining the future.

At a quarter past two, Donald got up to use the bathroom. The bedroom curtains hung limp and motionless in the hot, humid air.

He looked into Sally's room. The girls were sleeping on top of the covers, arms and legs flung out in angles of trust and abandon. Donald's breath caught and shuddered in his chest. When he realized that Sally had only this one childhood, he hated Stella.

Moving around the bed, he thrust the dimity back from the windows so that the meagerest breeze could find its way to the girls.

A pencil line of light showed beneath the guest-room door. "Stella?" he called softly and turned the knob.

Still wearing her housedress, awake but unoccupied, Stella sat on the bed, her back against the headboard.

"Stella? You're still up? It's after two."

"I don't feel like sleeping."

"That's because you slept this afternoon. Your days and nights are turned around. You need more exercise."

She didn't tell Donald that staying awake at night, waiting for the sky to grow light, was a vigil she kept. If she fell asleep in the dark, she woke in the dark. Sleep never lasted till morning. And waking in the bowels of the night was the worst. The worst of all worsts. When she woke in the middle of the night, she couldn't remember who she was.

When Sally and Lark climbed the steps to the Stillmans' apartment the Sunday after Thanksgiving, they had just left the Majestic Theater where *The Great Dictator* with Charlie Chaplin was playing to full houses.

Above Harvester, the sun glittered like flashy gilt against an intensely blue sky, but a sly, chill breeze blew grit along the gutters and against the doorsteps. The Stillman apartment, dim, soft, and down-at-the-heels, was cozy after the glinting, gritty street.

"Is Hilly sleeping?" Lark asked Helen Stillman.

"He's resting."

"Will he have tea with us?"

"I don't think so," Mrs. Stillman told her, dipping and raising the tea ball. When she had poured the tea, she sat down in the old wicker rocker and spoke softly, as one does when trying not to wake the baby.

"Hillyard is sad these days," she told them. "It's the war. He tries not to know about it, but it's hard."

"But *he* won't have to be a soldier again," Sally said.

"No. But the other war comes back to him now. He saw so much during the Great War. He was decorated, you know, by both the French and the American governments." She did not boast but, rather, indicated in this delicate way the extent of Hilly's service. "He saved the lives of many soldiers, and he suffered . . . wounds." She fell silent, staring into her teacup, forgetting the girls.

Sally and Lark sipped tea and munched cookies to fill the hush, which seemed a silence not to be broken with words.

They were relieved when the light outside began to fail, and they could leave without seeming rude.

When she came home from the Stillmans', Sally gathered up *Little Women* from her room and went along to the guest room where her mother now slept every night, except when the grandparents visited.

Sitting down on the slipper chair beside the bed, she told Stella, "Lark and I went to see Mrs. Stillman and Hilly after the movie. Hilly is sad, Mrs. Stillman said. On account of the war."

"I'm sorry," Stella said, and she was. Because she had rescued Hilly that time, out on the road to the cemetery, and because he was a shut-in like herself, Stella felt a strong tie to him, as if they were members of the same forbidden society.

"Lark says Hilly's getting his sanity back and that's why he's sad. Anyway, that's what Mrs. Erhardt thinks. He's remembering all the things he wanted to forget."

Seeing tears gather in Stella's eyes, Sally opened *Little Women* to chapter 25 in which Meg married John. Although Sally had read the chapter ahead of time to get the gist of things and "rehearsed" the scenes in order to bring drama to them, when she looked up after three pages, Stella had "disappeared."

When the chapter concluded ". . . and so Meg's married life began," Sally gave Stella a kiss, pulled the covers up to her neck, and went along to her own room with time to spare before her bath.

Climbing onto the bed, she arranged herself against the pillows and extended a hand in a gesture of invitation. "Would you like to climb up here beside me, Sally?"

Pause.

Smiling, she exclaimed, "What a wonderful reading. You

made me see the little wedding and the cake and the girls in their silver gray gowns. And Aunt March . . . you acted her part so well, for a minute I thought you were a persnickety old lady!"

She crooked an arm as if gathering an invisible child to her. "When I'm done with the Change, I'll tell everyone, 'If it hadn't been for Sally, I'd have ended up in St. Peter.'"

When he heard Sally drain the tub and, a little later, climb into bed, Donald lay aside M. L. Hansen's *The Atlantic Migration* and went up to say good-night. Sally was sitting up in bed with her book open in her lap.

"I've never read Louisa May Alcott," he told her, settling himself at the foot end of the bed. "Is *Little Women* good?"

"It's my favorite."

He laughed. "You say that about every book."

"Do I?"

"It's all right."

"*The Wind in the Willows* is my most favorite," she told him, "but *Little Women* comes right after that. Sometimes it's sad," she confessed, glancing down at the book.

"Do you read the sad parts?"

"Oh, yes."

"That's brave."

"No, it's not."

"No?"

"I especially like the sad parts," she said, laying a ribbon on the page and closing the book. "The sad parts never last a whole book, but they show that it's right to hope things will get better, because they *do.*"

She set the book on the table, continuing, "Sometimes I think of the good things I want to have happen, and I rehearse them. It almost feels like they're happening. Is it sensible to do that?"

Sensible was her new word. Grandma Elway who had visited at Thanksgiving used the word a good deal, and Grandma made it sound important, as if sensible could be one of the Commandments. Thou Shalt Be Sensible.

"Eminently."

"Does that mean yes?"

He nodded.

When Donald had kissed her good-night and switched off the lamp, Sally lay back against the pillow smiling and whispering, "Em-in-ent-ly. Eminently sensible."

After Mass the next Sunday, Lark pulled Sally aside in the vestibule of St. Boniface, cupped her hands around Sally's ear, and whispered, "I've got a wonderful secret. Promise you won't tell?"

Sally nodded.

"Mama's saved enough money to buy the lot for the Cape Ann!" Aloud she squealed, "Isn't that wonderful?"

"Why're you whispering?"

"Mama doesn't want Papa to know until she puts the money down and signs the papers," Lark said softly so that Mr. Erhardt wouldn't overhear. "Next spring the carpenters will start building our house." She squirmed with delight. "We can talk about it tomorrow at recess," she said and hurried to catch up with her parents.

Donald and Sally had walked the several blocks to church, and now they walked home. Overcast and still, no snow yet lying on the ground, the day felt like early November instead of December. Sally imagined herself and her father spending the afternoon curled up in armchairs reading the Sunday paper and listening to *One Man's Family.*

"How do you build a house?" she asked.

"What do you mean?"

"I mean, if you wanted to build a house, how would you start?" Within Sally's memory a handful of homes had been built on the fringes of town, but she had seen them only once or twice during construction, as she passed in the car.

"Well, first you'd talk to Mr. Rayzeen at the lumberyard about the kind of house you wanted. You'd probably have a plan in mind, you know, a layout. He'd tell you about how much it would cost to build, and then you'd go to the bank and ask them for a loan to pay for the house. Of course, you'd have to have saved some money on your own or the bank wouldn't loan you the rest."

That human beings could actually *make* a house seemed fantastical, complicated beyond imagining, something only God ought to be able to do. But she was glad it was humans, not God, because she did not find God reliable when it came to doing what needed doing.

"The first thing the builders do is dig a big hole for the basement," Donald continued, "and they line it with concrete."

Maybe Mrs. Erhardt would let Sally watch as the Cape Ann was being built. Sally had a lot of questions to ask Lark's mother. When were they going to start building? How long would it take to build the house? When she was grown up, could *she* learn how to build a house?

Out in the street, raking a last scum of oak leaves from the gutter was Constable Wall, who with Mrs. Wall lived catty-corner across the intersection of Second Street and Third Avenue from the Wheelers. He was not wearing his uniform, but Sally felt diffident nonetheless. She'd been told often enough that policemen were her friends, but she was always shy with Constable Wall and, if she was alone, usually crossed the street to avoid him.

"Don," he greeted Sally's father, tipping his billed cap with the earflaps toward Sally.

"Gus." Donald tipped his hat.

"Figure this may be the last chance I get to clean the gutter before the snow flies."

"I wouldn't be surprised."

Donald was scrambling eggs and Sally setting the kitchen table when the town whistle blew. She looked at the clock. A little past one, not time for the whistle to blow unless there was a fire and the whistle was calling volunteer firemen to the firehouse.

Donald turned from the stove. He and Sally looked at each other, puzzled. The blasts didn't sound like a fire alarm. They were all long blasts, and they went on and on.

Stella, in her nightdress, appeared in the kitchen doorway, one hand lying gracefully on her breast as if she were about to inquire regarding something inconsequential, such as, was there coffee?

"War," she said instead.

"What're you talking about, Stella?"

"We're at war."

"Why do you think that?"

"Don't you hear the alarm?"

"We don't know what that means," he told her.

He took her arm, leading her to the table. "Sit down. I've made breakfast."

"Will you have to go, Donald?"

"Go?"

"To war."

"Sally, run ask Gus Wall why the whistle's blowing," he said, buttering the toast. He eyed Stella, sitting calm and withdrawn.

On Monday, Congress declared war against Japan, and on Tuesday night, President Roosevelt spoke to the American people over the radio. Although the Fireside Chat did not begin until nine-thirty, Grandma Wheeler, who had arrived for a timely visit Monday morning, allowed Sally to stay up to listen.

Sally liked the sound of the president's voice. She liked his accent, which was different from her own. He sounded like someone who was smart and kind and had no doubt that things would eventually turn out all right. He didn't say that everything would be fine any day now. No, he said, "We must be set to face a long war . . ." But she appreciated his candor. You knew what was what with someone like that.

At school, in the stores, and at the post office, people talked war, war, war. A current of horrified excitement ran through the community during those first weeks after Pearl Harbor. Shock and fear made people feel related to each other.

At the Wheelers', lights were on in the house when Sally came home from school on the dark December afternoons. The kitchen was neat and clean, and an after-school treat was laid out on the table. Grandma Wheeler made meat loaf and fried chicken; she baked frosted chocolate-drop cookies and spice cake.

By Friday of the first week of her grandmother's visit, Sally was growing used to talking about what had happened at school; used to playing rummy in the evenings after her homework was done; to having a closetful of clean, pressed clothes and fresh-smelling, mangled bed linen.

When she climbed into bed Monday night, she ran her hands over the smooth sheets and pillow slips. They made her feel happy and important.

A year and a half ago, Grandma and Grandpa Elway had bought Stella the mangle as a little inducement to "take hold." It had remained in the corner of the kitchen with a sheet thrown over it, pulled out and used only when the grandmothers visited.

As the days passed and the first flurry of house cleaning, clothes-washing, mangling, ironing, baking, and mending subsided, Grandma Wheeler's work settled into a pattern of everyday routine, and she had more time to worry about Stella.

Stella had not come downstairs since she had announced the war, and she did not speak more than half a dozen words in a day. Irmgard Wheeler was shocked. In weekend visits she had not grasped the degree of the problem. She had known that Stella was bad. She hadn't known that she was *this* bad.

Irmgard was a tenderhearted woman, but even a tender-hearted person grows impatient when the well-being of those dearest is threatened. She was torn. One minute she wanted to hold Stella close and croon to her. The next, she wanted to shake her.

Instead, she sighed and clucked and shook her head while whipping soiled sheets from beds and slamming cupboard doors upon freshly scrubbed shelves. Now and then her brow puckered, her shoulders heaved, and she fumbled for the hanky tucked between her breasts.

All this was while Sally was at school. When Sally was at home, Irmgard was persistently cheerful. She oversaw the child's homework; listened with her to favorite radio programs; played cards, Monopoly, and Parcheesi with her; even sat on the floor and played Ginger Rogers paper dolls.

She couldn't prevent Sally from seeing how Stella was going downhill. But she would see to it that Sally didn't go down the hill with her.

Saturday afternoon, Donald took Sally downtown to buy her new patent-leather shoes at Lundeen's. Her old ones were too small, his mother told him.

Snow had fallen during the week and was banked along the curbs on Main Street, but a good many people were out and about, doing weekly marketing. In Lundeen's, Donald and Sally headed for the shoe department at the back of the store. Here and there, little knots of customers bent their heads together, speaking in low, buzzing tones, one or two shaking their heads.

When Sally was settled on a brown leatherette chair with a salesman's stool before her, Hy Johnson, the store manager, who often clerked on busy Saturdays, asked, "School shoes?"

"Mary Janes," Sally told him.

He straddled the stool, measured Sally's foot, then rose and appeared to hesitate before turning toward the curtained doorway leading to the storeroom.

When the shoes were decided upon, the box wrapped, and the sale concluded, Mr. Johnson again hesitated, at length asking Donald, "Have you heard? About Hilly Stillman?"

"Heard?"

Mr. Johnson bent his head sideways, indicating that Donald might want to step away from Sally a few paces to hear this news. Donald obliged.

"My God," Sally heard him murmur moments later as Mr. Johnson said something that she could not hear. As Donald turned away from the store manager, his face was blank as a washed slate.

"What's wrong, Daddy?"

He took her hand and they walked down the long center aisle to the front door. Outside, enormous white flakes had begun to fall, slowly, touching everything with lace.

"What about Hilly?" Sally asked.

"He's dead," Donald said quietly, stepping off the curb to cross Main Street, heading home.

Stella wasn't in the guest room or bath. He found her sitting on the edge of the bed in their room. She'd dressed herself in a wrinkled blue skirt and a white blouse, buttoned askew.

"Stella?"

"Arlene Erhardt called your mother."

"I heard about it downtown," he told her. "Would you like to come downstairs?"

She shook her head. "I'll wait."

"Wait?"

"For Arlene."

"Yes, all right." What now? "Would you like company?"

Again she shook her head.

"Well, I'll get out of my coat then," he told her, backing out of the room.

Arlene Erhardt arrived about five past one, eyes red and face puffy. She wondered if she ought to have shown up in this state. Lark had told her that Donald's mother was visiting, and Arlene guessed it was because of Stella. No one was supposed to know how bad Stella was, but of course everyone knew. Still, people pretended when they saw Donald or Sally.

"Come in, Arlene," Donald told her.

"I won't stay long," she said, as if visiting a sick friend.

Stella had heard the doorbell and was coming down the stairs. Arlene was grateful to be getting out of her coat and removing her boots because it gave her time to cover her shock. Stella looked . . . Well, Arlene had seen people lying in coffins who looked better. Her clothes—the blouse was buttoned all wrong, and the blue skirt was on backward.

Donald led Arlene to a wing chair. Irmgard Wheeler, Sally beside her, appeared at the dining-room door, asking, "Would you like a cup of coffee?"

"No, thank you. I can only stay a minute."

Stella sat on the sofa, Donald beside her. Sally arranged herself on the twin of the wing chair occupied by Mrs. Erhardt. Arlene glanced at Donald. Should she speak in front of Sally?

"Sally knows that Hilly killed himself," he told her.

Stella asked, "How did he . . . ?"

"He shot himself with a gun he had from the war," Arlene told her.

"Where'd he get bullets?" Donald wondered.

"Mrs. Stillman told me once that Hilly had come home from the war with so little, except pain, she couldn't bear to throw his things away. She doesn't know how he ever found the bullets. She kept them hidden. I guess, when people are desperate. . . . Pearl Harbor upset him."

Stella sat straight and still with her hands folded in her lap like Sally's. She seemed to be taking in what was said, but Arlene wasn't sure. The three Wheelers appeared not to breathe. Their eyes never left Arlene's face.

"I'm on my way to Helen Stillman's, so I'll know more later. I'll call you . . . about the arrangements and funeral, you know. Later this afternoon or after supper."

Rising and grabbing her coat from a bench beside the door, she yanked it on, murmuring, "I'll call you later." She snatched her boots from the newspaper beneath the bench and pulled the door open before Donald could get to it.

Arlene called at seven and Donald answered. "The funeral's Tuesday at ten in the morning at the Methodist church." Her voice was hoarse with tears and anger.

"Methodist?"

"The damned Catholics won't bury him because he killed himself," she said. "I'm sorry . . . I know you're Catholic, but I'm mad enough to chew tacks." Arlene was herself a convert. "Anyway, there'll be a luncheon buffet after the burial at Bernice and Bill McGivern's house. I hope you'll come."

"I have to be on the road, Arlene, but Sally says she's going to the funeral. I can't say about Stella. She says she's going but, well, we'll see." The line was silent. Then, "My mother wants to send food," he said. "Should it go to the McGiverns'? And what should she make, she wants to know."

Arlene thought for a moment. "A pot of baked beans? Could she do that?"

"Yes, of course."

"I'll pick them up Tuesday morning about nine and take them over to Bernice's." She paused. "It's nice of your mother, I mean, I know she's Catholic. Tell her thank you."

"It's quite all right."

"I'm sorry I rushed out the way I did this afternoon. Well, I'd better let you go, I suppose. You know, when something like this happens, it's like a light comes on. No, it's more like the light comes from a different direction, and things look different. I guess that's what they mean when they say, 'She saw things in a different light.'"

When he heard the click at the other end, Donald stared at the receiver for several seconds, then turned to his mother.

"Baked beans. Mrs. Erhardt will pick them up Tuesday morning."

December 22, 1941

Stella's emergence at the time of Hilly's death was a little rocket shooting into the air, sputtering and falling to earth again. At the end of the week following his burial, she was failing to bathe, refusing to leave the guest room, and ignoring food.

The shock of Pearl Harbor was followed by the shock of Hilly's suicide. Then, on the twenty-second of December, the first Monday of Christmas vacation, Lark telephoned Sally, asking if she could play at the Wheelers' that afternoon. "I'll bring my Myrna Loy paper dolls," she said without enthusiasm.

Lark never asked to play at Sally's house, not anymore. She invited Sally to the depot instead. When Grandma Wheeler heard that Lark was coming, she said, "Isn't that nice," and then "Is your room picked up?" But Sally dragged upstairs, sullen and worried, and lay down.

When Sally closed the bedroom door behind them, Lark revealed why she had come.

"Papa lost five hundred dollars playing poker, and Mama can't build the Cape Ann," she said. "Mama and Aunt Betty are moving to California without Papa, and I have to go too."

"When?" Sally asked in a stunned whisper.

"The middle of next month." Lark knelt on the pink rag rug and began to cry.

Sally knew she ought to put an arm around her friend and comfort her. But she couldn't. She was filled with rage. Lark was going to California and leaving Sally in Harvester with her mother.

Sally threw herself on the bed, pounding the mattress with her fists. "Go away! Go away! Go away! I can't stand you. I don't want you here!"

"Sally . . ."

"Go away!" she screamed. "I hate you!"

Sally was still knocked sideways by Lark's news when Harry Wheeler and the Elways showed up for Christmas. With their arrival, family meetings were held, serious meetings.

"A hysterectomy first. Then, if that doesn't help, committal," Herb Elway said, clearing his throat. "Time hasn't healed her." He looked at his wife. "Now we'll try something else."

Donald nodded, closed his eyes, and let his head fall backward in a gesture of weary, relieved submission. He was grateful to Herb for making the decision. It was Herb and Edna's *right.*

But Edna flared, "She needs to get away! Am I the only one who can see that? A trip out west, Arizona, or *something.* You know what happens to women who have hysterectomies. They grow mustaches and get deep voices, and, and, they're not . . . womanly." Her small fists worked in her lap. "And I won't allow Stella to go to St. Peter." Her eyes darted from one of them to another, searching for an ally. "She's not a lunatic!"

Christmas was on Thursday. On Sunday, they sat around the dining-room table, a barely picked-at roast beef growing cold before them, the silence of firm, unhappy decision lowered over them.

Edna Elway stared at an untouched cup of coffee and hated the others: Irmgard in the kitchen, tidying self-righteously; Harry soon to drive his poor-but-honest-man's Ford back to Worthington; even Herb with his maddening, innocent patience.

She knew what they thought. They thought she cared only

about what people would say. Well, that wasn't true. When it came down to it, she didn't give a damn what people were going to say. She simply couldn't bear to think of Stella, her sweet Stella, in one of those places with crazy people. And *her* somehow responsible. Oh, she'd read the articles. She knew these things were traced back to a mother who'd planted a poisoned seed in her child's brain.

"Mother?" Herb said. "It's time to leave." Rising and crossing to her, he patted her shoulder.

She could not recall her husband ever calling her "Mother" before. Under the circumstances, the word felt like an accusation.

Donald and Herb cajoled Stella into a dress and coat, then led her insistently out the door and down the walk to the Elway Lincoln. Several times she glanced back at the house, trying to pull away from the men.

"It's not for long, Stella," Donald told her, sick at his stomach. "Only for a visit."

Sally stood on the front stoop beside Irmgard Wheeler, observing her mother's departure as if it were a movie. But when Donald closed the car door after Stella, Sally ran down the walk, jerked open the door, and threw herself across her mother, screaming, "I love you! Don't go!"

Shrugging off Donald and Irmgard, Sally climbed the stairs to her room and closed the door. At the bureau mirror she dragged the rouge pad down her cheeks and smeared the old lipstick across her mouth until her lips were exaggerated and lewd.

Yanking the lace curtain from the box at the back of the closet, she whipped it 'round her head and shoulders, then scrabbled in the bottom of the box for the lint-coated candy cigarettes.

At the mirror again, she puffed elaborately on a cigarette, then held it away from her, between index and middle finger, the remaining fingers splayed and curved in a manner she'd noted in *The Women*.

Striking one provocative pose after another, poses from *Photoplay* or *Screen Magazine*, she rattled off biography like Ann Sheridan or Virginia Mayo.

"Harvester, Minnesota.

"A pretty little house . . . beside a brook.

"My darling dog, Fala, and my canary, Caroline.

"Daddy looked like Walter Pidgeon.

"Mommy died when I was nine. Run over by a crazy woman."

January 8, 1942

As she ladled out hot oatmeal into a bowl for Sally, her grandmother asked, "When is your friend Lark leaving for California?"

"Next Monday." Sally spooned sugar on the cereal.

"My stars, it's already Thursday. Are they giving her a going-away party at school?"

Sally nodded.

"Would you like to ask her to come home with you this afternoon? I could make cookies."

Sally shrugged. "Can she stay for supper?"

"If Mrs. Erhardt doesn't mind." She poured herself a cup of tea and sat down opposite Sally.

"Beverly?"

"Well, yes, I suppose."

The girls were settled into the breakfast nook with glasses of milk and a plate of homemade spritz cookies decorated with red and green sprinkles.

Holding up a cookie, Beverly wanted to know, "How's your grandma make the cookies like this?" Each cookie was in the shape of a knot.

"She's got a little tube that's called a press, and the dough goes in, and then it gets squeezed out," Sally told her, rising to find the tube kept in a drawer by the sink. "See?" she said, laying the cookie press on the table in front of Beverly.

"Mama's got one of those too," Lark observed. "It'll probably have to stay here when we go to California, 'cuz she said we can't take much."

"D'ya think she'd give it to me?" Beverly wanted to know.

Lark considered. "I don't know. I could ask her." She thought it was rude of Beverly to ask for the cookie press, although she didn't know why. "Some stuff she's packing'll get sent to California after we get settled. When we have enough money to send for it. But if she doesn't pack the cookie press, you could probably have it." She didn't want to fight with Beverly. There was so little time.

"My ma don't make cookies any more, 'cuz she does so much cookin' down at the Loon," Beverly explained. "But maybe I could learn how to do the press." Off on another tack, she sighed, "Godsakes, I wish I was going to California."

Beverly was always wishing that she was going to California. She had it in her mind that she could be a movie star. Lark and Sally never pointed out that she was homely as a mud fence, skinny and freckled, with hair like dried grass.

"When I grow up, I'm going to Hollywood," Beverly went on.

"When I grow up, I'm going to live in Harvester, Minnesota," Lark told them with a note of defiance.

"And me and Sally'll come visit you here!" Beverly chimed.

"Will you be married?" Sally wondered.

"I'm going to build the Cape Ann, and maybe I'll get married. There's a boy named Phillip in my old *Happy Stories for Bedtime* who's nice and I like him." In the story, the boy, who wore short pants and a dress shirt and tie, sat in a window seat gazing pensively out across the sea, waiting for the return of his father who was fighting the Hun. Phillip's elegant profile and serious air spoke of intelligence and sensitivity.

Beverly snorted and slapped the table. "Godsakes, you can't marry a boy from a story! He ain't real."

"Maybe he is," Sally said, not liking to see Lark ridiculed.

"Can we bring somebody with us if you got enough room?"

Beverly wanted to know. "I'm gonna bring Mickey Rooney. Who'd you bring?" she asked Sally.

"I might bring Daddy," Sally told her, reticent to suggest Walter Pidgeon.

"Yer *dad?*" Beverly exclaimed, though when she'd thought about it, she found it not so outlandish.

"What about your mama?" Lark wondered.

She lifted her shoulders and twisted her head sideways in an ambiguous gesture.

"Is your mama still in Mankato?" Lark asked, knowing that Arlene would want to know.

"Yes." Sally got up and returned the cookie press to the drawer.

"Is she coming home pretty soon?"

"I don't know. She's going to have an operation next week." Sally stood looking out the window above the sink, her back to the others.

"Really?"

"What kind?" Beverly wanted to know.

"I'm not sure. They're gonna take some stuff out of her."

"Out of her head?" Beverly wondered. That seemed the most likely.

"No." Though, come to think of it, Sally didn't know what they were taking out. Maybe it *was* from her head.

Abruptly changing the subject, Lark told Beverly, "When you come visit me from Hollywood, it'll be summertime, and we'll eat corn and tomatoes and onions and peas and all those things out of my garden. Did you ever eat one of those little yellow tomatoes fresh out of the garden? They're as sweet as candy. Grandpa calls them 'God's candy.' Hilly and I were going to pick tomatoes and peas and eat them in my garden behind the Cape Ann." As abruptly as she'd begun, she stopped.

"When we visit, I'll pick flowers and put 'em in a vase," Beverly told her. "I never picked real flowers, only weeds. But weeds are pretty too," she asserted, daring anyone to deny it.

"You want more cookies?" Sally pushed the plate toward Beverly, then Lark, feeling a strange compulsion to reward the two girls, for what she was not clear.

"You'll probably come back to Harvester real soon," she told Lark. "Your mother will hate California and wish she'd never left here. Don't you bet that's what will happen, Beverly?"

Mrs. Erhardt came to fetch Lark at seven-thirty. Despite Irmgard Wheeler's admonitions, Sally followed them out the door into the cold, clear night. In a black sky, frozen stars glittered.

When they reached the old pickup, she pulled from her pocket the two notes she'd written, one to Lark and the other to Mrs. Erhardt, and thrust them at Mrs. Erhardt, saying, "Promise not to read them until you're on the train."

Arlene Erhardt slipped the notes into her purse and climbed up into the truck. Even through her heavy coat, the seat was icy. She pulled out the choke and, tromping on the gas pedal, turned the key in the ignition.

If she'd been alone, Arlene thought, she might have opened the note from Sally. As it was, she waited until the train west had carried her and Lark and Betty beyond Minnesota.

Digging in her purse, she found the notes, wrinkled but still tightly folded. She handed Lark hers and opened her own.

"Dear Mrs. Erhardt," it said, "please don't forget me."

January 22, 1942

Donald called Sally from Mankato on Thursday night of the following week.

"Mommy's okay," he told her. "She had the operation this morning, and they let her have Jell-O for supper. I gave her your love when she woke up."

Stella did not talk to Sally that night, nor did she in the ensuing days, although Donald called several times from Mankato during her recuperation. On weekdays he was out on the road for Fidelity, but on the weekends he headed to Mankato, never offering to stop in Harvester on his way and pick up Sally.

Valentine's Day fell on Saturday. Trudging through a fresh snowfall to the post office, Sally found several items in the Wheeler box with her name on them, including a slip of paper advising her to call at the window for a package.

"I'd say you're a pretty popular girl," Mr. Kretzmarsky told her when she passed him the claim slip.

Outside, Sally sat on the bench where Mrs. Erhardt had told her that Hilly used to sit after he came home from the war. Opening her mail, Sally found a lacy card from her mother and father, the message written in Donald's hand telling her that they loved her and that they hoped she was minding Grandma Wheeler. Taped below the message was twenty-five cents.

From Grandma and Grandpa Elway she received another pretty card informing her that she was loved and that she should look for a little package in the mail. Tearing the wrapping off the package and opening the tiny box, Sally found a delicate bracelet made up of Black Hills gold rosebuds.

For lunch, Sally and her grandmother had tomato soup and Ritz crackers spread with pimento cheese.

"Tomato soup," Irmgard told her, "because it's red like a valentine heart."

"Grandma?"

"Yes?"

"Is Mommy coming home?"

"I honestly don't know."

"Is she over the operation yet?"

"Well, I don't really know that either."

They would tell her if her mother was dead, wouldn't they?

"I brought my skates," Beverly announced, arriving half an hour early and just in time for dessert, which was valentine sugar cookies. "You wanna go skating?" Shucking her jacket, cap, and mittens, she settled herself at the kitchen table.

"Get Beverly a glass of milk," Irmgard told Sally.

"These're good cookies," Beverly told Sally's grandmother. "How'd you make 'em like that?"

Irmgard showed her the cookie cutter.

"And how'd you get the frosting pink?"

Irmgard got down the bottle of food coloring from the cupboard.

"Godsakes," Beverly breathed admiringly. "Mrs. Erhardt gave me her cookie press before she left town, but I don't have anything to make dough with."

"You bring your press over someday," Irmgard told her, "and I'll teach you and Sally how to make spritz." The child was as transparent as a windowpane, but what could you do?

The warming house was crowded as the girls changed into their skates, and the rink was teeming with skaters when they emerged. The ice had been swept free of the new snow, but a desultory dusting of giant flakes continued drifting down, like an afterthought. The day was perfect for skating. The sky was low and windless, the air warm.

"You got the best coat of anybody," Beverly told Sally as they started around the rink together.

Sally had grown until the sleeves of her gray coat had been half way up to her elbows when Edna Elway came at

Thanksgiving. At Christmas, Grandma had brought Sally a cardinal red coat, cut along princess lines, with a black plush collar and deep cuffs that looked like seal fur. A matching black plush toque came with it.

"Them white skates look really good with it," Beverly added, taking some pride in being with the most smartly dressed girl at the rink.

After a couple of turns around the ice, Beverly said, "I'll skate backward and you hold my hands and steer me." So they skated in this fashion once around, then changed sides and Sally skated backward.

A high-school girl skimming past called, "That's real good!" and Sally and Beverly giggled in a pleased, self-conscious way.

Perhaps the compliment put them off their guard, for when Delmore Preuss slammed into them on purpose, they went down in a heap, the blade of Sally's left skate catching Beverly's wrist and opening it up.

Furious, Sally scrambled to her feet and skated after the boy, overtaking him two-thirds of the way around the big oval. Coming up behind, she threw herself against his back, knowing that she would go down with him, but too angry to care.

Delmore flew forward and coasted across the ice on his stomach while behind him Sally landed on her hands and knees. Hustling onto her blades, she dashed toward him, screaming, "You're a stupid bully! A stupid bully!"

A small crowd was gathering, among them Neddy Barnstable, who had just emerged from the warming house. Sally noticed no one as she stood over Delmore Preuss. He turned over on his back, pulling himself up onto his elbows, smirking.

He couldn't tell her that he'd done what he had because he liked her. He didn't know that he liked her. But he knew that people were standing around hearing her call him "stupid," and because he suspected that she was right, he yelled,

"Your ma's crazy as a loon, and they put her away in the bughouse!"

Tramping up the back walk from the alley, the girls heard the phone ringing in the kitchen, and as Sally flung the door open, Grandma Elway held out the receiver.

"It's your daddy."

"Mommy's not in St. Peter, is she?" Sally demanded. Something that humiliating simply could not happen.

"What makes you ask?"

"Someone told me she's in St. Peter."

"Who?"

"Just a boy at the skating rink."

In a tired voice Donald explained, "We took her yesterday, Grandpa and Grandma Elway and I."

"Can I visit her?"

"Not for a while."

"How long is she going to be there?"

"I don't know."

Behind the exhaustion in her father's voice Sally heard something else. A resignation, even relief, a distancing of himself from her mother and the burden of her illness.

"I have to go now," Sally whispered, hanging the receiver back on the hook.

The next morning, Irmgard, wearing her good navy blue challis, stood at the door of Sally's room.

"Grandma, I don't want to go to Mass," Sally pleaded. "My head hurts."

Irmgard crossed to the bed and lay a palm against Sally's brow. "You don't have a fever."

"But my head hurts."

Her grandmother eyed her with suspicion. "Granddad and I're all dressed and ready."

"Couldn't you go without me?"

"I don't like to do that."

Beverly, who had spent the night, sat up in bed. "I'll stay with her," she volunteered.

"There ought to be an adult," Irmgard told her.

"We'll stay right here in bed till you come back," Beverly suggested. "We won't even go downstairs." Beverly didn't see what the fuss was about. She and Charlie and Baby Delores often had to stay alone when their mother was working.

Irmgard looked doubtful.

"It's okay, Grandma. Beverly and I'll go back to sleep till you get home."

"Do you promise?" Sally's grandmother asked, holding her right elbow in the palm of her left hand and stroking her chin in a fretful manner. "I don't know."

At length, Irmgard left with Harry, Irmgard still not satisfied that she was doing the right thing. But these days she needed the serenity and reassurance of Mass.

Crossing herself with holy water in the church vestibule, she felt as if she were annointing herself with love. She was filled with calm and the confidence that, beyond the heavy doors leading into the nave, God was waiting for her, prepared to hear her concerns.

Genuflecting beside a pew halfway down the aisle, she thought, Here I am, God, come again. How welcome she felt, how much a member of the family. Slipping into the pew and kneeling and crossing herself, she trembled with relief. Yes. Yes, it was as it had always been. Nothing had changed since last Sunday. Singapore was under siege and about to fall to the Japanese; the Italians had bombed Alexandria, Egypt; but here it was always the same.

Closing her eyes, she breathed deeply and prayerfully air infused with supplications and incense, wet wool and Smith Brothers cough drops. Mass was a warmly lighted house on a winter night, a house whose windows drew one longingly, and whose door — O, miracle! — was never latched.

The morning sun burned through the stained-glass windows, melting their fulgent colors and splashing them across the congregation, like jewels tossed down to the faithful.

Crossing herself once more at the end of her prayers, Irmgard settled back in the pew, a child, light and blithe, relieved of adult cares for an insular hour.

At an organdy-curtained window where frost glittered like crystal in the morning light, Sally stood staring down at the crisp, virginal snow whose brittle crust she could almost feel breaking beneath heavy galoshes.

"What d'ya think it's like in St. Peter?" Beverly asked.

Sally shrugged. "I don't know. I've never seen it. Daddy says it's a hospital."

"Yeah, but for crazy people. D'ya think they're naked? Maybe they drink out of baby bottles. I wonder if they yell at each other all the time, like Grandma Strunk yells at everybody."

"Daddy says Mommy doesn't talk at all, so I don't think she yells." Sally was embarrassed to be discussing this, but Beverly was insistent, fascinated.

"You hungry? I'm hungry as a grizzly bear."

"We promised Grandma we wouldn't go downstairs."

"Oh, yeah. What d'ya think they feed them in St. Peter?"

Sally shook her head, swung around, and climbed back into bed. Facing away from Beverly, she pulled her cold feet up inside her flannel nightgown and tucked the covers close, insulating herself from the chill.

Monday morning, Sally descended the stairs still wearing her nightgown.

"Child, get dressed. You'll be late," Irmgard told her.

"I've got a headache," Sally said and indeed she did not look entirely well.

Irmgard felt the child's forehead once again, assured her that she had no fever, and insisted that she go to school.

"Please, Grandma?"

"No. I'll give you an aspirin if you have a headache, but you have to go to school. Now run along and let me make breakfast."

Slinking up the endless walk to the center doors of the school, Sally looked to neither side, but only down at the patch of snow-cleared concrete directly in front of her galoshes. If she saw no one, maybe no one would see her.

In the main floor hall, Miss Bailey smiled and waved just as she always had. Did she know that Sally's mother had been committed? Evidently not. By noon she'd surely have heard. Would she then wave and smile as now?

Sally hurried upstairs to the fourth-grade room and into

the cloakroom where she occupied herself in the far corner, ostensibly with a refractory buckle on one of her galoshes and, after that, with a worrying assignment in her language workbook.

Except for Beverly, who eventually warned her, "You better get to your seat. It's time for the last bell," no one spoke to Sally before class.

But, later, during spelling, while Miss Borgen wrote several extra-credit words on the blackboard, Ronald Oster and Delmore Preuss began giggling. Describing circles with their index fingers against their temples, they pointed to Sally.

Sally's face burned and the pulse in her neck and wrists beat painfully, as if her veins and arteries might burst from shame. She stared blindly at the front of the room, at the blur of Miss Borgen.

Only three days ago they had all exchanged valentines. She'd received a valentine from Delmore Preuss showing a boy with a heart-shaped pocket on his shirt, holding a bulldog on a leash. Inside it had declared, "Doggoned if I don't want you for my Valentine." Sally squirmed with misery now, recalling.

Although the lead in Sally's pencil broke as she wrote down the extra-credit words, she did not get up from her desk and walk to the pencil sharpener for fear of attracting unnecessary attention. When the bell rang for lunch dismissal, she dashed for the cloakroom, then sprinted out of the building before anyone could waylay her.

At home she entreated, "Don't make me go back, Grandma. My head really hurts."

"You'll have to face them sooner or later. Don't let them think they can get a rise out of you. If you don't answer back, they'll get tired of teasing." And, finally, "Hold your head up."

Holding one's head up wasn't a solution to Sally's problem, any more than armor was a solution to war. Each was a means of coming away without a mortal wound. If you were lucky.

Throughout the day, questions slithered, uninvited, beneath the gate of Sally's mind. When Grandma and Grandpa and

Donald had left her, had her mother cried? Was she frightened?

By afternoon recess everyone in Sally's class knew about her mother. Sally felt them looking at her and sometimes caught them, though she tried to avoid that, since it was terribly embarrassing to her.

"Sally's gonna get loony like her mother" their eyes predicted. "Wait and see."

Beverly told her, "Delmore Preuss's cousin, Minnie, cleans the offices over Truska's. One of them offices is Mr. Shane's. He's a lawyer."

Sally looked at her blankly.

"My ma says she figures that Minnie was snooping and found some papers about them putting your ma in St. Peter. Is Mr. Shane a lawyer for your dad? My ma says Minnie is sly, but I don't know what that means. And she says Minnie can't keep her mouth shut, either. So probably that's how Delmore found out about St. Peter."

Well, it didn't matter. Everybody knew, and that was what mattered.

When the final bell of the day rang, Sally leapt from her seat. She was among the first pupils out the school doors, Beverly close at her heels. They tore across the school yard through the snow, not bothering with sidewalks, but heading directly to Sally's house.

After running a block, Sally had a stitch in her side and slowed to a walk. She looked back, fearful that Delmore Preuss was following them, but she did not see him, so she paused to let the stitch subside before continuing on.

The two girls were heading down the alley behind the Wheeler house when Delmore Preuss, Ronald Oster, and Leroy Mosely jumped out from behind the Bofferding garage, hurling a fusillade of snowballs. They had taken a different route and sprinted all the way.

The soft, moist snow was packed hard and the balls felt like baseballs. The boys were laughing and calling the girls "Crazy Wheeler" and "Ugly Ridza."

Sally stood, beaten, letting the snowballs pelt her. Beside her, Beverly tossed her books down, scooped up snow, and bounding toward the boys, hurled it. In their midst she swung her fists in every direction. Heavily outnumbered, she was soon thrashing on the ground and Goddamning the boys who stuffed snow down her jacket and washed her face in it.

Seeing Beverly overwhelmed, Sally flung herself at the boys, kicking and pummeling and pulling hair until they turned on her, giving Beverly time to scramble to her feet. Snowballs forgotten, arms and legs flew.

The girls were about the same size and strength as the boys, but no sooner had they overpowered two of the boys than the third would launch himself at them.

Sally didn't quite understand the outcome. Suddenly Delmore Preuss, with whom Beverly had been in hand-to-hand combat, cried out, clutching his crotch and stumbling backward. Without Delmore, Ronald Oster and Leroy Mosely didn't want to fight. The three began retreating up the alley, Ronald and Leroy singsonging back, "Craaazy Wheeeler's craaazy old lady's locked up in a loony bin! Craaazy Wheeeler" and so on until they turned onto Fourth Avenue and disappeared.

Sally's lip was cut and starting to swell; a gash above Beverly's right eye was bleeding. Still, as they gathered up their books and slogged toward the Wheeler backdoor, Sally could not help feeling a flicker of pride in her wounded lip. She threw an arm around Beverly's waist, and though it hurt, she smiled for the first time in days.

February 21, 1942

Sally was asleep when her father pulled the car into the garage the following Friday night. Exhausted, she'd turned the radio off after *I Love a Mystery* and climbed the stairs without being told.

The next morning, she woke to the scrape of the snow shovel against the sidewalk in front of the house. Wandering to the window, she gazed at a modest new accumulation of snow that Donald was shoveling.

"Sit down and eat your pancakes," her grandmother advised when Sally came into the kitchen. "By then your daddy'll be done with the walks." She pulled a plate of pancakes from the oven where they'd been keeping. "He stopped in St. Peter on his way home. He'll tell you about it. Mind, that plate's hot," she said, placing it on a hot pad in front of Sally and pushing the can of Log Cabin syrup across the oilcloth toward her.

Irmgard had told Donald that Sally'd balked at going to Mass and school after being teased about Stella, so following break-fast, he loaded Sally's sled in the back of the Dodge, insisting that they drive out to Bacal's Hill, beyond the football field.

In the car he told her, "Your mother's being evaluated. That means the people at the hospital are studying her to see what she needs."

"When's she coming home?"

"Depends on how fast she gets better."

"But she's going to get better."

"The doctor I talked to thinks there's a pretty good chance."

Donald didn't tell her that when he'd last seen Stella, she had been unresponsive, as if she didn't hear people talking to her. She'd moved to a new, more distant place in her mind.

Donald and Sally dragged the Flexible Flyer up the hill. Around them others were doing the same.

Donald noted with surprise that Sally was nearly a head taller than other fourth-grade girls. He saw, too, that she was beautiful, even with the scabbed lip she'd got falling on the school steps. Of course he'd known that she was beautiful, but it was newly borne in on him.

How purposeful and controlled her movements were, as if she sensed people watching her. Had she always moved this way? The way she rode the Flyer down the hill was not like the others, but like an actress performing for an audience.

With Stella in the hospital, he would have time on the weekends to get reacquainted with Sally, he thought, stamping his feet and hunching his shoulders, though he was not actually cold. But what about the weekdays?

Donald sighed. His mother couldn't help out indefinitely. The old man needed her, and she missed her own place. He'd have to look for another job, one here in Harvester, though nothing here would pay as much as the road job.

Some distance away, Brenda Barnstable watched Neddy fling himself on the sled and skim down the hill. "Careful!" she called.

At the foot of the slope, Neddy fell in step with Sally, and they climbed to the top together. Donald noted that unlike most girls who were tall for their age, Sally didn't stoop and duck her head, but stood straight and held her head high.

Brenda Barnstable called, "Time to leave, Neddy."

"We've only been here a little while."

"Forty minutes. And my feet are frozen."

"Five more minutes? Please?"

"No." She put an arm around his shoulder, corralling him. "My feet are frozen," she repeated, a steely note in her voice.

"I could bring him home," Donald offered.

Brenda glanced up at him, and for a second, her features seemed paralyzed. Then she flashed a fulsome smile, explaining hurriedly but with overmuch cordiality, "No, really, he has a piano lesson."

"Not for an hour," Neddy complained.

"But you have to get cleaned up and changed. Come on," she insisted, taking hold of his mittened hand and pulling him along. "Thanks, anyway," she sang out over her shoulder.

Sally and Donald stood watching the two leave. "She didn't even let him go back down the hill on his sled. He had to walk," Sally observed. Turning away, she dragged the sled back to the rim of the hill and launched herself down its icy hump.

Neddy's mother must think that being crazy was catching, like measles, Sally speculated. Sally had caught it from Stella, and Neddy might catch it from *her*.

Donald shrugged, reflecting that Brenda Barnstable hadn't figured out how to talk to someone whose wife was in the state hospital for the insane. Arlene Erhardt would have known how to talk to him.

His eye wandered over the town, nearly all of which could be seen from Bacal's Hill. It didn't really feel like home today. The half-dozen church spires and the gray, sleepy, midwinter Main Street were vaguely unfamiliar, provincial and foreign, like a picture postcard from Czechoslovakia or somewhere, if picture postcards could any longer be sent from Czechoslovakia.

"Did I get a letter from Lark?" Sally inquired as she skinned off her snow pants.

Irmgard shook her head. "They're busy getting settled in California, Sally, and Lark's got a new school to get used to. You'll hear, don't worry."

"But it's been a month," Sally complained, "a whole month."

"Be patient."

Sally had written Lark two letters and didn't know where to send them. She'd even confided the news about her mother to her. Lark would have something reassuring to say, if she ever received Sally's letters.

After supper, Irmgard talked Sally into accompanying her to the Majestic to see *Pride and Prejudice*, which was late reaching Harvester. She, like Sally, needed to get out among people and grow used to their glances. Also, she wanted to give Bub and his dad a chance to talk.

"Would you join me in a bourbon?" Harry asked Donald when Irmgard and Sally had left.

"I'm not sure I've got any," Donald told him.

"Hell, I've got some," Harry said and fetched the pint bottle of Schenley's down from the kitchen cupboard where he'd put it earlier. "Neat or water?" he called.

"Water, thanks."

They sat on either side of the silent console radio, Harry in a wing chair, Donald on the sofa.

"I'm thinking about looking for work here in Harvester," Donald told his father, "so I can look after Sally." He held his glass on his knee. "With a wife in the asylum and a child to look after, I'm going to have to sit out this war."

Harry nodded. "They'll never draft you, under the circumstances."

"People will call me a draft dodger."

"Oh, hell, nobody who knows you would say that."

Donald shrugged, not quite convinced. Returning to the subject of work, he said, "Jobs here don't pay anything is the problem."

"What kind of work were you thinking of?"

"I don't know. Damned near anything. Beggers can't be choosers." He smiled ruefully.

Harry hitched himself around onto his left haunch. "I'd like to see you use your education."

"Doing what?"

"Hell, couldn't you teach? There's going to be men from the high school going to war. It doesn't pay a whole helluva lot, but it'd be a living."

"What do I know about teaching?" Funny thing was, the idea kind of excited him.

"I expect you could learn." A grin further creased the round, deeply lined little face, the face of a snowplow operator or telephone lineman (*his* old man had been a gandy dancer), though Harry was registrar of deeds in an office in the county courthouse and proud to wear a tie to work.

They were companionably silent.

Later, Harry asked about Stella, questions both practical and informed. "I read a while back in *Hygeia* that they're having pretty fair success with shock treatment. D'ya think they might try that with Stella? Could be she'll be out of there, you know, within a few months. What d'ya think of the place?"

Donald gave him his own impressions of the doctors and the hospital. The place, by its nature, had a taint to it, the same as a prison. No. Worse than a prison, he thought. But you gave both a wide berth.

Harry held his glass by the rim and twisted his wrist to set the ice cubes swirling and clattering. "Maybe it's wrong of me, but I can't help wondering why the Elways don't offer to put Stella in a private place. Wouldn't she get more personal looking after? They could afford it, couldn't they?"

Donald didn't answer at once. He shifted position, crossed one leg over the other, and stared at his glass. "It was discussed," he said finally. "If it had been up to Herb, I think they would have. Maybe they will yet. They know I can't afford it."

Again, he fell silent.

"Well, what happened that they didn't?"

"Edna. She can't stand to have Stella where she can't get to her in a few minutes. St. Peter's, what? maybe fifteen minutes away. Edna . . . It's like Stella's a child again, and she might come down with polio or diphtheria or something."

He put both feet on the floor, propping his elbows on his knees. "I didn't push the Elways to pay for a private hospital. Maybe later, when Edna gets used to things. Maybe Herb'll talk her into it then."

He looked at Harry. "Am I right? Am I doing the right thing? Should I have come out and asked them to?"

"Hell, Bub, there isn't any 'right' or 'wrong.' It's a 'damned if you do, and damned if you don't' kind of a deal. How about another?" he asked, rising. "I'm going to have one myself."

St. Bridget County began yielding up its young men to the
armed services. Some were drafted; many enlisted: farm
boys with muscled arms and ruddy faces, though many of
them could have qualified for deferment and some were
deferred until fall when crops were harvested; young men
from behind gas pumps and store counters; draymen and
tinsmiths; lawyers and teachers. Danny Navarin, who drove
a truck for Sinclair Oil, enlisted in the navy, and his mother,
Desiree, organized Red Cross volunteer work in a spare room
at the library.

The county was not so large but what many faces appearing
in the *Standard Ledger* were familiar — Junior Schuneman and
Francis Kretzmarsky, among others — and most of the names
were. The war became personal now.

Donald had worried needlessly about being called a draft
dodger. At forty-two, he was above the draft age and most men
of forty-two were not petitioning their selective service boards
to get into the military.

He mulled over Harry's question "Could you teach?" and a
few weeks later walked over to the school to talk to Bill Engel
the superintendent. Donald did not have a degree in education.
He had not taken courses at college in how to teach, but excep-
tions were being made. Three men from the high-school faculty

had enlisted, among them Mr. Hjalmer, who taught history and coached the baseball team. Donald had pitched for his high-school team, and under the circumstances, that seemed sufficient to qualify him for Mr. Hjalmer's position, especially since he had a degree in history from Gustavus Adolphus.

In reviewing his application, the school board was not unanimous in its pleasure. "His wife. Well, it might interfere with his performance," Reggie Albers, Katherine Albers' father, ventured. Discussion ensued and at length an impatient Dr. White pointed out, "The man is bright, likable, has a degree in history, and we need him." So on the Tuesday following Labor Day in 1942, Donald began teaching history and coaching baseball at Harvester High School.

By that time Sally had received and answered a number of letters from Lark, the first of which had not arrived until mid-March. The themes of that first letter would appear again and again in Lark's missives.

March 14, 1942

Dear Sally,

Mama and Aunt Betty rented a house in a housing project for defense workers. The project is in Pacific Beach. Pacific Beach is on the edge of San Diego. Mama got a job at a place where they make airplanes.

Where we live isn't really a house because it's two places stuck together. But it has a living room, two bedrooms, a bathroom, and a kitchen with a place for a table and chairs.

We can't afford any furniture yet so we sleep on the floor in the living room, but we're going to get beds pretty soon.

I go to a stupid school that's all on one floor, and I don't have any friends and I don't want any. There's a girl in my class named Shirley who walks home from school the same way that I go, but she is not nice at all. She's from Yoming. I probably didn't spell that right, but I don't have a dictionary. She swears all the time and she's mean and she doesn't wash once a month.

I hate it here and I'm going to run away when I get some

money. I will come to Harvester and see you. I'm not afraid to
run away. Don't tell anyone that I told you about running away.

Theres no trees and grass where we live. Just sand and sand
flees and I've got a hundred bites. There's only one good thing
about here. The people who live in the house that's connected
to ours are named Fanny and Garnett Dugan and they have
two English bull dogs named Sesil and Persy. Fanny and
Garnett and Sesil and Persy are nice. But you and Hilly are my
best friends even if he is dead. Please write to me.

Love xoxoxoxoxoxoxox

Lark Ann Browning Erhardt

p.s. Also I like Beverly.
p.s. Could you send me a picture of you?

Late in the spring, in a subsequent letter, Lark wrote:

Dear Sally,

An awful terrible thing happened to me but I can't tell you
what. It's too scarey and embarussing. I wish I was in
Harvester. Constabel Wall would arrest the boys who live in
the project and they'd never get out of jail . . .

Sally could not imagine what had happened. Although letters
continued back and forth, Lark did not reveal the "awful, terrible thing."

Much later in the year, because Fanny was not strong, Lark
accepted a job walking the Dugan's dogs, Percy and Cecil.
"They protect me from The Boys," she wrote, "and Garnett
pays me so I'm saving money to run away."

Although Sally longed to see her friend, she worried about
Lark's dangerous notion of running away. "When I take off, it
will be on a box car. I know plenty about railroads and 'riding
the rails.'"

Donald worked hard reviewing what he'd learned in college
and supplementing it with materials Desiree Navarin helped

him find at the library. He taught five classes: two in American history, two in world history, and one in civics. Three preparations were a heavy load but not unusual, and by the time baseball coaching duties began in late winter, he would have a handle on the teaching, he hoped.

As a member of the coaching staff, Donald felt it behooved him to show support for his fellow coaches. He began attending home games of the high-school teams. Now it was football; basketball would follow, and so on through the year, and through the several varsity sports. Sally, and usually Beverly as well, accompanied him.

After the Harvester/Red Berry game on a warm, brilliant Saturday afternoon in early October, he dropped Beverly at home, then headed for Worthington, Sally beside him in the front seat, chattering about the home team's 13 to 7 victory.

The maize light of October bathed the harvested fields flowing away endlessly in all directions. Farmyard trees and groves were washed with yellow, gold, and red and, here and there, the earthy brown of oak or beech.

When Sally had said everything she had to say about the football game, she rode in silence, scouting the pastures for horses and sheep. Donald began humming "Praise the Lord, and Pass the Ammunition," and she glanced at him, taking up the tune herself. She noted for the first time and with a clutch of panic that he was graying. How old was he? Pretty old, she supposed, but too young to be turning gray.

Home from his Saturday half-day at the courthouse, Harry was kneeling in the garden, cutting winter squash from the vines when Donald drew to the curb in front of the small white clapboard house.

Set in the middle of a great, square yard, the house looked as if it might be consumed in the red and yellow conflagration of surrounding maples and birch. Already the air was filled with the perfume of leaf-burning from the season's first raking.

After carrying her overnight bag up to the little yellow bedroom under the eaves where she always slept, Sally ran downstairs and out the backdoor to the double glider in the grape arbor.

"Are you hungry?" Irmgard called out the backdoor. "We'll have an early supper." She was convinced that most people arrived hungry, even if they wouldn't admit it. "Sally, pick Grandma a few tomatoes."

Later, as she and Sally cleared away dinner dishes, she noted, "Have to pick the last of the tomatoes tomorrow. Don't want the frost to get them."

"Some of them are still green," Sally pointed out.

"We'll pull the bushes out and hang them in the back hall. They'll ripen up."

"Did you can tomatoes?" Donald inquired, stirring cream from the top of the milk bottle into his coffee.

"Oh, my, yes. Nearly fifty quarts. They're put away in the fruit cellar." She brought out a fresh-baked apple pie and set it on the table.

After Mass the next day, Sally helped Irmgard bring in the remaining tomatoes, and following lunch, she trailed her granddad out back to clean the little barn, which years ago had been given over to sheltering his car. She swept the floor, then climbed the ladder to the haymow where items no longer used but too good to throw away were stored. Opening the loft door through which hay had once been loaded into the barn, she called down to her grandpa where he stood in the drive, examining a rake whose comb had come loose.

"Look at me, Grandpa."

"You be careful you don't fall and break your neck," he advised, his brown little face smiling up at her.

Those were the exact words that Sally had known he

would say, and their familiarity and certainty reassured her.

Around three, when she had swept the drive and raked the frill of leaves from the still-green grass into a pile in the back driveway, Sally and her grandpa stood watching them burn, breathing in their final gift, the perfume of their going.

"Better take a bath after all that dust and smoke," Irmgard called, and Sally headed upstairs to the bathroom, which, like her bedroom, was under the eaves. Rising from a long soak, she had to duck her head so as not to hit it on the sloped ceiling.

The bath made her drowsy. Toweling off and dusting with DuBarry talcum, she pulled on a skirt and blouse and lay down across the bed to rest for a minute. At the window, elm leaves, pale yellowy green, brushed delicately against the panes.

Waking, Sally saw that the sun slanted sidewise through the tree. The clock on the bureau said four-thirty. She rolled over onto her back, yawning and stretching.

Shadows of the lacey tip-ends of the elm boughs danced on the yellow walls. Up from the kitchen wafted the smell of pot roast slow-cooking in the iron Dutch oven on the back of the stove.

The voices of her father and his parents droned. Words drifted up through the warm air register in the corner of the bedroom, a holdover from the days when a wood stove heated the kitchen below.

"I hate her," Donald rasped.

Sally lifted her head from the pillow, propping herself on her elbows.

"I look at her, sitting on a bench, staring at a wall, at another patient, at me, and it's all the same to her. No difference. I want to hit her, shove her against a wall, and scream at her, what the hell does she think she's doing to Sally and me."

Coming up through the register, her father's sobs sounded metallic and strangled, as if they were strained by the metal grille through which they struggled.

"On the way home I'm so ashamed, I have to pull off the

road. I know I haven't been kind to her." He broke down, weeping harshly, choking on his tears. "But when I'm there, I want to kill her."

Dropping her head against the pillow, Sally put both hands over her ears and rocked from side to side in a monumental *no.*

October — December 1942

The fall grading period was galloping to an end, and for the first time, Donald had to draw up, administer, and score what were deemed important tests — the six-week examinations. When he'd scored them, he had to tot up final grades for the period; enter them on report cards, along with attendance figures and comments on each student's attitudes and progress; then turn the records of grades and attendance into the principal's office. He'd done less paper work as a salesman.

Because he was entirely unschooled in the systems and methodology, and because he was on probation as well, he labored painstakingly, sweating over the least quiz, agonizing over the records. Next grading period would be easier. This time he must prove to the principal, the superintendent, and the school board that he could do what the others did.

Days and weeks slipped by and with them milestones: Stella had been hospitalized for six months, nine months; fifth grade commenced for Sally and rolled inexorably toward Halloween, Thanksgiving, Christmas.

Sally wrote regularly to her mother, feeling like an archer shooting arrows into a starless night, hoping they would find the target. Stella did not write back. Although she was disappointed, Sally was not surprised.

Eavesdropping on adult conversation and snooping in family correspondence, Sally knew that her mother had had shock treatments, whatever those were, and that she had responded, then slipped once more out of reach.

Although Donald had spoken earlier of taking Sally to visit her mother, he did not. Instead, he offered excuses that were plausible and sometimes even true.

Lacking any real idea of the hospital, Sally imagined an idyllic setting for Stella, a place like Sherwood Forest in *The Adventures of Robin Hood*, starring Errol Flynn, which she had seen at the penny movies.

Sylvan and sheltering, with golden sunlight falling in shafts through dancing leaves, it embraced at its heart a structure half crenellated castle, half ivied university, and in a room where gossamer draperies stirred at tall Gothic windows, Stella lived in a state of not unpleasant revery.

Now that Donald was home during the week, he and Sally developed routines for cooking, cleaning, yard work, and shopping.

The first year of "batching," rather than haphazardly keeping abreast of all the household chores, they allowed one or two areas to slide, then worked furiously catching up. Thus, they cooked and marketed and ran the Hoover for several weeks, ignoring the laundry, until neither had a clean sock or ironed shirt. Or the refrigerator emptied down to a single half jar of Limburger cheese spread while the closets and drawers filled up with fresh clothes, bed linens, and tea towels.

About once a month, the grandparents traded off visiting, and the grandmothers unerringly detected the lapsed chores, falling upon them greedily and dispatching them with satisfaction. Had nothing required putting to rights, they might have departed feeling useless. Few things are more cheering, they each knew, than going to bed exhausted, putting small matters to rights, when large matters will not yield.

When she came for the holiday, Irmgard Wheeler spent half of the day after Christmas, which was a Saturday, letting down the hems of Sally's dresses and skirts. Edna Elway, seeing the stack of clothes to be let down, exclaimed, "My word, Sally, you need some new things."

Irmgard bristled. "There's nothing wrong with wearing things let down." She knotted a thread and stabbed the needle into a hem. "Think of the Russian children in Stalingrad freezing to death."

"I just hadn't noticed that Sally'd outgrown her dresses. I must be blind."

The two grandmothers sat opposite each other in the wing chairs while Sally and Beverly sprawled on the floor, playing rummy. The men had driven Donald's car to the Sinclair station to find out what was causing a grinding noise in the front left side, down about where the wheel and axle met.

Irmgard was sorry she'd taken umbrage about the hems. Edna wasn't as pert and confident as she'd once been. She'd put on weight and while she still wore expensive clothes, she was less aware of them. Yesterday she'd had a run in her stocking, though of course these days plenty of women did, what with good hose so hard to find. Still, it had shocked Irmgard.

Irmgard had taken to wearing cotton stockings from the Lane Bryant catalog. She knew they made her look like an old lady, but she was sixty after all and had never been one to put on a show.

"Would you like a cup of tea?" Edna asked.

"That would be nice. I don't mind it weak." Everything except home produce was so hard to get, Irmgard made things stretch as far as they would go.

Edna's jaw was starting to sag, Irmgard noted. That would provoke her. Or maybe not. Maybe it meant no more to her than the laddered stocking. She had been through the wringer.

"How about a game of bridge when the men get back?" Irmgard asked as Edna set the teacup and saucer on the table beside her. "You and me playing partners."

Sunday afternoon Sally returned to Mankato with Herb and Edna. "Tomorrow you and I'll drive to the Cities and find you a new coat," Edna told her granddaughter, eyeing the length of wrist showing below Sally's cuff. "You're going to be taller than your mother, I shouldn't be surprised." Edna's voice caught. Pulling her gloves on roughly, she embraced Donald, telling him, "We'll bring her back next weekend."

Sally's watch, a Christmas gift from the Elway grandparents, read five past seven when Herb pulled the Lincoln into the drive of the four-bedroom Tudor that faced on a little triangular park.

Sally managed her own bag, lugging it into the front hall and setting it beside the open stairway. Shucking coat and cap, she wandered into the big living room and flicked on a lamp beside the sofa.

Grandma Elway's house had a wonderful smell, Sally thought—decades of Grandma's perfumes mixed with countless fires in the living-room grate, plus some unidentifiable element having to do with the comfort that proceeds from prosperity.

"I'll fix us a bite," Edna told Sally. "Why don't you get into your flannel nightdress."

In her bedroom—Stella's room when she was growing up—Sally changed into the flannel gown, crossed to the window, and stared out at the dark twisted forms of winter trees, silhouetted against the light of street lamps, the sharp, shadows of their limbs falling across the snowy park.

This was what her mother had seen in winter when she looked out. Sally tried to imagine herself as the young Stella, tried to imagine the thoughts Stella might have had as she stood at this window. Had she known that she was going to be crazy? Did a person see it coming, like shadows moving across the lawn?

Sally and Edna set out for Minneapolis early the next morning, Edna driving her own car, a blue Buick. The day was overcast but showed signs of clearing.

They were not long on the road when a water tower loomed up with the name *St. Peter* written large on it. That they would be passing through the town where Stella was hospitalized had not occurred to Sally. She was shaken and lay a hand on Edna's arm. "Can we go see Mommy?"

"We can't see her today," Edna said without explanation. Catching her lower lip between her teeth, she looked quickly at Sally. "We could drive by the hospital. Do you want to do that?"

Sally nodded, breathing shallowly and clasping her hands tightly together. She was going to see where her mother lived. An awful tension stretched her tight: she wanted to know what the hospital looked like, yet she feared seeing it.

Edna turned left, driving up a broad, inclining street, desolate in late December. Sally's boots bore hard against the floor, as if she would halt the car by main force.

"This is it," Grandma was saying. "Is it the way you imagined?"

Sally sat on her folded knees, staring at the various buildings. No, it wasn't as she had imagined. It was just bricks and bricks and bricks, and lawns, and trees. Like the hospital in St. Bridget, repeated many times. No Sherwood Forest, no turrets and banners. It looked like a place where they kept the temperature at sixty-five in the winter.

"Your mother sleeps in that building," Grandma pointed out, but Sally was staring ahead, willing the car away.

By the time they stopped for an early lunch at the Saint Paul House in Shakopee, part of Sally regretted not having paid more attention to the hospital. When I try to imagine Mommy, all I'll be able to remember is all those bricks, she thought. But another part of her was gratified to maintain the moated castle and the sheltering forest washed with golden light, to add to it regularly small details of amenity and security, to imagine her mother happy, though captive.

While Edna checked them into the Curtis Hotel, Sally surveyed the bustling lobby with its elegant appointments, Oriental carpets, fireplace, and fine furniture. She took an instant liking to it because it made her feel like Greta Garbo in *Grand Hotel*. Very sophisticated.

Unpacking in a double room overlooking Eleventh Street, Edna turned from the closet, her eyes distant with reminiscence, and told Sally, "Your mother and I stayed in this hotel when she was a girl, when we came to Minneapolis shopping." Suddenly she was knocking bottles over and spilling face powder, hastily emptying her cosmetic bag on the vanity, shoving perfume and nail polish this way and that, to no purpose.

With the last bottle righted, she ushered Sally out of the room and the hotel, onto Tenth Street, and grasped her granddaughter's mittened hand tightly in hers, suggesting, "Let's walk to Nicollet Avenue."

The clouds had moved east and the day was bright. Sally skittered along the sidewalk like a long-legged bird, poking into a doorway here, a restaurant there, craning to glimpse the upper reaches of the Foshay Tower. Edna was winded keeping up, but she would not let go of Sally's hand. My God, she thought, what if Sally were to run into the street? She shuddered, forced a smile, and wished she'd worn her other shoes.

In the shops and department stores, Edna fluttered and chattered and dashed back and forth, waylaying and belaying, pinning clerks to the dressing-room door with her questions and prattle. By midafternoon, when they paused for a pastry and tea, Sally was dazed.

Grandma Elway explained to the waitress from what towns she and Sally came, in what hotel they were staying, what was the purpose of the trip, and what success they had thus far enjoyed. At the cash register, she repeated everything for the cashier while Sally glanced away, shifting her weight from one foot to the other and chewing the end of one of her braids.

Noting that several customers were waiting in line behind Edna, Sally at length tugged on her grandmother's coat sleeve. "We'd better go now, Grandma."

Late in the afternoon as Sally tried on coats, Edna began contending with a clerk about the color of a particular garment. The clerk had referred to it as "plum," and Edna said that it wasn't anything like plum, it was in fact "puce." Her tone offended the clerk, a senior salesperson who was in line to become buyer for the department as soon as Mr. Ames, the current buyer, enlisted in the Coast Guard, which he planned to do in January, right after inventory.

"If you would care to see the stock sheet, madam," said the clerk, "you would find that the manufacturer designates this color 'plum.'"

"Are you disputing my opinion, *Miss?*" Edna demanded, her face thrust forward, cords in her neck straining above the collar of the seal coat.

"I am only pointing out the manufacturer-designated color," the clerk said, not retreating an inch. "If you like, I could provide you with that company's address, so that you could take it up with them." The woman's voice was rather awful in its quiet, impersonal manner.

Sally who lingered, forgotten, in the doorway of a dressing stall, waiting to model a coat for her grandmother, backed into the room, closed the door, and stood pressed against it.

Beyond the partition, Edna was insisting, "I want to speak to your superior."

Sally sat down on a stool, covered her ears, and began humming. When she lifted her hands, a man's voice was murmuring, "Here is the stock sheet. Hmmmm. Yes, I see that the manufacturer designates this color 'plum,' as you will note. If you wish to take the matter up with the manufacturer, I will be happy to provide you with his address." The voice was weary but firm.

"I have no intention of taking the matter up with the manufacturer," Edna was saying. "All I wanted was civil, helpful treatment. I asked to see this clerk's superior," she went on, her voice tearful, "but you're not *anyone's* superior. I will write a letter to the president of the store."

Edna's voice trailed off, crying to no one in particular or anyone who would listen, "People are impertinent. It's the war. It's ruining everything!"

The clerk and her boss conversed in increasingly indistinct voices as they moved away from the stalls. Slipping out of the coat she'd been trying, Sally pulled on her own coat, then her cap and scarf.

Outside the dressing room, she looked around. Edna was nowhere in sight. Sally crossed the Girls' Department, headed toward a bank of elevators. Edna was not waiting there, nor was she in the ladies' rest room opposite. Beside the elevators were several chairs, and Sally sat down in one to wait. Maybe her grandmother had gone looking for the president of the store.

Sally's watch said four-forty. She did not want to leave the third floor to search for Edna, for fear her grandmother would return from the president's office or wherever she'd disappeared and find Sally gone.

Twice, women asked Sally if she was waiting for someone,

and she'd told them her mother was trying on a dress. When the rest-room matron whom she'd questioned about Edna came out and headed toward a service stairs, she asked, "You find your grandma?"

"Yes, thank you."

"Well, you have a good evening then," the woman called back, withdrawing into the stairwell.

Sally glanced at her watch. Five-twenty. The store closed in ten minutes. Clerks began straightening merchandise, returning goods to racks and shelves, covering tables with muslin sheets, and studying their sales pads. They discussed the sort of day it had been, and Sally thought she heard the "plum" versus "puce" clerk talking about Edna and speculating on whether Sally's grandmother could do her any harm when it came time for promotion to buyer.

A man who looked like a floorwalker came reconnoitering through the third floor, casting a fish-eye about, making certain no detail of closing-up had gone unattended to. Sally stood and pressed the "down" button for the elevator. In another minute the man would accost her, wanting to know why she was hanging about.

On the street, where darkness had already fallen, Sally waited by the revolving doors, observing everyone who came out of the store. Street lamps, headlights, and illumination from store windows lit the sidewalks only dimly as the city observed wartime "brown-out."

An overcoated policeman stood at the corner, answering questions, giving directions, and occasionally stepping into the street to unsnarl a knot of cars. Several times he glanced toward Sally, standing alone in the cold.

Again Sally looked at her watch. Five-forty-five. She would wait until six. And then? Ask the policeman what streets would take her to the Curtis Hotel? Would that get her grandmother into trouble?

Her feet were cold. She stamped up Nicollet Avenue, away

from the policeman, but not so far that Edna would miss her should she still be in the store and come searching. Trying to look casual and unworried, as though she often waited for her grandmother like this, she studied the store-window displays and passersby. But along with the cold and damp of the night, fear overtook her.

What if something had happened to her grandmother? What if she'd been hit by a streetcar? How would Sally find her, or even find out? How would she pay for food? For despite her apprehensions, she was hungry.

Six o'clock came. Somewhere not too distant, church bells rang the hour. Well, *now* what was she going to do?

At a quarter past six, a taxicab screeched to the curb, its back door was flung open, and Edna jumped out. Tears streaming, arms thrown wide, she dashed toward Sally, scooping the child to her breast and sobbing, "My baby, poor baby! Oh, my God, what's wrong with me?"

Mindless of the taxi waiting, she stood crooning and rocking Sally in her embrace for several minutes before holding her away and crying, "You must be frozen. Get in the cab."

In the hotel lobby, people turned to stare as Edna, still weeping and with her hat askew, hurried Sally to the elevators. With the door of their room closed behind them, she helped Sally out of her coat, chafed her cold hands, then removed her boots and shoes and rubbed the child's feet as well, all the while gabbling half incoherently about the monster she herself was, not fit to have child or grandchild.

Clutching Sally in a ruthless embrace, she cried, "Darling Sally, will you ever forgive your grandmother?"

"Graaandma," Sally pleaded, extricating herself and studying Edna's tear-swollen face, her ruined makeup. "It's okay. I'm all right." To see her elegant, self-possessed grandmother reduced to this bawling, distraught child chilled Sally worse than the cold night.

"Take off your coat and hat," she told her grandmother. "Where did you go?" Pulling back the bedding and arranging the pillows, Sally crawled beneath the covers and sat in bed watching her grandmother shrug out of her coat and drop it on a chair.

Edna said nothing, but great wracking sighs shuddered up from her breast as she removed a hat pin, yanked off her hat, and pressed the pin back again into the blue felt. Tossing the hat down on top of the fur coat, she slipped out of her shoes and turned to face Sally.

"Where's your hanky?" Sally asked.

For a moment Edna seemed not to comprehend the question. But she crossed to her purse, thrown on the floor beside the bed, and extracted a handkerchief from it, wiping her eyes and nose. Then, sitting at the foot of the bed and staring at the square of linen in her hands, she shook her head slowly as one might, emerging from a lengthy and profound daze.

"I don't know what happened to me today. I'm so ashamed." She looked at Sally. "I forgot . . . I *forgot* about you. I ran out of the store and forgot that you were with me." Twisting the handkerchief, she went on, "I can't explain. I must be crazy."

"You're not crazy!"

Edna regarded her. "No. No, of course not. I didn't mean 'crazy.' I meant 'upset.' 'Beside myself.'"

Arms folded across her breast and brow pinched with appraisal, Sally contemplated her grandmother. "You're not crazy. Mommy's crazy. *You* have to pay attention. People who aren't crazy have to pay attention. You can worry about Mommy when you go to bed at night," she pointed out. "You can't do it when you're driving the car, otherwise you might run over a dog like Mommy did. And you can't do it when you're buying a coat. You have to do it at night when nobody'll get hurt. Do you understand, Grandma?"

"Who told you all this?"

"Nobody. It's just . . . *sensible.*" She flung the bed covers back with a snap, complaining, "I'm hungry. Can we get something to eat?"

Edna stared at her for several seconds, then began giggling. In a moment they were both bent double laughing.

When Edna had washed her face, combed her hair, and reapplied her makeup, the two took the elevator to the first floor and ran up a considerable bill in the dining room.

The next morning, Edna and Sally tackled Young Quinlan's and Dayton's in search of a coat. Coming out of Dayton's, Sally darted away, up Nicollet Avenue in pursuit of two retreating figures. "Neddy!" she called.

Neddy and Brenda Barnstable turned.

"Sally!"

"What're you doing?" Sally wanted to know.

"Visiting Grandma and Grandpa Shelborne," Neddy told her. "What're *you* doing?"

"Buying clothes."

"I'm Sally's Grandmother Elway," Edna told the well-dressed woman and her son, recognizing the name Shelborne and making one or two assumptions. "We were about to stop for lunch. Would you join us?"

"I'm Brenda Barnstable," the woman said in a voice heavy with disinterest. "I'm not sure about lunch . . ."

"Say yes, please?" begged Neddy who had been trailing his mother from one millinery department to another all morning.

"The Fountain Room at Young Quinlan's?" Edna suggested.

Neddy's glance at his mother was gray and resentful. Brenda grudgingly assented, though she had no inclination to lunch with Stella Wheeler's mother and daughter. Brenda was not a snob, but really, being with people who were, well, part of a very unhappy situation was uncomfortable. What could you talk about? An aura of taint — was that too strong a word? — surrounded them, didn't it?

The waitress's shoes, uniform, underwear, and stockings all

whispered of petit bourgeois propriety. Recording their orders on a pale green pad, she was simultaneously helpful, friendly, and discreetly appraising. Many years in the Fountain Room had honed her sense of customer status. With an astonishing degree of accuracy, she could tell you how much a woman's husband earned or how many dollars her hat had set him back.

Sitting opposite each other, Sally and Neddy ignored the two women and discussed what they'd got for Christmas and how many extra-credit library books they'd read during Christmas vacation.

They talked about Lark and what Sally knew of her life in San Diego. "Something awful happened to her. I don't know what, but don't tell anyone. She doesn't want anyone to know." Neddy was the only boy Sally would trust with such information. "If you want to write her sometime, I think she'd like it. She says she's going to run away and come back to Harvester, but I hope she doesn't because I'm afraid something awful might happen."

Neddy nodded.

"She's saving up all her birthday and Christmas money and the money she makes walking the neighbors' dogs. When she has enough, she's going to run away. Do you think she really will?"

His face was serious and not disbelieving. Sally was relieved to have someone she could share her fears with besides Beverly, who couldn't comprehend anyone wanting to run away from California.

"Mankato. My husband's a doctor there," Edna was explaining.

Brenda Barnstable was polite. "My Uncle Henry's a doctor at the Mayo Clinic. Heart. Treated crowned heads." She sipped ice water, glancing around the room for any of her many cousins or sorority sisters. She'd telephone this afternoon, find out what was going on. This time of year there'd be parties, some place to wear her new clothes. She wouldn't go back to

Harvester until she'd *done* something, until she had something to talk about. Nothing ever happened in Harvester. People expected her to return with stories, she was sure, with little escapades, adventures, and gossip, something about the mayor or the scion of a department-store fortune. God, what was life coming to, if she couldn't regale what passed for society in a whistle-stop like Harvester?

She shuddered and turned her attention to Edna who was filling the void of Brenda's indifference with chatter not quite desperate, but nonetheless labored.

Like someone standing on an embarrassingly bald spot in the carpet to prevent its being seen, Edna was self-conscious and oddly resentful. On the other hand, *she* had importuned this woman to join her for lunch. It was her own vanity, which challenged her to prove that she could swim with the big fish. And it was her own vanity, that caused her now to feel misjudged and ill-used.

"Have you read *The Moon Is Down*?" she asked Brenda, certain that the woman hadn't, but in need of a score.

"Who wrote it?" Brenda asked, unabashed.

"Steinbeck."

"No. I don't like Steinbeck. *The Grapes of Wrath* was interminable. I gave up halfway through. I don't think novelists have any right to string you along like that, just going on forever, and all of it sordid and sad, as if all you had to do with your time was read them. It's a nerve." With utter equanimity and genuine appetite, she launched into her salmon croquette.

So bald-faced was Brenda's response, Edna could imagine no suitable riposte, none consistent with her Episcopal school upbringing at any rate. And so the score went to Brenda, who doubtless was unaware of any competition.

Driving out of the city the next morning, Edna asked Sally, "Do you hate shopping?"

Sally considered. "No. Why?"

"Your mother hated shopping when she was a girl. I had to bribe her to go. I thought when she got into high school, she'd take an interest," Edna went on. "But she didn't. Didn't take any interest in boys either. Just wanted to read and dream. I worried she wouldn't get enough fresh air and exercise. My people believed in fresh air and exercise. Kept girls from getting dreamy."

Sally liked shopping with her grandmother. She liked pretty clothes. Pretty clothes were something she didn't have to envy other girls. Pretty clothes and a pretty face. Boys could tease her about Stella being crazy, but they couldn't tease her about her clothes or her face.

"You were raised Catholic, so you never joined Job's Daughters, but I sort of pushed your mother into it. They had parties and little dances once or twice a year. I thought it'd do her good to have to ask a boy to a party."

"Did she? Ask a boy?"

"I practically had to ask them for her. She just didn't want to be bothered. But, you know, I didn't want her to be an old maid, so I saw to it that she went to the high-school prom and that kind of thing. If a girl doesn't develop social skills by the time she goes to college, she'll end up a nurse or a school-teacher," she said.

While this wasn't a *sin,* her tone implied, it was surely a shame.

July 1943

Because he needed two summers, carrying full course-loads in education, to earn his teaching certification, Donald enrolled at Mankato State Teachers' College the second and third summers of Stella's hospitalization. Edna and Herb insisted that he and Sally stay with them; indeed, they could not have been more pleased with the arrangement.

It was the only way that Donald could manage financially, carrying sixteen credits a summer. At that, he worked part-time at Brett's Department Store, eschewing a loan from Herb.

Although Sally missed Beverly, Mrs. Stillman, Mrs. Navarin at the library, even Neddy Barnstable, for three months neither Delmore Preuss nor Ronald Oster could humiliate her. People were able to forget a good many disgraces, but Stella's being in the asylum wasn't one of them.

To be Clara Hennessey wouldn't be as bad as being Sally Wheeler. Clara Hennessey had failed fifth grade, ending up in Sally's class. She was big for her age and already had breasts and b.o. Everyone said Clara was slow, and Sally guessed that she probably was, but she felt sorry for the girl because boys called her Clarabelle the Cow, due to her prematurely large breasts. And the first week of fifth grade she'd been discovered to have head lice and ringworm.

Still, being slow and having to stay out of school until your ringworm and head lice were cured seemed preferable to having a crazy mother. Sally had mastered an icy, aloof face, which she directed toward anyone who seemed slighting, but every taunting reference to Stella, every shoulder turned against her for whispered gossip was as startling and painful as the first. Collected in her memory, they were a swarm of endlessly stinging bees.

The first summer in Mankato, Sally's mother was allowed to visit them one weekend. She was not ready to live away from the hospital, but the doctor had agreed with Edna that a short furlough would likely do no harm. With the war on, hospital staff was stretched thin, and Stella's absence for the weekend meant one less patient for the attendants in the Psychopath Building.

Friday, July 9th, Donald drove to the state hospital after his last class. Heat and humidity were caught in the sharp elbow of the Minnesota River where Mankato sprawled. Westerly breezes skimmed over the embanking hills without scooping the heat from the valley.

The sleeves of Donald's white shirt were rolled high on his arms, the neck was open, and the front windows of the Buick, which Edna had pressed him to take, were rolled all the way down. Still, he felt choked as he drove north out of town, headed for St. Peter. Summer heat did not normally affect him. All his summers had been lived in heat not so different from this. Yet he tugged at the open collar of his shirt and adjusted the vent windows.

Stella looked cool in the plain, square-neck beige and white chambray dress sent her by Edna. She smiled shyly, crossing the little lobby of the Psychopath Building to meet Donald, but flinched when his hand touched her arm as she slid into the car.

On the road, she lay her head against the back of the seat and closed her eyes, luxuriating in the wind washing over her face and neck, lifting and tossing her hair.

"Tell me if that gets too breezy," Donald told her.

She nodded but didn't speak, nor did she respond as Donald

spoke desultorily of classes at the college, the part-time job in the men's department at Brett's, or Sally's learning tennis. He thought that she was absorbing and comprehending what he told her, but withholding response as a way of giving him to understand her limitations, which must be part of the weekend, and best accepted early on. That was okay. He'd made a list of small talk, bits of minor news that would not upset her. She did not open her eyes until they turned into the alleyway leading to the garage behind the Elway house.

Sally, who had been forewarned and instructed by Edna and Donald, waited in the living room. Wearing a flowered cotton dirndl skirt and embroidered peasant blouse, she stood by the mantel, crossing and uncrossing all her fingers, clearing her throat, and rocking onto the sides of her loafers. She had been told not to rush at Stella, but to wait for her mother to approach her.

Behind the closed door of her bedroom, she had rehearsed at the tall mirror, trying on different smiles, and choosing at length the Mrs. Albers, closed-mouth smile, which seemed least threatening.

How to greet her mother? "Hello, Mommy," she'd said to the mirror, then, "Hi, Mommy," then, simply, "Hi." The last sounded too casual, too unsympathetic, so she opted for "How are you, Mommy?"

Now the creak of the screen door drifted in from the kitchen and a subdued, murmured greeting between Stella and Edna, which Sally could not make out. Moments later, three pairs of feet made their way down the central hall toward the front of the house, Donald leading the way, saying, "I'll carry Stella's suitcase upstairs." Sally wiped her palms on the dirndl skirt.

As Stella and Edna appeared in the archway, Edna smiled meaningfully. "Don't rush. Don't blurt," the look reminded. The two women paused, framed in the door.

"Mommy," Sally whispered, "how are you?" Memories of

early childhood—a brief Eden of misty recollection, before Stella began weeping—rushed at Sally, nearly obscuring her mother's face. Nudging them aside, Sally smiled the closed-mouth smile and moved across the room, slowly, lest she startle her mother. "Mommy?"

Stella studied the child. Sally had grown, far beyond her expectations. Despite the sprawling, indeterminate boundaries of time that hospitalization had assumed, Stella had failed to envision how much Sally might change.

Sally's body had lengthened out and stood pressed against the onset of adolescent curves; the manner in which she carried herself and held her head, with a daunting queenliness, hinted of a rod of mettle running down her spine.

Stella felt robbed and repudiated. Too much had changed while her back was turned. Sally was no longer a little girl. Donald was teaching. They were not the people she had known.

She would not think about this. Thinking would make her sad. She had her ways of eluding sadness.

Although Sally was reluctant even to look at her mother, for fear of distressing her, unconsciously she grasped Stella's hands, placing them, one on either side of her own face.

Stella held her daughter's cheeks in this way for several moments, warming her cold hands on the child's hot, flushed face. At length she removed them and crossed to the sofa, waiting for Sally to sit before seating herself a foot or more distant.

Donald came into the living room, lowering himself into a club chair opposite his wife. Edna, who'd been standing by the door, watching the reunion between Sally and Stella, took the other chair facing the sofa, though not before straightening a lamp shade and moving a dish of candy from an end table to the coffee table.

Edna's hands, folded around each other in her lap, twitched like small, high-strung animals. "I'm cooking pheasant for dinner. Your favorite. Dad got them out of the locker this morning," she added, referring to the Elway locker in the cold-storage plant downtown. Crossing and uncrossing her legs, she observed, "Dad had good luck hunting last fall, shot a lot of nice ducks and pheasants. A deer, too, later. Sam Burch at the cold-storage plant butchered it for us. With meat-rationing, it's come in handy. Your father likes meat, you know."

She rose and offered the dish of bridge mix to Stella, then Sally and Donald. "I tried to think of something you wouldn't have at the . . . in St. Peter. I didn't think they'd probably have pheasant, and of course I remembered how much you liked it. They do raise chickens on the farm there, I know, and nice vegetables. Am I right?"

Having put several pieces of bridge mix into her mouth, Stella nodded.

Edna half rose from her chair. "Did you say something, dear?"

But Stella shook her head and reached for more candy. She rarely had candy. The attendants in the Psychopath Building were kind to her. They often gave her cookies, but not often candy. If she remembered, she would ask to take candy back with her. She missed the Psychopath Building and Eunice who shared her room. Eunice didn't talk. Stella didn't mind. It was soothing. Anyway, Stella herself rarely spoke. Sometimes, like Eunice, she didn't speak at all. Sometimes she didn't even think. She disappeared then.

Once, when she had disappeared, she'd awakened in the infirmary with a tube in her arm. Back in the Psychopath Building, an attendant had told her that the tube was there because she hadn't been eating.

She liked the Psychopath Building. It wasn't so very big, not like the building with the flats, which was too big and frightened her. The Psychopath Building was friendly. Only women worked there. She liked that. And the women were pleasant.

Usually, when patients first arrived at the "bughouse," as many called it, they were housed in the Psychopath Building for a few weeks, or perhaps months. But later they were moved to the larger building. A few were kept on in the Psychopath Building. Stella wasn't sure for what reason, but she thought it was because the women who worked there liked them and simply "forgot" to move them along. She was grateful not to have been moved, and she often thanked the attendants. She'd told Mrs. Korn, the night matron, that God would carry her directly to heaven when she died — no purgatory or anything like that — because Mrs. Korn allowed Stella to remain in the Psychopath Building.

Stella thought that Mrs. Korn had been startled, since she was unaccustomed to Stella's speaking much. And really, Stella, too, had been startled to hear her own words.

Stella had the notion that her very words could make her sad. Or make someone else sad, which was the same thing. She'd been assured that that wasn't so, but she wasn't convinced. She had words and thoughts in her head that, she knew, were *wrong*.

Sometimes she thought that moving around could make her sad as well, so she sat very still. She would do anything not to feel sad, including disappearing.

"I want to lie down," she told her mother.

Edna and Donald rose simultaneously. "Of course, you do," Edna exclaimed, hurrying toward Stella as if she were an invalid requiring assistance in order to rise and move about. "You must be exhausted."

"Where?" Stella wondered.

"Why, in your old room," Edna told her, taking her arm. Believing that Stella would feel more at home in the room of her childhood, Edna had moved Sally into a guest room while Stella visited.

Withdrawing her arm from her mother's grasp, as she had flinched from Donald's, Stella crossed to the stairs. She believed that touching people made her sad or made them sad, and she tried not to touch anyone or allow them to touch her. When she disappeared, nothing touched her and she did not touch anyone. But she was going to try not to disappear while she was here. If she was not to disappear, however, she would have to protect herself and the others. She would have to be careful not to talk too much or think too much or touch. She had touched Sally, but Sally had touched her first, so maybe that had been all right. This once.

While Edna and Donald helped Stella settle into her old room, Sally remained on the sofa, hands clasped tight together in her lap. Stella hadn't wanted Sally to touch her. Sally had felt it. Her mother had stiffened when Sally took her hands, and she had waited for Sally to sit on the sofa before seating herself, putting obvious distance between them. Her mother had been more interested in candy than in Sally.

Sally set her jaw, tossed her braids over her shoulder, and rose, shoulders squared. Her grandmother and Donald were on the landing, so she slipped soundlessly through the house and out the side door that did not creak. She had a quarter in her pocket that granddad had given her that morning. She'd walk down to Front Street and buy a movie magazine.

In the drugstore, standing beside a couple of Mankato high-school girls poring over a copy of *Photoplay*, Sally suddenly turned away. From the display boxes on top of the candy counter she grabbed a bag of Brach's bridge mix, then tossed it back, choosing gumdrops instead, recalling that when she was small, before Stella had begun weeping, her mother had been partial to gumdrops.

Pausing in the living-room doorway and wiping her eyes with a lace-edged handkerchief, Edna wondered aloud, "Now, where did Sally disappear?" After a moment she picked up the candy dish from the coffee table and carried it to the kitchen. As she stood in the pantry, pouring out bridge mix into the dish, a tear dribbled from her chin, landing on a chocolate-covered peanut. Wiping her cheek with the back of a hand, she identified the wet nut and fished it out, reminding herself to buy more candy to slip into Stella's suitcase before she left.

June 6, 1944, as Donald was launching into the second summer of classes, a massive Allied force landed at Omaha Beach in Normandy.

"Isn't it *something?*" the young woman behind the counter in the registrar's office gushed the following morning. Sunlight poured through tall, mullioned windows, backlighting natural blonde hair. Limpid blue eyes, empty and innocent as cloudless morning skies, looked out from a dimpled, pep-rally face. "D-Day," she chirruped as if it were homecoming. "My boyfriend says it's the beginning of the end," she told Donald, shrugging her long hair back over her shoulder.

The girl's unsullied ebullience rubbed Donald the wrong way. "The end" was not all that close, he wanted to assure her. Before the end, thousands were going to die horribly. Maybe her boyfriend.

However, he wasn't here to set her straight. He was here to beard the bureaucracy, in an effort to have his practice teaching requirement waived. He'd *practiced* for two years.

Later, racing down one of Old Main's wide hallways toward an ed theory class, he felt silly. Who the hell was he to take offense at a girl's excitement over the Normandy invasion?

Sally's sense of the war came in part from Lark's letters: Arlene was working in an aircraft plant; servicemen ate Sunday dinner with them; and blackouts in San Diego were not uncommon. How different from southern Minnesota, Sally mused, envying the Erhardts their exciting new home with its harbor and naval base, its Camp Pendleton and Camp Callan nearby.

You'd feel part of the war if you lived there, she thought. In Harvester and Mankato all you could do was collect scrap metal, paper, and rubber for War Drives or buy War Bonds or write to servicemen or something like that. Hardly ever did you see soldiers or sailors, unless they were recruiters or home on leave. Sally felt left out of the war.

Her father had his maps of the war zones tacked up on the walls of the sewing room in Harvester and his history books that "put him in the picture." The sewing room in which Stella had seldom if ever sewn, Donald had converted into an office. There he tracked the war: the European, Pacific, and North African "theaters," as they were called.

Soon after Stella had been hospitalized, he'd bought a small secondhand radio for the office. He listened to the news, then marked battle sites, advances, retreats, wins, and losses on his maps. To Sally, he pointed out where El Alamein, Singapore, Bataan, Salerno, Stalingrad, and Essen were. Even so, she found it all too remote, too academic. She yearned to be with Lark, where antiaircraft guns daily shook the southern California coast with deep, thrilling "booooms" as they practiced shooting at targets.

On that day after D-Day, a letter from Lark lay waiting on the table in the foyer at Grandma Elway's. Letters from Sally's friend were increasingly rare, and those that came were little different from the first: Lark hated life in San Diego; she couldn't bear the snowless climate; she had no friends; the school was jerry-built, the teachers a ragtag bunch who didn't know how to teach arithmetic or geography.

In the past six months, Lark had spoken disparagingly of her mother. Sally had been shocked and mystified, but like much of what Lark had hinted at during the past two and a half years, no details or explanations accompanied the little flare, fired across two thousand miles.

Standing her tennis racket against the hall table, Sally carried Lark's letter upstairs. With the door closed, she settled into a chair by the window, tore open the envelope, and withdrew a number of sheets of lined paper.

Dear Sally,

I'm sorry I haven't written in such a long time. I can't even remember what I told you.

You know that Uncle Stanley's in the army. He was in Italy the last time Aunt Betty got a letter from him. We knew he was in Italy because he called one of his army friends paesano in the letter, and Aunt Betty says that's an Italian word. Lucky for us, the censors missed it. Sometimes half his letter is blacked out by the censors.

Anyway, Aunt Betty is still working at Gilpin's Department Store and she's had several raises and promosions. She says it's because so many men were drafted but Mama says Aunt Betty is a whiz at merchandizing. Anyway, she's the main Buyer now for women's clothes and stuff and she gets to take the train to New York sometimes.

She writes to Uncle Stanley just about every day and he writes to her a *lot*. I think she writes so much because she feels bad that she doesn't love him as much as she used to. He's crazy about her. It's very complacated. Mama says if he loved her so much, how come he stayed away so long when he was painting sceenery in Hollywood? Mama writes to Uncle Stanley too. She says its because it's her duty. I'm not going to love any men when I grow up. It makes you awful. Well, Aunt Betty isn't awful, but it makes some people awful.

Papa is still saying he's going to get a judge to take me away from Mama. I don't think it's going to happen because then Mama would never speak to him again as long as she lives. To tell the truth, I don't want to live with ether one of them.

I have saved up a lot of money from taking care of Cecil and Percy and from Xmas and birthdays. Pretty soon I'll be able to buy a *ticke*t to Harvester. Really.

Fanny who lives next door and owns Cecil and Percy is very sick. I think she might die but I don't tell anyone because I don't want Garnett who is her husband to find out. He's just crazy about her.

My worst enemy is still Shirley. She practically lives here because of our piano. Aunt Betty pays for Shirley to have lessons with a very important teacher because it turns out Shirley is a prodijy. Anyway I have to listen to her practise all the time and it's making me crazy.

Please write and tell me about Harvester and everybody there.

> Your friend,
> Lark Ann Browning Erhardt

p.s. I am sorry I used the word Crazy.

p.s.s. Please tell Mrs. Stillman and Beverly hello when you see them, and tell them it won't be long before I am back.

p.s.s.s. I know I told you a long time ago about the oil painting I got at Trustworthy Second Hand. The picture of the farm I'm going to have some day. Shirley wants that picture!!!!! I'm afraid she's going to steal it. She has a key to our house because she practises the piano here. If she ever steals it, I will kill her.

A frown creased Sally's brow. She rose, tossed Lark's letter on the secretary, and paced up and down. Lark sounded—Sally didn't want to *think* the word—crazy. She hid the letter in one of the empty suitcases at the back of her closet.

At dinner, Grandma Elway asked, "How's Lark?"

"She's fine," Sally lied, spreading jam in the fold of a Parker House roll. "Mrs. Erhardt bought a secondhand piano." This was the kind of thing that Grandma liked to hear.

"Does Lark play?"

"No, but her Aunt Betty does."

Grandma nodded. "Would you like a piano?"

"I haven't got a musical bone in my body, Grandma, so don't waste your money."

Grandpa laughed.

Sometimes Sally felt as if she were playing her family like a piano, sensing which keys to play and which not. She could make them laugh, prevent their worrying, and occasionally, cause them to forget that Stella was in the bughouse.

October 12, 1944

The slanting topaz light of October poured through the west windows of the library. In the reference room, Sally hunched over an encyclopedia, researching Mark Twain for a theme due the following week in Miss Kemp's English class.

The afternoon was unusually warm for mid-October, and since the storm windows were not up yet, Mrs. Navarin had raised a couple of sashes. Outside the reference-room windows, bumblebees droned single-mindedly among asters and mums, gathering the last of the nectar.

A block away, in the street behind the schoolhouse, the marching band struck up "Anchors Aweigh," rehearsing patriotic routines for half-time ceremonies of the next afternoon's homecoming game against Red Berry. The music drowned the hum of the bumblebees.

Out at the athletic field, at the foot of Bacal's Hill, Donald was assisting Mr. Armstrong, the football coach, drilling the boys in defensive plays. When she didn't have homework, Sally sometimes wandered out to watch, fascinated by the drama of the grunting and wheezing, of helmets crashing; whistles blowing; and men shouting across the generous, open spaces.

At four-thirty she rose, returned the encyclopedias to the shelf, shuffled her notes together, and gathered up her schoolbooks, along with a biography of Twain she intended to check out.

Browsing through shelves of fiction in the larger, main room was Laurence Lundeen, natty and sleek. The owner of Lundeen's Dry Goods waved to Sally, and she waved back. She was not sure why, but he seemed to take special pains to be nice to her, as if they shared a secret. She speculated whether it was because they were both good-looking. Handsomeness was the only feature of their lives that she could imagine they had in common.

Sally thought the prematurely gray-haired Mr. Lundeen mysterious and sophisticated. That he'd lived in New York for a number of years confirmed his extraordinariness.

Laurence Lundeen turned back to the fiction shelves. Was he in a Balzac mood? he wondered. No, he thought he'd like to reread *Kristin Lavransdatter,* all three volumes. God, what a tale that was. Anyone who thought Scandinavians were a cold, colorless lot ought to give it a try.

He'd first been drawn to the trilogy because of his name, Laurence — Lavrans. Both sides of his family were Scandinavian, his mother an Anderson from up near Taylors Falls.

On a trip that was to celebrate their fifteenth wedding anniversary in 1915, his parents had been killed when the *Lusitania* was torpedoed.

Ten years old and without siblings, Laurence was taken in and raised by his father's parents. Then, when he was a junior at St. Olaf, his Grandfather Lundeen had dropped dead of a heart attack on Main Street as he came out of Lundeen's Dry Goods, and Grannie Lundeen had taken over running the business as if she'd been born to dry goods.

Laurence was twenty-five and living in Greenwich Village when his grandmother wrote, asking if she should donate the house to the town for a library. What she was asking, as much as anything, was did he think he'd be coming back to Harvester.

Laurence wasn't getting rich in New York, but he was paying his way, painting watercolors for the tourist trade. In 1930, early days of the Great Depression, making a living with watercolors wasn't easy. But Laurence was good, and he was canny. He painted the cityscapes tourists liked to believe they had seen.

"Give the place away, Grannie," he'd encouraged her. "Build yourself a bungalow. Everything on one floor."

And she had. But in '33 she'd suffered a stroke and could no longer oversee Lundeen's Dry Goods. Laurence packed up his watercolors and took the train back to Harvester to look after her and run the store.

She'd passed away three days after Christmas, and people wondered what Laurence would do. Selling a home and business in a little burg like Harvester in '33 was damned near impossible. If he kept them, he'd have a living.

Laurence wasn't worried about a living. He'd made a living in New York and could again. But he stayed. Why, he didn't know.

He'd created a jewel box out of his grandmother's bungalow, Harvester women said. He was sharp in business, Harvester men noted. From somewhere, he'd found Hy Johnson to manage the store. Without relinquishing much control, Laurence had got himself an able, honest Baptist to shoulder the day-to-day tedium.

The only quarrel the town had with Laurence was his being a bachelor when Harvester produced so many lovely girls who went off to the Cities each year to find husbands. You'd think one of them would take Laurence's fancy. Or one of the young teachers up at the school.

Nonetheless, Laurence was invited to dinner or bridge as often as anyone in the county. The Whites and Barnstables and people like that wouldn't throw a party without him. He was witty, willing to sit on committees, and not afraid to bid a grand slam.

Sally cast a backward glance at the angular, tweedy-looking businessman, wondering how old he was. Younger than her father. She wished he would fall in love with Miss Bailey, the second-grade teacher who'd years ago cast Sally as the narrator in the Christmas Program. The two were friends. Mr. Lundeen sometimes escorted Miss Bailey to the movies. But Miss Bailey wasn't what was called seductive, and when Sally'd observed the two together, they'd looked more like kin than kissers. They laughed a lot, but the laughter had no lovey edge to it.

Ahead of Sally in line were Mrs. White and Neddy Barnstable's mother. As Mrs. Navarin date-due stamped John Steinbeck's *The Moon Is Down* for Nadine White, Mr. Navarin thrust open the outer door, then the inside door leading from the vestibule. The skin around his staring eyes and parted lips was a milky color. His eyes sought his wife's, and his hands, the knuckles grimed from mechanic's work at the Sinclair station, came together in an anguished, spastic clasping at his breast.

Desiree Navarin's dark, hooded gaze took him in, and she steadied herself against the desk, date-stamper still gripped in her right hand. It had just printed *Oct 26, '44* inside the cover of the Steinbeck. A twisting of her mouth begged her husband, "Don't say it."

Nadine White hurried behind the desk and held the librarian. Brenda Barnstable reached to take the date-stamper from her hand. "I'll take over for Desiree," Laurence Lundeen told them, crossing the room.

He opened the front door and watched as the Navarins shuffled out to Joe's truck at the curb, climbed into it, and sat staring, not at each other, but through the windshield.

Laurence drew Brenda's books to him.

"'Oh whence, I asked, and whither?'" he recited. "'He smiled and would not say, / And looked at me and beckoned / And laughed and led the way.'"

Recalling himself, he stamped the first of Mrs. Barnstable's books. "Housman," he said. "Let's hope that's how it greeted Danny."

"Death?"

"Death." He stamped the second book and slid the two volumes toward her.

Brenda was tempted to ask who Housman was, but she didn't like making a fool of herself in front of Laurence Lundeen. "I'd better get home and make a hot dish to take to the Navarins."

Sally hadn't known Danny well. An only child, he'd been a sunny, teasing young man who winked at girls and sometimes played bassoon in the summer band. He hadn't yet become the person he was going to be.

She lay the Twain biography on the desk, then chafed the goose bumps on her arms. Though the sun clung to the tree tops, evening was creeping from house to house.

The following Wednesday, sitting at a reference-room table again, Sally wrote her mother, "Daddy let me go to the bonfire out by the football field last Thursday night."

Naturally, she did not mention the news about Danny Navarin, but went on to say:

The cheerleaders held a pep fest and the coaches talked about how hard the boys had been working to get ready for the Homecoming Game and how we were going to win—and guess what—we did! It's a good thing we didn't play St. Bridget for Homecoming because we wouldn't have beat them. Daddy says that's why we didn't play them.

The bonfire was so big I think you could see it in Ula.

Daddy gave a pep talk at the bonfire because he's been working on defense with the team. Beverly said Daddy looked handsome. Anyway you would have been proud because his little speech was funny and I could see that the football players liked it.

I think Daddy looks younger than he used to. It's because of all the athletic stuff he's doing. He says he should be as strong as the boys if he's going to show them how to do things.

I'm really busy with all my classes—and with trying to remember my locker combination *and* take my gym romper home and wash it every month!!! Ugh. Did you have to wear a gym romper when you were in 7th grade? They are so ugly. Beverly says they're the color of vomit if the person who's vomiting has been eating grass—you know—a hidious green.

Miss Benoit made Katherine Albers take gym class even tho she had her period and had terrible cramps. Miss Benoit said the exercize would be good for Katherine's cramps but by the end of class, she looked worse than her gym suit (thats what Beverly said and I agree) and you could see she was trying really hard not to cry. Katherine gets really bad cramps. I used to think I wanted to be her, because she's perfect and her dad gives her *everything*. To tell the truth I'd rather be Beverly living upstairs over the Loon Cafe with hardly any furniture. Beverly says periods are nothing to worry about for godsakes (haha). Beverly says Mr. Albers makes her feel icky even if he does give Katherine everything. He does have a really red face like he's mad all the time. But he's a lawyer so I guess he must be o.k.

I'm glad I didn't get my period yet. I hope mine will be as easy as Beverly's. I hope you don't think it's bad for me to write you about periods and things like that. To tell the truth, when Grandma Elway told me about periods, she was so embarrassed I thought she would die. She gave me a sanitary belt and a big box of Kotex and a book and she said it was just one of those things women had to put up with and I should be filisofical (I'll look up the spelling).

The last time I saw her she said had I got my period yet and I said no and she said But you're so tall. I laughed out loud because if tall had anything to do with it, plenty of high school boys would be wearing sanitary belts.

Anyway, except for you I only really talk about periods and things like that with Beverly. She'll talk about *anything!!!* I told her I'd be too embarrassed to go into Eggers drug store and buy Kotex when I finally get my period and the box from Grandma Elway runs out. Beverly said if I gave her the money she'd buy them for me. She is not afraid of anything.

Daddy said I should tell you about my school work. Well I like Miss Kemp's English Class and I like Art Class, but I hate American History and Math. I also don't like gym class mainly because of Miss Benoit and the stupid things we do most of the time—for instance push-ups! I am getting A's so far except in gym class.

Beverly and I went to *Going My Way* with Bing Crosbey and Ingrid Bergman. We really liked it. It almost made me feel religious. Well of course I am religious and I like Father Delias and I go to church because otherwise Grandma Wheeler would get after me, so don't worry about that. OK?

Anyway Bing Crosbey was really cute. Not handsome like Walter Pigeon who is my favorite man Movie Star but cute anyway. Ingrid Bergman was very beautiful and she acted very well. I would like to be in a movie. I think it would be wonderful to pretend you were somebody else, a nun or something. Beverly and I played nuns after we saw the movie but we weren't very good. I guess 7th grade is pretty old for dress up. Anyway it was fun. We pretended I died because I was so holy and tried to save a little girl from drownding and I got neumonia. But when Beverly was saying a rosary over me she farted and we laughed so hard we couldn't get back in the mood. I hope you don't mind my saying farted. I picked it up from Beverly.

Afterward we made fudge which Grandma Wheeler taught us how to do. Sometimes it turns out as hard as a rock but Beverly and I eat it anyway because it still tastes pretty good and we have strong teeth. Beverly gets the sugar from her mother who gets it from the Loon Cafe so don't worry about us using up all our sugar stamps.

Well Mommy, I'd better end this because it's getting really long. I hope you come home soon.

Love xoxoxoxoxoxoxox

Sally

Sally always told her mother that she hoped she would come home soon. But when she thought about Stella coming home, her stomach seized up, and she felt nauseated. Although Delmore Preuss and people like that still teased her, it didn't happen so often as it had, and sometimes she almost forgot that her mother was alive and crazy.

Sally rose and went to the desk in the main room where Laurence Lundeen sorted through returned books, piling them on a trolley.

"How do you spell *philosophical?*"

He printed the word on a slip of paper and handed it to her.

"Was I ever wrong!" she laughed, stuffing the paper in the pocket of her skirt. "When is Mrs. Navarin coming back to work?"

"I'm not sure," he said, slipping a card into its pocket inside a book cover. "A month, maybe." He piled several books on the cart. "Danny was the sun that keeps the planets from flying off in all directions. Right now, the Navarin planets are loose."

Sally was startled by the intimate, revelatory nature of Mr. Lundeen's words. He spoke to her as though to another adult, and not just any adult, but one whom he trusted. Her face flushed with pleasure, and she had to bite the corner of her mouth and furrow her brow to keep from smiling.

"Is there anything I could do, you know, to help? I mean, should I go by her house or anything?"

He considered this. "Would you take her a book?" From beneath the desk he pulled *Emma*. "Jane Austen's like an aspirin. Temporary relief of pain." He handed Sally a slim, leather-bound book, which she thought was probably his own. "I have to warn you, Desiree looks like something in a Greek tragedy."

Sally nodded. She knew nothing about Greek tragedy, but she preferred being talked to above her knowledge rather than beneath it.

The Navarin house at the north edge of Harvester sat low on an acre of land, screened by tall evergreens in back and apple trees, now heavy laden and winey, in front. Sally walked the bike up the long gravel drive, smelling the hundreds of apples unharvested beneath the trees. Beside stone steps leading to a broad, screened porch with pillars of softly rounded river rock, she dropped the bike. The house was brown shingle with deep stone foundations, and looked like a year-round lake cabin.

Sally knocked and, when no one came, knocked again, wondering if she ought simply to leave the book inside the screen door. But she was curious to see how someone in a Greek tragedy looked.

Through the glass portion of the door, she saw a shadowy

figure moving slowly down a hallway toward her. A barefoot Desiree Navarin, wearing an old aqua robe and, Sally observed, little else, opened the door. Mrs. Navarin looked blankly at Sally and did not clutch at her gaping robe. Her long black hair hung down, untended.

"I . . . I brought this book," Sally stammered.

"Book?" Mrs. Navarin's voice was husky, as though these were her first spoken words of the day.

"*Emma.*" Sally held the book up.

Desiree reached out a hand and ran fingertips along Sally's cheek, as if only now realizing who stood at the door. Instantly she withdrew the hand, and a look of dislike or profound resentment passed over her features. "Thank you for bringing the book," she said, taking it from Sally.

Sally looked around, disconcerted, and bit nervously on the tip of an index finger. "I, well, could I use your bathroom? I should have gone before I left home," she apologized.

". . . back here," Desiree said, leading Sally down the hall and through the kitchen to a tiny pine-paneled lavatory off the back entry.

Along the hall were hung photos of Danny, beginning with baby pictures and going on, through grade school, high school, and the navy. On a shallow shelf below the pictures were ribbons he'd won—a purple one with gold letters for First in the High Jump at the District Track Meet. The others Sally did not have time to read as she passed.

When Sally came out of the lavatory, Mrs. Navarin had disappeared. A few breakfast dishes still sat beside the kitchen sink. The Navarins didn't eat much, it appeared.

The house didn't look trashy the way Sally's often had when Stella was going cuckoo; it looked forgotten, as though the Navarins had moved into other quarters, leaving this place behind, untended.

Sally started back down the hallway, which was now quite dim. Passing the archway to the living room, she saw Mrs.

Navarin in a chair beside the stone fireplace, sitting at a three-quarter angle to the front window, so that her profile presented itself to Sally's view. Her hair was carelessly thrown back over her shoulder, revealing the high cheekbone and firm jawline. Down the side of her face streaked great dark lines, as if they'd been scratched there with red crayon.

Sally paused, finally saying softly, "'Bye, then."

Mrs. Navarin did not respond, so Sally let herself out.

Reaching the Navarin mailbox, she glanced back at the dark house set amongst the trees, and a thrill of comprehension shook her, starting at her scalp, which seemed to contract, and running down her spine to the very soles of her feet inside the scuffed saddle shoes. Suffering. A sense of the word, nearly as strong as an experience of it, gripped her. She trembled, and raised a hand to her cheek, scraping her nails down the smooth skin.

"Will there be a funeral?" Beverly asked.

Mrs. Stillman, who was the girls' source of expertise where matters military were concerned, poured more tea into their cups.

"Well, I don't really know. Of course, there's no body, so you couldn't have a burial. Still, it doesn't seem right not to have a ceremony, does it?" She set the teapot on a trivet. "How difficult it must be for families who have no body to bury. Almost as if the person hadn't *quite* died.

"Priests tell us that the body is only dust, that it came from dust and returns to dust, and we should not revere it when the soul has departed. But priests don't give birth. And when you come to think of it, the people who wrote the Bible probably didn't either.

"The place where Hillyard is buried is not about dust. It's a meeting place for Hilly and me." Cup in hand, she gathered wool for a moment. Then, "Maybe there'll be a memorial service for Danny," she speculated, returning to Beverly's question. "There was for Ernie Quilley, you remember."

Beverly and Sally did not remember. They had not known Ernie Quilley or the farm family he came from. Having taught school for so many years, Mrs. Stillman knew a raft of people they had never heard of.

"Is Mrs. Navarin back at the library?" the old woman asked. "I haven't been in this week."

"Mr. Lundeen's still running it," Sally told her.

"It'll take a while," Helen Stillman observed. "You have to decide finally what *you* believe about death before you can find any peace. You can't take someone else's word for what it is. You must invent a death you can live with, taking into account the clues you pick up along the way. For instance," she said, warming to this new tack, "I believe in ghosts. For me, they're a clue."

"Really? You believe in ghosts?" Sally asked.

Mrs. Stillman nodded and passed the plate of cookies. "I'm not saying I've seen one, but my cousin in California has."

"Honest?"

"Many years ago, when Hillyard was just a baby, and I needed someone to look after him while I taught, my cousin, who was only a sixteen-year-old girl, came in from the farm to stay with us and help out. She thought that living in town would be exciting." Mrs. Stillman shook her head and leaned back in the chair, recalling.

"Well, the long and short of it is, she got into trouble with some fellow here in town, wouldn't tell us who he was, and had to leave Harvester. I believe the fellow must have given her some money because my cousin didn't have any of her own, and she paid for a ticket to California. I sometimes think California is the Nod they talk about in the Bible, the way people go there when they get into trouble.

"My cousin . . . her name was Elvira . . . wound up in Oxnard, taking care of an elderly lady with quite a bit of money and property. Elvira had her baby, a little girl she named Mary Ann, and they made a nice life for themselves.

"Then, one night . . . oh, it's many years ago now . . . a man appeared to Elvira. Well, not a man but a ghost of a man. She was living in her own place then. The old woman she'd cared for had passed on and left Elvira a nice little house. Mary Ann was grown and living in Cambria, but Elvira had a couple of schoolteacher boarders staying with her. And they were right

199

there in the house that night, sound asleep, when Elvira woke up and saw the man who had got her into trouble.

"He was standing in the doorway of her bedroom, wearing one of those cream-colored summer suits with a matching vest and soft, cream-colored shoes and spats. His shirt was a shade darker than the suit, she said, and his tie a pale green jacquard. She said she was amazed how real everything about him was. She'd always imagined ghosts were like gauze curtains. With his right hand he held a panama hat against his thigh, and the thumb of his left hand was hooked into his watch pocket so that Elvira could see his watch chain. A tiny gold steamship dangled from it.

"He raised the panama like this." Mrs. Stillman demonstrated the way a man who is carrying his hat will sometimes put it to his head and then raise it in respectful salutation. "Then he said, 'I've come to tell you I'm sorry, Elvira,' and just like that, he was gone.

"Right away Elvira wrote me about it. It had affected her, she said, in a deep way. His appearing like that had told her he'd been thinking about her all those years. It wasn't that she'd been pining for him; she'd had to get over that a long time before. But they hadn't had any touch with each other since she'd left Harvester, and over the years, she'd just naturally assumed that she was dead to him. Still, a person doesn't like to think that she could be erased from somebody's life without a trace. A person likes to think she's left some engraving on that other person.

"And, now, he'd come to let her know that she'd been in his thoughts. He'd made a special journey to tell her." Mrs. Stillman lay a hand on her cheek in a gesture of wonderment. "Elvira said it gave her such a feeling of freedom. Like she could flap her arms and fly.

"She described it all to me. I may have left out some of the details. What he had on and what he did. At any rate, I recognized the man immediately. I'd seen him a thousand times, and I knew he was wearing that outfit she described on the day he died.

"I didn't say anything to Elvira about recognizing who he was. Keeping her secret all those years was a great source of pride to her. She wore that secret like a diamond ring."

"Who was he?" Sally and Beverly chorused.

"I couldn't tell. It wouldn't be right."

"But you said he's been dead for years."

"It's not my secret to tell. It's Elvira's."

"Godsakes, it's like a movie," Beverly exclaimed.

Sally pressed, "There's no way she could have known what the man was wearing when he died?"

"None."

"So, then, he really was a ghost."

"Yes. And that's why I say that each person has to figure out for himself what death is. They have to arrive at what's true for *them*. How else could people endure?"

Sally felt that she and Beverly had crossed the border into the country of Mrs. Stillman, a fantastical place, with startling revelations at each turning.

In the gloom of the gymnasium at three-thirty in the afternoon without artificial light, the red crepe-paper streamers looping and cascading around the walls reminded Sally of blood. Hot, flushed cheeks, sweaty underarms, and faintly buzzing ears reminded her of blood. Her own.

Well, she'd known that "a visit from her aunt" was inevitable. But, today? The day of the class party? She'd awakened feeling swollen. The skin of her stomach and chest were taut, uncomfortable, and her nipples were tender. Although she did not normally perspire much, her face and body felt moist and, worse, greasy. Breakfast had sat heavy in her stomach and queased as she bent to pull on her boots.

On another day she might have stayed home from school. After all, she was coming down with *something.* But today was the seventh-grade class party. If she stayed home, it would look as if she were afraid to go to the party. Two or three girls in the class weren't going. They didn't have a pretty dress or they were Baptist or they were afraid no boy would ask them to dance and they'd look unpopular.

Sally was going, whether or not any boy asked her to dance. She would stand up straight and hold her head up and, if no one asked her to dance, look disdainful or amused.

For the past week the phys. ed. teachers, Mr. Vargo and Miss

Benoit, had instructed seventh-grade boys and girls in social dancing, preparing them for the party. Beverly said it was the most pitiful thing she'd seen since Ronald Oster threw the Meyers' cat in front of the snowplow. "Tryin' to teach them clodhoppers to fox-trot is as hopeless as tryin' to teach a snake to sing."

Three-thirty was the hour for the party, because the seventh-grade advisors had all agreed that twelve- and thirteen-year-olds were too young for an evening party.

"Stupid," Sally complained to Beverly. "You have to wear your party clothes to school in the morning or keep them in your locker all day, getting wrinkled, and then change in that hideous girls' shower room after school."

No one went home to change because, MotherOfGod, Sally thought, the party lasted from only three-thirty to five-thirty, and you'd miss half of it if you went home to change.

Having the party on April 11 was also stupid, because the weather was completely unpredictable. Well, naturally, it turned out that a dusting of snow lay on the ground when the seventh graders woke that morning. And the sky was threatening. The girls who planned to wear their frilly Easter dresses, purchased with an eye to summer, would freeze their elbows off in the gymnasium at three-thirty. But what could you expect of April?

During third-hour study hall, Sally felt an uncomfortable clutching sensation down in That region. By the time the dismissal bell rang, she sensed a warm ooze between her legs. MotherOfGod, what would she do? She daren't stand up for fear blood had seeped through to the back of her skirt. One more thing for Delmore Preuss and Ronald Oster to tease her about. At least her party dress was safe and unsullied in her locker. But how to get out of study hall?

"Katherine!"

Katherine Albers turned.

"Come here. Please." Sally and Katherine weren't all that

close, but any port in a storm. Sally motioned Katherine to bend down so she could whisper into her ear. "I got The Curse. It's the first time. What'll I do? I don't want to stand up."

Katherine bent close, pretending to point out something in their English literature text. "I'll stand right here. You get up, and I'll get behind you and walk real close, with my hands on your shoulders, as if I'm being silly and sort of steering you down the hall. Head for the lavatory. Here, hold my books for me, okay?"

Sally nodded and, glancing around to be certain no bane of her existence was present, took Katherine's books and started out the door and down the hall. People turned to look at them. Sally laughed, calling out to Katherine, "All right, all right, Katherine, I'll never call you Miss Priss again." Not very clever, she knew, but the best she could manage on short notice.

Katherine steered her into the girls' lavatory and back toward the last stall where they wouldn't be bothered by worldly girls from the upper grades, should any happen in.

"I'll get you a Kotex from the machine," Katherine whispered, shoving Sally into the cubicle. "Check the back of your skirt and see if it's okay."

"Do you have a nickel for the machine?"

Katherine nodded and turned away.

Sally's skirt was all right, but her slip and panties were stained. She dried them as best she could with toilet paper and took the Kotex pad Katherine passed her under the door of the stall.

"You can go home at lunch and change," Katherine whispered through the door.

With the bulky-feeling pad pinned in place, Sally emerged. "You'd better get to class or you'll be late. I'll get a Late Slip at the office. And thank you. You saved my life." She waved the other girl off to English class.

Katherine bent to pick up her books from the floor. Peering

up from beneath long, curved lashes, she whispered, "Do you, well, do you think I'm Miss Priss?"

Miss Kemp, one of the chaperones, removed "Don't Fence Me In" from the turn table and slipped "Sentimental Journey" onto the phonograph spindle.

Along the east wall of the gymnasium, girls sat on metal folding chairs or stood in nervous little knots of two or three, tittering, balling damp handkerchiefs in their fists, peering slyly across the great echoing expanse, and debating how many Ladies' Choice numbers Miss Kemp might call.

On a folding table against the north wall, just below the stage apron, Mrs. Albers' punch bowl, filled with red Kool-Aid punch, beckoned those desperate to look occupied. Beside it, paper plates loaded with store cookies emptied as boys grabbed five and six at a time.

Now Mr. Vargo was moving among the boys, exhorting them to "Get out there and dance if you want to stay on my good side."

Sally and Beverly, determined to get some cookies before they were all gone, were leaning against the stage apron, pulling apart vanilla sandwich cookies and eating the frosting inside.

"These're the worst cookies I ever ate," Beverly said, wiping frosting from the end of her nose.

Sally nodded, glancing with bold amusement at the cluster of eight or ten boys gathered on the west side of the gym, calling each other "Romeo" and shoving one another in the direction of the girls. "Pitiful," she said.

"We should just dance with each other," Beverly opined.

"We'd look desperate."

"I'm not coming to another one of these dumb things if those hayseeds are going to stand around with their mouths open catching flies."

Sally straightened, thrusting her shoulders back. Her breasts, still only suggestions of breasts, hurt as they rubbed against the stiff, cold taffeta of her dress. Otherwise she didn't feel too bad, a little sweaty, once in a while a bit light-headed.

"I love your dress," Katherine Albers told her as she filled a paper cup with punch. "Yours, too," she told Beverly.

"It's Sally's; she let me wear it," Beverly explained, rubbing her poverty in Katherine's face, then regretting it because she did feel oddly sorry for Katherine. "Thanks. I like it too. The color's neat," she added.

Sally was aware of being nearly a head taller than the other two girls, but when she caught herself slumping, she'd recall Grandma Wheeler's words, "People will assume that you're confident if you stand straight and hold your head up."

She was taller than most boys in the seventh grade too. And dancing with a girl half a head taller made boys feel like runty little kids. Well, she wasn't going to ruin her posture for the likes of Delmore Preuss.

Clara Hennessey, who had been sitting on a folding chair, off to one side, away from the other girls, clomped over to the punch table and ladled out a cup of Kool-Aid. Her shoes were men's, and although Clara was the biggest pupil in the seventh grade, they were three sizes too big for her, slopping up and down as she walked.

Headed once more toward the cookies, Ronald Oster called out, "Hey, Clarabelle the Cow, where'd ya get the gun boats?"

Clara looked at him blankly and edged away, sensing mortification.

"Well, at least she don't have your problem," Beverly spoke up. "Must be hard for your folks, finding a store that'll sell 'em two left shoes." She glanced at Sally and Katherine. "You seen him *dance?*"

The other two girls giggled. Ronald grabbed a handful of cookies and swaggered away, laughing rather too heartily over his shoulder, "Better call the rendering plant, 'cuz it smells like something died around here." This in reference to Clara's body odor.

Clara, tentative but grateful, smiled at the three girls.

"Don't let dopes like that getcha down," Beverly told her.

Clara nodded and clomped back to her folding chair.

"I wonder why she came?" Sally ventured.

"She's got the right," Beverly said.

"It can't be much fun, though."

"Maybe she likes Kool-Aid and cardboard cookies, or maybe her ma made her get out of the house."

"Why would she do that?" Katherine asked.

Beverly looked at her for a moment. "You don't know?"

Katherine shook her head, sorry she'd asked, as she sensed something coming that she didn't want to know.

Beverly moved closer, glancing around to be certain no boys were in hearing range. "Her ma's a whore."

"What's that?" Katherine asked.

Beverly rolled her eyes but whispered, "She does it for money."

"Does *what?*" Sally demanded.

"Godsakes, you two are dumb as doorknobs," she said with forbearance.

"She lets men put their thing in her *down there,* and she charges them."

Katherine jerked her head back as if Beverly had hit her with a fist.

"*Whaaat?*" Sally demanded, incredulous, hands on her hips.

"I have to go to the bathroom," Katherine breathed and, whirling, ran toward the girls' shower room.

"What got inta her?" Beverly wondered.

Ignoring Katherine, Sally pressed, "He puts his thing in her? *Why???*"

"You are barely smarter than a rock," Beverly told her.

"I'm serious, Beverly Ridza. You tell me why," Sally insisted.

"'Cuz men like ta do that."

"MotherOfGod." Sally was revolted. Could this be true? "Are you making this up?"

"Godsakes, no. That's how ladies get babies. The guy puts his thing in them."

"I don't believe that."

"Well, it's true."

Sally needed to sit down. "Who told you?"

"Godsakes, everybody knows. That's how your ma got *you.*"

"Oh, stop it!" Her father wouldn't do something like that.

Miss Kemp announced Ladies' Choice, and Beverly said she was going to ask Leroy Mosley. "Why don't you ask Neddy?"

Sally shook her head and bore off like a sleepwalker toward the girls' shower room. Inside, she looked up and down the rows of gym lockers, but did not see Katherine. She had not meant to track her down, only to get away from Beverly and her superior knowledge of men putting their thing inside ladies. But not finding Katherine, she began searching the curtainless showers, the only place remaining where she could be.

In the last shower, Katherine huddled on the floor in the corner. Although she'd doubtless heard Sally's footsteps, she did not look up or open her tightly closed eyes. Her hands were clasped over her mouth.

"Katherine? It's Sally." Sally bent as if speaking to a small child. "It's really icky, isn't it, what Beverly said about Mrs. Hennessey and . . . men. But don't let it upset you so much. Just remember, you don't ever have to do that if you don't want to. Try not to think about it, okay?"

Katherine did not respond.

"Katherine, can you hear me?"

The girl nodded so slightly that Sally was unsure that it was a nod. She went on, "It's so icky, I'm not going to think about it for a whole year. The two of us won't think about it together for a year, okay?"

Katherine opened her eyes, but stared straight ahead at the gray metal shower wall, opposite.

"You want to go over to my house? This party's dumb."

"I can't."

"Why?"

"My dad's picking me up."

"We could call him and tell him to pick you up at my house."

Katherine shook her head slowly. "He'd get mad."

"Why? Just tell him the party was dumb."

"I can't do that."

"*Really?*" He must be incredibly stupid, Sally thought. "Well, come out with me and we'll dance. I can lead 'cuz I'm tall."

Again Katherine shook her head.

"You want to just stay in here for a while?"

She nodded.

"Okay. But, well, okay. But if you change your mind, I'll still dance." She began to back away. "I'm really sorry you're upset."

Out in the gymnasium, Mr. Vargo was saying, "All right, every boy has to ask a girl for the next number. And that means *every* boy."

The wire mesh-enclosed clock said a quarter to five. Would Katherine stay in the shower room till five-thirty? Sally wondered.

"Sally? Want to dance?" Neddy Barnstable asked.

A record of "Long Ago and Far Away" was playing.

"I guess."

None of the seventh-grade boys was a good dancer, but Neddy at least didn't pump her arm up and down as if he were chopping wood with it.

"Pretty boring party, huh?"

"Yah."

"My mom said I could have a party at our house sometime and play the phonograph, so we could practice dancing. D'ya think anybody'd come?"

"Sure. Beverly and I'll bring fudge."

She sounded as if she'd actually come, he thought. On the other hand, if she liked him, wouldn't she sound a little—shy or nervous or something? God knew, *he* was nervous. Asking her to dance had used up his supply of guts for the next year. He'd spent half the afternoon thinking of things to talk about and now he couldn't remember one of them.

"How's your mother?" he asked at last. "Do you ever see her?" The moment the words were out of his mouth, he rued them. Her mother was probably the last topic she wanted to talk about.

"You're the only person in the class who's ever asked me about her, except for Delmore Preuss and Ronald Oster when they were being stupid and didn't really want to know." She looked off in the direction of the girls' shower-room door. Katherine hadn't emerged yet. Maybe she should have stayed with her. "I guess she's okay. I see her three or four times a year. Mostly she doesn't talk, so it's hard to visit. And I get the feeling she's uncomfortable when we come, like she wants to evaporate. But the doctor thinks there's hope, and we shouldn't give up. I write to her so that when she comes home, she won't have so much to catch up on. And also, so she knows that it's okay to come home, that we want her to come home."

Talking to Neddy about Stella felt good. She shouldn't dither on, though. People mustn't think that she was, well, strange. She knew from people's faces that many were waiting for her to show signs of looniness. *It's in the blood, you know.*

"I think you're pretty brave," Neddy told her.

"Brave? Me? Oh, no. I'm the least brave person you could ever meet."

"Well, *I* think you're brave, and nothing you say will change my mind," he blurted, unable to prevent himself from acting like a damned fool.

"Thank you."

He could not tell if she thought he was the stupidest person in the world or not. The song ended, and he walked her back to the folding chairs.

"Would you like to dance again?"

"I guess."

Beverly plopped down on the folding chair. "Was he any good?" she asked as Neddy wandered back across the floor to where the boys milled around like penned animals.

"He only stepped on my feet one time, so that wasn't bad."

Duane Steiner asked Sally to dance, and Leroy Mosely led Beverly out to the floor for the third time. The other boys hooted at him, so he danced her backward toward the girls' side, away from the razzing.

When Mr. Vargo called, "Last dance!" and Miss Kemp put "Goodnight, Sweetheart" on the phonograph, Neddy Barnstable again asked Sally. They discussed plans for the possible party at his house.

"After supper on Friday?" Neddy wondered. "Could you come then? My dad could give you a ride home. Beverly too."

As the gymnasium began emptying, Katherine appeared. Slipping into her coat and looking neither left nor right, she gathered up her mother's punch bowl from the table. As Sally and Beverly pushed their way out the doors into the cold late afternoon, Katherine was at the curb where her father waited in the Cadillac.

Stowing the punch bowl in the back seat, Katherine opened the front passenger door and slid in, staring straight ahead. Mr. Albers, always red-faced, as if his collar were too tight, put the car in gear. And the Cadillac slid away from the curb.

"See you in the funny papers," Sally called chummily, but Katherine did not turn her head.

Late evening, April 11 — 12, 1945

"I finally got The Curse," Sally wrote her mother that night.

Will my chest get bigger now? I don't see why girls have to get The Curse. Couldn't God have thought of an easier way?

Beverly told me and Katherine Albers how ladies get babies. I'm still not sure I believe her. It's so icky. If Beverly's right, that's another thing God could have done better.

Is it a sacrilege when I say bad things about God? Lark said it was a mortal sin to talk bad about God, even when he deserves it. He must be Very Strict. Even President Roosevelt lets people say bad things about him.

The Seventh Grade Class Party was today. I wore the red taffeta dress that Grandma E. gave me at Valentines. The party was really boooorrrring. The boys in our class are so stupid and most of them couldn't dance if they were getting paid. I don't know why we can't have cute boys like they have in the ninth grade. The only boy in Seventh Grade who isn't toooo ugly or mean is Neddy Barnstable. He at least tries to dance.

When I'm old enough to go on "dates" I think I'll go with boys who are older than me. Is that a good thing to do?

If you were here, I might not be brave enough to talk to you like this, but in a letter I'm not as embarrassed. For instance, I might not tell you about Katherine Albers getting upset when Beverly told us how ladies get babies. It spoiled the whole party for her. It made me kind of sick too but I didn't let it spoil the party. I told Katherine that I'm not going to think about it for a year and she shouldn't either, but she couldn't seem to get it out of her head. I don't like Mr. Albers. He's not very friendly and he really thinks he's the cat's pajamas. The truth is he's nothing to write home about. He's getting plump and he has a red face most of the time. Grandma W. says that people's faces eventually get to look like what's on their consciences.

Did you eat all the candy we sent you for Valentines? I asked Mrs. Anderson to stick in extra black gum drops because I know you like them.

If you ever feel like writing to me, I'd like to get aletter from you. It doesn't have to be long just whatever you want to write.

Love and kisses,
Sally

The next afternoon during Miss Dickie's home ec class, as the girls struggled with lumpy blancmange, the town whistle blew, not pausing for longs and shorts as it did when summoning the Volunteer Fire Department, but blowing steadily, on and on, until it knelled inside your heart, Miss Dickie thought, just as it had that Sunday when the Japs had bombed Pearl Harbor.

The trembling excitement that attends tragedy ran through the home ec kitchen, and Miss Dickie could not settle the girls down with warnings of curdled pudding. The intercom clicked on. A charged, tantalizing hum ensued. A throat cleared at the other end of the line, and the voice of Superintendent Engel informed them, "We have received sad news. President Roosevelt has died of a stroke. Teachers may dismiss pupils at their earliest convenience. There *will* be school tomorrow."

Looking around, Sally found that most of the girls, including Beverly, were in tears. Even Miss Dickie with her finical ways, her narrow, hunched-in shoulders, and her hands that were twenty years older than the rest of her, was biting her lip.

"Turn off your stoves," she said. "Put your aprons away. I'll clean up. Go home." Wheeling, she marched toward the pantry, barking her bony hip on the corner of a work counter as she hastened away.

Sally had a cold, empty feeling in her stomach.

"Now that President Roosevelt's dead, who'll look after us?" Katherine Albers wondered.

Home was not where Sally wanted to go. She wanted to go where people were talking about President Roosevelt.

"Where you goin'?" Beverly asked as they stood at their open lockers, unsure what to take home and what to leave. Oughtn't they to leave everything, as they would if someone in the family had died?

"The library, I guess."

As they crossed the first-floor hall toward the front door, Sally saw Miss Bailey sitting at her desk, collapsed against the back of the chair, arms hanging at her sides, as if someone had shoved her down.

"Miss Bailey," Sally called, turning toward the second-grade room, "Isn't it terrible?"

Pegeen Bailey sat up slowly and leaned across the wide oak desk toward the girls. "Yes. It's terrible." She sounded angry. "He worked so hard, and now he won't see the end of it.

"And Eleanor . . ." She went on, speaking of Mrs. Roosevelt as of a girlfriend whose welfare concerned her, "what will she do now? So much talent there." She looked up at the two young women standing at the other side of the desk. "Talent wasted is . . . a slow death. Don't forget that," she said, expelling a sighing breath. Testing the phrase for soundness, she said, "A wasting disease. Yes, that's it."

Outside, making their way down the walk, the girls turned as Miss Bailey threw open a window and called after them, as if she might never see them again, "The president did not waste his talents. Eleanor, either. Don't you."

They put it down to Franklin Roosevelt's sudden death.

The president's death had struck Mrs. Navarin a new blow. Returning to the library after New Year's, she had worked a reduced schedule, with Laurence Lundeen spelling her. She seemed to Sally hollowed out and dried up, like a plant still standing in cold November; she was *there*, but not really alive.

Now she seemed further attenuated. The great, dark concavities of her eye sockets were like the empty windows of a vandalized house. Yet she filed cards resolutely, the nearly rote act mooring her to life.

She took no note of Sally and Beverly when they entered, nor of Mr. Navarin who stood close by, stooping, protective. When the news had come on the radio at the station, he hadn't stopped to scrub off the grease and grime of an engine overhaul, but had jumped in the pickup to be with Desiree. In his grimed hands he held the forest green cap with the "Sinclair" script across the front. Lifting first one foot, then the other, he checked the pale oak floor to see if he'd tracked in grease. Dark, alien fumes of oil and gasoline hung in the air around him.

Beyond Mr. Navarin, in the reference room, Laurence Lundeen leaned across the book trolley, staring blindly at the school across the street. Straightening, he extracted a handkerchief from his trousers pocket and wiped his eyes.

Sally had expected the library to be full of people, talking about the president's passing. Instead, three silent figures stood apart from each other in rooms where news of death echoed.

The two girls exchanged glances and tiptoed toward the old sofa at the back of the main room. Above the fiction shelves hung two portraits, one of Andrew Carnegie, the other of Franklin Roosevelt.

Sitting down, Beverly stared up at the picture of Roosevelt and felt her throat tighten. She wasn't one to cry, but she felt pretty bad, as bad as she could remember feeling, as bad as she'd felt when Hilly Stillman had blown his head off.

Mr. Roosevelt had been the only president of her lifetime, sort of like God. No. Better than God, because he talked to you on the radio and made you feel like if he met you, he'd *like* you, and you'd have lots of things to joke about. If God was like that, she'd go to church oftener.

Beside her, Sally regretted coming to the library. Apart from the ticking of the clock, Beverly's snuffling was the only sound in the building. And the snuffling was deafening. If Sally didn't get out of there, she'd explode.

At length, the workings of the clock whirred, bonging the half hour, and Sally sprang up without a word, dashing to the front door and out, passing the unaltered Navarin tableau on the way. Outside, she gulped earthy April air and hurried home along streets strangely empty.

In the living room at 301 Second Street, Donald sat on the sofa listening to funereal music on the radio. He looked up as Sally came in. "Baseball practice was canceled," he said.

Stamping her foot, Sally stood in the doorway. "Why did he do it? I hate him for doing this!"

From the top of the Ferris wheel, Sally and Beverly were able to see all the way to Bussey's Corner, or they would have if the grain elevators by the depot had not stood in the way.

"Look over there," Beverly insisted, twisting around in the seat.

Sally turned toward the northwest.

"Those trees . . . 'way off there . . . are by Sioux Woman Lake."

"Are you sure?"

"Yeah, 'cuz, see, there's Elwood Hanson's farm."

"Who's he?"

"He's sweet on my ma."

"Really?" Rose Ridza was not Sally's notion of a woman anyone would be sweet on. Plain as a mud fence. And no style. Of course Rose had never had any money for style, but you knew by the way she wore her hair that she never gave a thought to fixing herself up.

"He takes her to dances."

"Really?"

"He even took her to *Mildred Pierce.*"

"How old is he?"

"Pretty old."

"As old as Daddy?"

Beverly considered. "Yeah. Maybe even a little older. 'Y' can't really tell, 'cuz he's real bald."

"Is he going to marry her?"

Beverly shrugged. "Who cares?"

"What do you mean, 'Who cares?' *I'd* care if it was my mother."

"Ma says I'm going t' be in eighth grade this year, and pretty soon I'll be gone from here. And that's true."

"So? What does that have to do with it?"

"Well, if Elwood did ask her to get married, what skin would it be off my nose? If I'm in Hollywood?"

"You don't understand," Sally huffed. "Don't you love your mother? Doesn't she love you?"

"What's that got to do with it?" Beverly was getting a little impatient with this conversation.

"Well, it'd be disloyal of your mother to get married again, I think."

"Disloyal to who? Ren Ridza? Look at them scars on Charlie's arms sometime." Beverly knew that her grammar was going to hell in a handbasket. She wanted to talk like Sally and Katherine Albers, but when she got excited or mad, she slipped back into the old ways.

"No. Disloyal to you and Charlie and Delores. If she's running around with Elwood Johnson . . ."

"Hanson."

"Hanson. If she's running around with him, she's not thinking about you as much as she used to, she's thinking about him. And she's giving him some of *your* love, the love you should be getting. Don't you see?"

"Nope." Beverly rocked the seat back and forth as the wheel sped 'round its orbit. Half standing, she peered off to the southwest, a hand to her brow, shielding her eyes against the neon cerise of the horizon. "Hey, I can see Hollywood. There's Mickey Rooney! And Judy Garland!" Her face illumined by the Technicolor glow still bathing the tops of trees and buildings and people on the Ferris wheel, she sang out to Sally behind her, "Yup! I can see Merle Oberon too!"

Before and behind them, up and down the broad Main Street, Harvester Days flowed like a river of Kool-Aid gaiety, awash with colored lights. A Ferris wheel, merry-go-round, tilt-a-whirl, kiddie cars, and one or two other rides whirled like Catherine wheels or snaked like electric animals, giving off energy and permission. Booths of chance and food and of fortunes told lined the sidewalks where farm families and town families and folks from as far away as St. Bridget milled and laughed and shouted, spilling popcorn, drinking soda pop, and stuffing themselves with delights sold from church booths: wurst and kolache and poppy-seed cake and fried fish and watermelon.

Because of the war, the town had not celebrated Harvester Days the past three years. But with the Germans surrendering in May and the end of the war seeming to lie just ahead, the town council had voted to resume the festival.

Then last Monday, the United States had dropped a special bomb on a place called Hiroshima and, on Thursday, another on Nagasaki, and people were saying the war was all over but the shouting, wasn't it wonderful?

"Is your dad coming downtown?" Beverly asked. She and Sally, standing in line to ride the tilt-a-whirl, plucked feathery wisps from cones of cotton candy, laying them on their tongues to feel the strange evanescence.

"He's going to the penny movie. They're showing *Mr. Deeds Goes To Town.* Maybe he'll come later."

"Look, up there," Beverly told her. "It's Mrs. Stillman."

The curtains at Helen Stillman's open bedroom window were drawn to one side, and she sat leaning against the sill, listening to the calliope music and watching the parade of people below.

"Mrs. Stillman!" Beverly called. "Down here! It's Beverly!" Jumping up and down, she flung her arms in a wild arc above her head.

Helen Stillman smiled and waved and blew the girls a kiss.

"She must get lonesome," Sally speculated.

"Hasn't got chick nor child," Beverly said, borrowing an

expression of her mother's. "But she never acts sad, ya know? Seems like she enjoys every little thing. Stuff we'd think was practically *nothing* is *something* to her, like sitting up there watching us down here. Doesn't she look happy?"

Sally nodded and waved again to the woman at the window. The tilt-a-whirl had stopped and the riders were coming down the steps. She handed her ticket to the boy at the gate and followed Beverly up to one of the crescent-shaped leatherette seats.

"Heh, Neddy," Beverly called to Neddy Barnstable when he and Leroy Mosely and some other boy the girls didn't know slid into a seat opposite. "Hi, Leroy."

"Are you boy-crazy?" Sally teased, wishing she could be that casual with boys. The boys in her class were so dopey, she could never think of anything to say to them. Except Neddy Barnstable. He had the good sense to lead the conversation so she didn't have to wrack her brain every time for something pointless like "Some geography test, huh?"

Billy Rabel, who was in the eighth grade, ninth this fall, was easy to talk to. Sometimes, if he didn't have football or baseball practice, he fell in with her on the way home from school. He talked about sports and his dad's meat market and his brother, Gerald, who was in the marines. He didn't actually expect her to say anything, so of course, she sometimes did actually think of something.

Billy Rabel was terribly cute. A lot of girls had crushes on him. He was sort of stuck on himself, but who wouldn't be if they looked like that? And being with a boy who was stuck on himself was easier than being with one who wasn't, because self-confident boys talked about anything they wanted to, and you weren't always worried about embarrassing pauses in the conversation.

"Neddy Barnstable wants you for his girlfriend," Beverly told Sally.

"What a dumb cluck you are. He talks to me because of Mommy. He feels sorry for me."

"Oh, sure," Beverly snorted.

"There's Katherine Albers," Sally pointed out, changing the subject.

"With her pa," Beverly said, making a face. "Why doesn't he let her do something by herself? He's always hanging around. Godsakes, even on the Ferris wheel."

The tilt-a-whirl started up, and Beverly bent her strength to making their car revolve faster than the others. Holding onto the bar in front of her, Sally leaned back, abandoning herself to the looping, centrifugal force pinning her against the seat. Eyes closed, black hair flying, she swam dizzily in an ecstasy of motion.

Tepid evening air rushing along the inner curve of her shoulders and against the nape of her neck raised goose bumps on her arms and down her back. Laughing voluptuously, she pressed her elbows against the sides of her waist in a convulsive little hug of pleasure.

When the machine stopped, Neddy and Leroy Mosely and the unknown boy scuttled amongst the flow of riders leaving the tilt-a-whirl, directing a course by unspoken agreement to intersect with Beverly and Sally's as the girls reached the steps leading away from the ride.

"So, you going on the Ferris wheel?" Leroy asked, not looking at Beverly or Sally, but away, toward Lundeen's Dry Goods—yet by some subtlety of voice, giving them to know they were being addressed.

"We been already," Beverly said without turning around.

"Wanna go again?"

Beverly looked sideways at Sally. Sally returned the glance, then looked down, as if absorbed by the litter in the street.

"Yeah, okay, I guess," Beverly told Leroy.

The third boy drifted away toward the airplane ride as the girls led the way, standing aside as Neddy and Leroy bought the tickets. Sally felt as though everyone at the carnival was looking at her and remarking that she was riding the Ferris wheel with Neddy Barnstable. Maybe everyone was wondering if Brenda Barnstable knew that her boy was with that loony Stella Wheeler's girl. Sally straightened her shoulders, stood tall, and thrust her chin high. If she looked snooty, so be it. Let them remark on that too.

She wished that Billy Rabel had asked her on the Ferris wheel. Neddy was nice, but almost-eighth-grade boys had a puny, undercooked look to them, all hands and wrists and collarbones.

Neddy followed her up the single step into the gondola. Sally was grateful he didn't have that sullen hangdog look so many boys got when they were embarrassed to be seen with a girl and were half-pretending the whole thing had been her idea. Neddy talked to her and didn't droop over his side of the gondola, looking as if he might jump.

"Did you get your lifesaving certificate this summer?" he asked.

"I got it in Mankato while Daddy was taking classes. You?"

He nodded. "I'm glad I got it," he said with real enthusiasm.

"Yes?" She looked at him. Most nearly-eighth-grade boys, when they could not avoid talking to a girl, spoke with an insulting lack of energy, as if they could just barely get the words out.

The warmth of Neddy's words was proof of his good manners and compassion—not a desire to have her for his girlfriend, as Beverly was always insisting. That was fine. She liked having him for a friend. But if she were to have a boyfriend, it would be Billy Rabel, with his swarthy, insolent good looks and self-confidence.

"Well," Neddy explained, "I like the idea of being able to help someone, don't you? I mean, if someone was drowning, I could dive in and *do* something . . . haul him to shore and give him artificial respiration. How many times does a person get to save somebody?"

"Well, I suppose doctors and firemen and people like that do it all the time," she pointed out.

"Yes, but I mean ordinary people like me." He colored and grinned. "Of course, maybe I just like the idea of being a hero," he admitted. He brushed back the hank of clean, biscuit-colored hair that fell over his brow.

Sally studied him. "No, I don't think you're trying to be a hero. I think you're a nice person who likes to save people," she assured him. "And anyway, what difference does it make why you save someone, as long as you do it?" Her natural pragmatism rebelled at scrupling over the intent behind good works.

"A nice person," she'd called him. He was certain that a girl *really* interested in him wouldn't call him "a nice person." "A nice person" was something her grandmother might call you. A girl really interested would be nervous, like he was. Sally was never nervous with him. She was as composed as she was beautiful. Look at the way she held her head, high up off her shoulders, like . . . a lily at the end of a tall stalk. And the way her eyes met the world straight on, not caring whether the world liked her.

Yet the tiny flame of hope he felt when Sally was around was not entirely quenched, and he allowed himself to imagine a day when she would moon over him. Well, not *moon*, but at least not call him "a nice person."

When they alighted from the Ferris wheel, Sally thanked him for the ride. "I had a good time," she said, and he felt as if feathers were falling all over him, tickling him and making him happy. "Me too."

Climbing down from the merry-go-round, Beverly said, "Look, there's your pa." She pointed to three adults standing outside Anderson's Candy and Ice Cream.

Slipping in and out amongst the throng and picking their way toward Donald, Sally and Beverly saw that the couple with him was the Navarins.

"Mrs. Navarin!" Beverly exploded as they came abreast of the little group.

A thin, indifferent acknowledgment briefly touched Desiree Navarin's lips, then died.

"I'm glad you came to Harvester Days," Beverly barreled on. "It's pretty neat this year. You should see the animals they got on the merry-go-round. Giraffes and tigers and even a baby elephant."

Joe Navarin gave Beverly a quick squeeze on the shoulder, relieved by her noisy exuberant presence. "You girls been trying the rides, have you?"

Beverly entertained them with details.

Standing between Donald and Desiree, Sally caught a breath of whatever it was Grandpa Elway had in his before-dinner libation, as he called it. She looked askance at her father and leaned a bit toward him. No. Must be Mrs. Navarin.

Stealing sidelong glances, she studied the librarian. Her hipbones jutted beneath the blue cotton dress, and her elbows were sharp as lances.

She'd always had those dark, hooded lids, which Sally thought mysterious and exotic. But once her skin had been the color of fine parchment, and now it looked waxen and preserved.

At the first break in Beverly's narrative, Desiree turned to Joe, suggesting, "I think we should start home." Nodding to the others, she put an arm through her husband's and walked away, carefully, planting each foot as though walking on ice.

Mid-August — November 1945

The following Tuesday, when the town whistle blew long and without pause, folks knew what it meant and they ran into the street and hugged each other without thinking about it. "It's over!" they laughed, or cried. And there was no difference between the laughing and the crying. Joy and sorrow were inextricably woven together. The boys who would now be spared and the boys who had been lost, in that moment, held hands around the town.

"I was so happy," Sally wrote Stella that night.

> I even liked Mrs. Bensinger. I wonder what life will be like without a war. Daddy says we won't need ration stamps and he'll buy new tires for the car. Except for the trips to Grandma and Grandpa Elway's and to St. Peter, we hardly ever use the car because the tires are so bad. Daddy's had them retreaded but he says you can only do so much with rotten old tires.
>
> The most important thing is that no more boys will get killed. We went to church last night and Father Delias said all the boys who died are in heaven. According to the Baltimore Catechism I'm not sure that's true but I trust Father Delias more than the Catechism so I'm going to believe it.

The school board had promised teachers who went to war that their jobs would be waiting for them when they came back. Consequently, Donald had never been certain of employment when peace came. However, Mr. Hjalmer, whose position Donald had filled, informed the board that he had married a San Diego girl and planned to stay there. Learning this, the board extended Donald's contract for the next year. Unfortunate about that wife, but his work hadn't suffered. He had the most detailed lesson plans of anyone on the faculty.

Donald and Sally drove to Mankato for Thanksgiving. He felt guilty never going to *his* folks for the holidays, but the Elways were near Stella. On the steering wheel of the Dodge his hands tightened and released, tightened and released. A muscle behind his right shoulder pinched, and he twisted his head, trying to relax it.

"Sorry you had to miss the doings at the Barnstables'," he told Sally.

"Mmph," she grunted, gazing across the fields, which wore a lace of snow.

"Would you like to give a party? At Christmas, maybe?" She shrugged.

Was talking to thirteen-year-olds always this tough? He had trouble recalling what he had been like at thirteen. Had he ever *been* thirteen or, for that matter, twenty-five? In the last eight or ten years, he had lived what seemed to him an endless life.

The morning after Thanksgiving, Sally and Edna set out for St. Peter to visit Stella. Donald and Herb would drive over on Saturday. Best to go two at a time, they agreed.

Sally had the bag of big gumdrops on the seat beside her. Except for her letters, the candy was all she could contribute to her mother's happiness. And gumdrops did make Stella happy. When Edna and Sally had visited her while Donald was away at the teachers' convention, Stella had giggled gleefully when she saw the bag. She had seemed more sanguine in October than in years. She'd spoken a little, answering one or two questions Edna put to her, and when they'd left, she'd waved, calling good-bye after them.

Now they waited in the lounge area of the Psychopath

Building while an attendant went in search of the patient. Minutes later, a shy but willing Stella followed the same attendant into the room, greeting Sally and Edna with a rare hint of smile. Like a proper hostess, she forbore to sit until they were comfortably seated.

"How are you feeling, Mommy?"

Stella did not answer at once. Her face was thoughtful as she considered. At length she replied, "I'm feeling well. Sometimes I have a little pain in my arm . . . here." She touched her upper left forearm. "I fell out of Grandma Elway's apple tree when I was seven and broke my arm there. The doctor says I may have some arthritis in it."

She spoke as to strangers, whether because she did not recognize them or because she did, they were not certain. Edna and Sally were pleased to hear her talk and at the same time frightened and hurt by her manner of speaking. Still, she looked well, better than she had in a long time, so they buttressed themselves with this comfort and mustered the courage to respond as strangers.

"Did it hurt a lot when you broke your arm?" Sally asked.

"I don't remember very well. I suppose it must have," she said. "Have you ever broken your arm?"

Sally shook her head. "No. I've never broken anything. I've been very healthy."

"That's good. I haven't always been healthy." She shifted in her chair, drawing herself up to tell them with some pride, "But I gained five pounds this year."

"That's wonderful," Edna exclaimed.

"Yes," Stella agreed, looking upon it as a personal accomplishment, which perhaps it was.

"That's a pretty dress," Sally said of the rather drab though once attractive garment her mother wore.

"Yes." She glanced into the corner of the room, tossing her head in a girlish and self-conscious manner. "Eunice says that I'm beautiful."

"Is Eunice talking then?" Edna inquired. The last she knew, Stella's roommate did not speak.

Stella giggled. "Of course, she's talking. She talks to me. She's my friend." A look not quite of panic but of circumspection passed over Stella's features, as if she had not meant to speak so freely of Eunice but had been carried away, vaunting the friendship unwisely.

She rose slowly, hands twined together in front of her, like a prim schoolteacher dismissing the class. "I have to go now. Thank you for coming."

A moment of confused silence followed, then Sally rushed forward to waylay her mother. "Here," she said, thrusting the bag of candy at her. "Your gumdrops."

Stella looked at the bag and at Sally as if she knew nothing of this. She made as if to hand the bag back, but Sally put her hands out to prevent her.

"Mr. Anderson gave me extra black ones," Sally told her, putting the bag in Stella's hands and backing away.

"Perhaps I'll see you again," Stella said, watching them leave.

November 25 — 26, 1945

At five-thirty Tuesday morning the phone rang. Sally heard Donald pad downstairs to the kitchen. Minutes later he flicked on the lamp and sat down at the edge of the bed.

Clearing his throat, he told her, "Your mother's . . . dead." After a moment, "A ruptured appendix. No one to blame."

Donald first called the principal and superintendant of the school. They would have to find a substitute to teach his classes for the remainder of the week.

Other calls followed: to St. Peter, to the Elways, to the Wheelers, to the local funeral home, to Father Delias, and so on and so on. In a mechanical, anesthetized voice, Donald made arrangements.

Sally was peripherally aware of it all, but remained in her room until Grandma and Grandpa Wheeler, distracted and disheveled, arrived midmorning from Worthington. Grandma Wheeler made a pot of coffee. Harry Wheeler carried in boxes of canned goods that Irmgard had hastily gathered from their fruit cellar as though they were heading to a remote outpost in an uncharted land.

"I sure as hell don't know why we brought these," Harry told Donald. "Your mother insisted."

Grandpa and Grandma Elway arrived late in the afternoon, haggard and silent. Overnight, Grandma Elway had grown frail, and she was unable to talk, communicating instead by quick little nods and jerks of her head. Sweet, blameless Stella, she thought, who had never harmed a soul. Where was fairness, where . . . God? The word *God* writhed and spat in her brain like something on a hot griddle.

Bewildered, Herb Elway sat staring at a gaping rent in the world through which his daughter had escaped. He lit a cigar and forgot it. Now and then he shifted his weight or shook her head. Clearing his throat, he rose and wandered to the kitchen or bathroom or to a window, though he did not actually see anything from the window, except that jagged, indecent hole.

Donald asked Edna to choose Stella's burial dress from among those he'd packed away in a trunk. Coming upon the wine colored wool dress, Edna lifted it out and held it against her breast, stanching the wound where her own life poured out.

Borne by hearse from St. Peter and arriving in Harvester late that same Tuesday, Stella's body was received by Voss Funeral Home. After a silent evening meal, laid out by Irmgard from the goods she'd brought, Donald and Edna drove to the mortuary to pick out a casket and other accoutrements of death. They would not see Stella until the next morning when she was brought to the house in the casket for visitation.

Archie Voss led them to a large room where a good many caskets were arranged in order, from least to most expensive. Edna broke away from Donald, drawn to the bronze casket at the costlier end.

"This one." She grasped the rim with her small hands, knuckles strained white.

"Maybe we should hear what Archie has to say about them," Donald suggested, fairly certain the bronze one was beyond his means, yet not wanting to stint. He was willing to pay more than he could afford, but this casket seemed indecent, insulting to Stella, as if she might have been the sort to demand such extravagance.

"This one," Edna repeated.

"Could we at least hear about the others?" Donald suggested.

"If it's the money," she said coldly, "Herb and I will pay."

A pink flush stained Donald's neck and face. His hands shook, and he thrust them deep into his pockets. "It's not the money, Edna. Well, maybe partly, but it's more that I can't imagine Stella wanting such an expensive casket. She wasn't like that."

Edna stiffened. "I think I know what she was like. Stella was quality. When I bought something for her, it was the best. Herb and I are paying for the casket," she said with finality.

Gall rose in Donald's throat, and a vein in his temple throbbed. He wanted to strike Edna, to hear her cry out. Instead, he turned and marched through the mortuary and out the front door.

He hadn't taken his coat off when he'd gone in, and now he was shivering as perspiration evaporated from his face and body. He paced the veranda, chilled and hunched in a knot of frustration.

"Ah, Christ," he sighed at last, shoulders heaving. He pulled the collar of his overcoat up against the cold night and stamped his icy feet.

When Edna emerged at last, he saw that she was a trembling old woman. The last remnants of his anger left him, and he didn't give a damn if she bought a secondhand Duesenberg to bury Stella in.

People began arriving at the house after dinner Wednesday. The days had grown short and the nights bitter. Visitors pulled off their gloves and blew on their curled fingers, then carried their coats upstairs to the guest bedroom as the front closet filled.

Stella, in her extravagant casket, was placed against the triangular wall down which the stairway balustrade descended into the living room. The sofa, which was normally lined up against that wall, had been pushed to the adjacent one and the radio into the dining room.

On a stand near the casket a guest registry waited for signatures. The smell of egg coffee infused the stifling warmth of the house; windows steamed, and the steam condensed, running like tears down the dark glass.

On the dining-room table, an array of sweets was laid out. Throughout the afternoon, neighbors and the ladies of Stella's long-ago sodality connection had carried in cakes, cookies, cinnamon rolls, caramel rolls, and kolache. Tomorrow, following the funeral, hot dishes and ham and scalloped potatoes and several kinds of Jell-O salad would appear on the table.

"Doesn't she look natural?" Mrs. Wall was remarking to her constable husband, Gus. Truth was, if she hadn't known it was Stella Wheeler, well, she wouldn't have known. Hair all done up by Pearl from Pearl's Beauty Parlor, rouge and lipstick painted on by Geneva Voss, Stella Wheeler looked like a chippy. Too bad. Mrs. Wheeler used to be a very pretty woman.

The Walls stood respectfully beside the open casket, noting the richness of the interior, the elegance of the exterior. Cost more than Gus made in a year, Mrs. Wall surmised. Whose idea had it been to get the most expensive one Voss had? The Elway woman likely. Well, a fool and her money . . .

Sitting on a straight chair near the casket, Sally greeted familiar faces — Rose Ridza and Beverly; Mr. and Mrs. Navarin, who had brought Helen Stillman; Mr. and Mrs. Albers and Katherine; the Barnstables; and so on.

How unfamiliar the faces seemed, Sally thought, and how *individual*, distinct, and removed from each other, like little islands floating past, each in its own little sea. Even those who touched one another, like Mr. Albers with his hand on Katherine's shoulder, were notably, appallingly separate.

Grandma Elway was talking to Laurence Lundeen with whom she was unacquainted but whose eyes were deep and sympathetic. "The worst is," she confided, her brown-spotted hand on his sleeve, "Stella was so much improved, nearly ready to come home. Oh, yes, almost her old self again when this happened."

Sally stared.

"Are you okay?" Katherine Albers asked, turning away from her father, who was disputing something with Father Delias.

"I'm fine."

Beside Sally's chair, Neddy Barnstable bent to say, "I'm really sorry." He lay a plain envelope on her lap and moved along to make room for Mrs. Stillman.

Sitting on the stairs with Donald, Mrs. Navarin spoke intently, eyes hot, hands flying up suddenly, like angry birds.

Half an hour later, Sally bolted into the kitchen, grabbed an old jacket from a hook by the backdoor, and let herself out. In the garage, she leapt into the backseat of the Dodge and curled up in a ball.

Until Tuesday, endless years had stretched ahead in which Stella would regain her sanity and Sally would forgive her for having lost it. Now those possibilities were dead.

An hour passed. The car door opened.

"Sally." Donald touched her sleeve. "Sally?"

Unable to relinquish her thoughts, she turned a vacant gaze on him.

"Sally!"

She started. His face was close, a strange, frightened face she'd never seen before.

He thinks I'm going to be crazy like Mommy.

Under the bedside lamp was the envelope Neddy Barnstable had given her the night of visitation. Almost daily Sally slipped it out, removing the lengthy note, and reading it.

"Dear Sally," it said.

> I am sorry your mom died. I didn't know her very well, but I liked her. My Grandma Barnstable told me it's good to share a memory of a person who has died, so I'm going to share a memory of your mom. I don't know how many years ago it was. Quite a few.
>
> Your mom accidentally hit the Rabel's dog with her car. He was a big old dog, but she picked him up and carried him to our house which was about six blocks away. She wouldn't drive the car again, she said.
>
> My mom looked at the dog and said right away that he was dead, but your mom asked to have my dad examine him anyway. I guess she didn't want to believe my mom.
>
> When my dad told her the dog really was dead, she cried for a long time. When she stopped crying, she and my dad talked and she told him that when she was young, she wanted to be a nurse so she could help everyone live until they were very old. She didn't think anybody should die until they were old and then they should die in their sleep in the middle of a beautiful dream.
>
> After she said that, she cried a little more, I guess because the Rabel's dog hadn't died in his sleep and also because she hadn't gotten to be a nurse.
>
> I felt bad for your mom and I liked her for saying that because it showed that she had a good heart. It always stayed in

my memory, about dying in your sleep in the middle of a beautiful dream.

I hope it doesn't make you sad to hear this story. If it does, I'm sorry.

Sincerely,
Neddy Barnstable

"Is coach home?" Billy Rabel stood on the back stoop.

"He's got junior varsity practice," Sally told him.

"Can I come in and wait?"

Sally let him pass. "Aren't you on the j.v. team?"

Billy pulled out a kitchen chair, tossing his jacket over the back. Collapsing onto the chair, he stretched out his long legs, crossing them at the ankles.

"Yeah. I hadda miss practice, and I wanta explain to Coach. I don't wanta lose my place in the lineup."

"You better brush your teeth or something. You smell of cigarettes."

"Yeah?" He looked concerned but not flustered. "You got a toothbrush I can use?"

"You can use my tooth*paste*," she said, going to fetch it.

Taking the Ipana from her and squeezing half an inch onto his index finger, Billy said, "You're not gonna tell Coach, are you, about the cigarettes?" His mouth twisted in a knowing grin.

Slowly and not looking at him, Sally screwed the cap onto the toothpaste tube. Billy's smile made her feel clumsy and kiddish. Although he was only in the ninth grade, a year ahead of her, he had the shadow of soft, unshaved beard along his upper lip and the intimation of presumptuous virility in his manner.

"You wouldn't want me to get kicked off the team," he said, sliding his right foot sideways across the linoleum till the side of his shoe nudged against hers. "Would you?"

"I won't tell. . . ."

"If?"

"If you teach me to smoke."

"I tried smokin' once, but Godsakes it made me dizzy," Beverly said one Sunday afternoon, months after Stella's death. Her back against the bureau, she sat on the floor in Sally's room, sketching her friend. "Hold still. You keep movin'."

"It made me dizzy at first," Sally said, "but not any more."

She puffed languidly on a Pall Mall, knocking the ash into a glass dish on the bedside table. Every other week when he got his allowance, Billy Rabel sneaked Sally a pack of cigarettes, an insurance policy against her tattling to Coach about his smoking. She wouldn't have, but she accepted the cigarettes, because it kept Billy coming around.

"It's cold in here with the window open," Beverly complained.

"I'm almost done," Sally told her, amazed at the way Beverly could carry on a conversation and sketch at the same time. Sally blew smoke out her nostrils and stubbed the cigarette out.

Beverly had always earned A's in art, but it was only lately, since she'd started baby-sitting and running errands for Mr. Eggers at the drugstore, that she had spare money to buy paper, sketch pencils, and charcoal. She was serious enough about drawing to send away for fixative and to slap together a makeshift portfolio to protect her best pieces.

"Let me see," Sally said.

"It's not done. You keep movin'."

"Well, let me see anyway."

Beverly held up the pad.

"That's really good. Is that what I look like? Or did you make it prettier so I'd like it?"

"I wouldn't do that," Beverly disdained.

"Well, it's really good. Can I have it when you're done?"

"If I like it."

"No, let me have it even if you don't like it."

Beverly shook her head. "If it isn't good, I want to keep it, so I can study what I did wrong."

"I wish I was good at something the way you are." Being

pretty or beautiful or whatever she was, wasn't enough. It was all she had, but it wasn't enough.

Beverly shrugged. "You're a good ice skater."

"Oh *really.*" Sally hooted, beating the bed pillow with her fist. "I'm pretty good for someone in a little burg like Harvester. I couldn't ever be a famous ice skater, and you know it."

"Well, just about every girl would like to have your looks," Beverly told her.

"That doesn't count. I didn't have anything to do with that. Let me ask you something. If you had to choose between being pretty and being good at art, which would you choose?"

Beverly was plain as a common sparrow, and she knew it. She'd always wanted to be pretty. She'd always wanted to be Sally. But if she had to choose, she'd choose to be good at art. Drawing made her feel, well, kind of powerful. Maybe being pretty made you feel powerful, too, but if Sally was any example, it didn't make you feel powerful enough.

"See? I knew it," Sally said and felt sad, though she spoke with an airy insouciance.

Changing the subject, Beverly told her, "Rose is getting hitched in June."

"Your mother's getting married? MotherofGod. Is she going to live on his farm?"

"Not just her. All of us."

"But what about the apartment? What about her job and *your* job running errands? How'll you make money? I'll never see you if you're stuck on some damned farm."

"I'll be coming to school on the bus, like the other farm kids," Beverly pointed out. "And Elwood says he'll pay me allowance if I help with chores. Charlie too. Charlie can't wait to move out there."

"And what about parties and movies? How are you going to get to them?" Sally demanded.

"Elwood says he'll drive me in. I can always stay over night with you, can't I?"

Sally didn't answer.

"Elwood says Ma can keep her egg money. She's been workin' so long, she needs to feel like she's got her own money. He's a pretty nice guy, really. And guess what? He says when I'm old enough and have my driver's licence, he'll let me drive the car to town for dances and stuff." She paused to let Sally acknowledge Elwood's generosity. When Sally said nothing, Beverly pointed out, "I'm not movin' to Wyoming, for Godsakes, it's only two, three miles outta town."

Gazing blandly out the window as if none of this was anything to her, Sally was sick with rage. And in June, when Rose sent Sally and Donald an invitation to her wedding at St. Boniface Catholic Church, Sally stayed away.

In ninth grade, Sally complained to Beverly, "Except for smoking and reading dirty books, this is the most boring year of my life."

Ninth-grade boys didn't ask girls for dates. If coerced, they would show up at parties arranged by girls, tiresome, self-conscious parties where the boys huddled in a corner talking and laughing amongst themselves, but fell instantly silent when expected to dance. Inevitably, one girl wept before the evening was over. Not always the same girl but the one whose crush had boiled to a froth during the current week and must inevitably spill over on the weekend.

In the bathroom, with the door bolted as if boys might storm it, she was surrounded by her friends, petting her and murmuring sympathetically, wringing out cold washcloths to freshen her face and offering such advice as "Just ignore him. If you ignore him he'll probably like you." But ninth-grade boys didn't notice if you ignored them. They expected to be ignored. When a girl who'd been leaving notes in their locker and making eyes at them across study hall ceased to do so, it was a relief, as if a buzzing fly had flown off to bother someone else.

Sally did not cry in bathrooms and was embarrassed by girls

who did. She was embarrassed, too, by the parties where these girls ended up in bathrooms. For heaven's sake, ninth-grade boys didn't even kiss yet. How could you cry over them?

At one of these occasions, a particularly dreary Saturday night in Angela Bussey's basement, half a dozen tenth-grade boys, including Billy Rabel, crashed the party. Billy, smelling of beer, grabbed Sally and began dancing with her, maneuvering her behind the furnace where he French-kissed her.

Tenth grade was not much better than ninth. Some girls, giving up on the boys in their own class, began dating upper classmen. Sally waited for Billy Rabel to ask her out and, when he didn't, reasoned that it was because she was Coach's daughter. She was going to have to throw herself at him.

Although Neddy Barnstable called several times to ask her out during the summer between tenth and eleventh grade, Sally declined without knowing why. She baby-sat sporadically but, unlike many girls her age, found infants questionably adorable. Maybe she was not maternal.

She also read: Cather, Hemingway, Steinbeck, Fitzgerald, and anyone both Russian and dead. Two or three afternoons a week she rode her bike to Elwood Hanson's farm to loll around with Beverly.

Because most of Beverly's chores were early morning or early evening, the two girls idled away long days under the trees in the front yard, Sally smoking and reading aloud Housman and Wilfred Owen, Parker and Emily Dickinson; Beverly sketching, both gossiping about movie stars, boys home from college, and Sheila Grubb who was said to be stepping out on her husband. Often they changed into swimsuits and pedaled down the dusty gravel road to Sioux Woman Lake.

Beverly spent a good deal of time talking about the future, discussing plans to be an artist, maybe in New York, trying it out on Sally.

"What about you? What're you going to do?" she asked more than once, disturbed that Sally never spoke of college or work.

One humid, breathless afternoon while sketching an arthritic-looking crab-apple tree, Beverly observed, "Seems like all the girls I know are hell-bent to get married."

Sprawled on an old patchwork quilt losing its batting through countless frayed spots, Sally scratched her thigh where a fly had settled to drink sweat. Turning page 103 of *The Grapes of Wrath,* she responded, "Hmmm."

"Are you?"

"Hmmm?"

"Are you hell-bent to get married?"

"I don't know," Sally murmured.

That was another thing that bothered Beverly. Sally might end up marrying some guy just because she was bored and looking to pass the time.

"Rose says you shouldn't get married 'til you have an education, cuz you could end up like her, marrying a mean drunk like my pa and having to cook at the Loon Cafe or something."

"Hmmm."

"You want to go to college or secretarial school or something, don't you?"

Sally got to her feet, inchmeal. Although the question had not eluded her, she brushed away a leaf stuck to the back of her arm and said, "I'm going swimming now."

Upstairs, tugging on a puckery elasticized green swimsuit, Beverly conceded, "Well, we're only going to be in the eleventh grade. There's plenty of time to decide about college."

She did not in truth believe that. Even if you didn't know what you wanted to be, you ought to plan to be *something.* You could always change your mind later. Without a plan, you might just drift.

Already dressed in a new two-piece pink and white check swimsuit, Sally leaned against the window sash, peering down into the farmyard where Elwood's old brown and white spaniel lay in the shade of a rusty pickup. The rutted drive and creaking windmill had a comforting lenience, like the dog and the rackety truck, not nagging you to make a plan, not worrying you about boys. Not giving a damn whether you were crazy.

When Sally was in the eleventh grade, she asked Billy Rabel to the Sadie Hawkins Day Dance, which in Harvester was not held in February on Sadie Hawkins Day but in October.

All the girls wanted to date Billy. He was the best-looking boy in the senior class and "built like a brick shit house," as Beverly put it.

Sadie Hawkins Day custom had the girl calling for the boy at his home. Most boys played this for all it was worth, letting the girls cool their heels while they combed their hair one last time, waiting for their dates to open the door, cheering as the girls shelled out money for dance tickets.

But when Sally offered to pick up Billy in Donald's car, he grinned, telling her, "I don't go for that girl's-in-charge crap."

"You *will* let me pay for the tickets?"

"Oh, yeah. That's different."

"Coach," Billy greeted Donald, smiling and rubbing his palms together rather like his father, with a merchant's practiced bonhomie, as if he were about to point out the virtues of the pork roast in the meat case.

"Have a chair," Donald said, settling himself on the sofa.

"Yes, sir." Billy sat deep in a wing chair, resting his right ankle on his left knee in a manly pose. "I figure Michigan'll go to the Rose Bowl this year," he began.

"I wouldn't be surprised."

"I figure they'll play California."

Donald nodded. "Have you made any plans for college?" he asked, prompted by mention of the Rose Bowl.

". . . thinking about a couple of years of business college, then coming back and going in with the old man." Billy undid the buttoned button on his tweed jacket and leaned forward. "The old man makes the best Polish sausage, frankfurters, and liverwurst in southern Minnesota, but like he says, he needs wider distribution. I wanta learn how that works." Again he rubbed his palms. "Someday you'll see Rabel's Meats as far away as Mankato."

Sally's nyloned legs appeared on the stairs. She descended, wearing a black velveteen skirt and a lightweight white sweater set, pink and blue embroidered flowers at the neck and down the front of the cardigan.

Billy rose and shook Donald's hand. "Coach. Good talking with you."

Fetching her coat from the closet and pulling it on, Sally called over her shoulder, "See you."

After the dance, Billy drove out of town on the Ula road and pulled onto a lane leading into Wes Adolphson's pasture where the car was shielded by a stand of red cedar.

Parking in the country was new to Sally, although she was aware that people did it, and she tried to appear knowing, even indifferent.

From the back seat, Billy grabbed a bottle of Coke, opened it, and drank off part of it. Then he reached across Sally, flipped open the glove compartment, and pulled out a pint of Old Granddad in a brown paper bag, pouring whiskey into the Coke bottle until the level of brown liquid rose again to the neck. Covering the top of the Coke bottle with his thumb, he turned it upside down, then right side up, and handed it to Sally.

"Ever had whiskey?"

"A couple of times," Sally lied, taking a tiny sip from the bottle, shivering, and handing it to Billy.

"Go ahead, take a real swig," he told her, pushing it back to her.

"Trying to get me drunk?"

"You think I'm that kind of guy?" he said with a tone of injury. Sally thought he was being sardonic.

"How do I know what kind of guy you are?" She tipped the bottle up and drank. The liquor tasted of darkness and defiance. She couldn't imagine drinking it in broad daylight.

In the dimness of the front seat, illumined only by the dashboard, Billy looked dusky and somehow Latin. He smelled of

243

Aqua Velva and now of Old Granddad and Coke. Laying an arm across her shoulders and reaching with the other hand for the bottle, his athletic bulk loomed over her. She felt surrounded by him and, beyond that, surrounded by the cocoon of the warm car. She could feel Billy's body heat, like an intoxicating fuzziness in which she might become trapped. He helped her slip off her coat, brushing her breast with his arm as he did.

When they had drunk all of the Coke, he set the bottle on the floor on the passenger side and as he straightened, lay a hand on her thigh, on top of her skirt.

"Nice," he said of the soft nap of the velveteen, and French-kissed her.

All this was quite pleasant, Sally thought, with a degree of objectivity that surprised her. However, she did not know where to draw the line. Girls *did* draw lines, she knew that. Different girls drew different lines. Some felt that whatever went on on the outside of their clothes was all right. Others claimed that anything above the waist was okay, and still others, that everything was allowable except going all the way.

On a first date, Sally decided, French-kissing was enough though she didn't make a big deal of it when removing Billy's hand from beneath her sweater. Rose had told Beverly that boys would naturally *try* anything. Girls had to take command, "firmly but not unkindly."

"Sounds like training a dog," Beverly had said.

In the front seat of Mr. Rabel's car, a great deal of French-kissing and hugging and squirming and pressing of bodies went on, with Billy calling Sally "honey," each time his hands wandered, as if calling her "honey" were a key he would use to "unlock her drawers," as Beverly would put it.

But obviously he wasn't too upset at not getting past first base on the initial date, because he continued asking her out. On the third date, she let him fondle her breasts, wondering as she did if these decisions were always so cut and dried.

After the Christmas Dance to which Billy invited her, he

asked Sally to go steady. From his jacket pocket he fished a dog-tag chain with his class ring on it and hung it around her neck, calling her "more beautiful than Jane Powell," a compliment Sally considered dubious.

Calling her beautiful, like calling her "honey," was a ploy, Sally perceived, meant to break down her resistance to going all the way. That fact notwithstanding, the little world of Mr. Rabel's car, with the heater humming and plenty of Coke and Old Granddad to drink, was a cozy little world filled with pleasures if not happiness.

Although Billy told Leroy Mosely's brother Daryl and a couple of other boys that Sally was an "easy" girl, she was *his* easy girl, and on Valentine's Day, 1949, he gave her his letter sweater to wear.

Billy's purple and gold sweater was the kind that girls flaunted—practically covered with "patches" for football, basketball, baseball, and track. On the sleeve were chevrons indicating that he had lettered in these sports since he was a freshman.

Some girls in Sally's class had earned their own letter sweaters with patches for band, glee club, or cheerleading, but Sally was not musical, and she'd never been interested in cheerleading, which seemed to be the province of short, cute girls who smiled all the time. Sally was already five feet eight, beautiful, and not all that smiling.

Except for Beverly, who knew better, most students presumed that because Billy was a senior and because he'd given Sally his letter sweater and class ring to wear, they "went all the way." After all, he'd told some of the guys that she was easy.

Billy and Sally did everything except go all the way. They petted until they both had come, and though she didn't know why, she would go no further.

Then one snowy night in March, sitting in the Rable car

listening to Hobbs' House on WCCO, Sally refused even to let Billy unbutton her jeans.

She'd asked him if he'd liked *Black Boy,* which she'd loaned him.

"I never finished it."

"How come?"

"Well, Jesus, it's about this nigger, and he works in a whore house. How'm I gonna be interested in that?" To put her on the defensive where she belonged, he added, "You must have a dirty mind."

In May, Sally broke off with Billy despite the fact that it would mean not going to the junior-senior prom.

In the back seat of his dad's Nash Ambassador on a warm, soft night, his hard-on collapsing, he asked in disbelief, *"Why?"*

"You never read anything, Billy." It was more than that.

"What?"

"You laughed when I asked you to read *Cannery Row.* You said I had a dirty mind when I gave you *Black Boy.*"

"Does Coach know you read that kind of stuff? Where're you getting it? You could get into trouble, you know." He opened the back door of the Nash, climbing out and adjusting his underwear. Sliding behind the wheel, he started the engine. "You gonna get in front?"

"I'll ride back here."

Shifting the car into gear and spraying gravel, he spun out of the Sioux Woman Lake parking lot, fishtailing onto the country road leading back to town.

Pulling to the curb in front of Sally's house, he cut the engine and, before Sally could jump out, asked in an aggrieved voice, "What d'ya *want,* for Chrissake? I take you to every dance. I let you wear my sweater and class ring."

"I'm sorry, Billy," she told him, feeling a panicked sort of re-morse for what she had to do. She'd never broken up with a boy before. Would he get really mad or maybe cry? "You're okay.

It's me. Most girls in school would give their right arm to go out with you."

"What d'ya want me to do? Tell me. You want me to read books, is that it?"

"I want you to *want* to read books, not do it because you *have* to."

"That's not fair. If I'm willing to read, what the hell do you care why?"

"It's not just reading books. I can't explain. It's too hard."

"Well, try."

"You know Laurence Lundeen?"

"Everybody knows him. So what about him?"

"I want to date someone like him. Only younger. Please don't be mad, Billy."

He hit the steering wheel hard with the palm of his hand. "Laurence Lundeen, Jesus. What the hell is that about?"

"Let's be friends, please?"

He snorted. "Oh, sure, we're real likely to be friends. You as good as called me a bonehead."

Sally opened the door.

Stretching round to face her, he said, "I was really serious about you. Really serious."

"I'm sorry."

"My folks said 'Her mother was nuts. Remember when she killed our Blackie? It's in the family,' but I went out with you anyway, didn't I?"

Sally closed the door, wheeled slowly, and headed toward the house. Behind her, the Nash squealed away from the curb, waking half the people on the block.

By the next afternoon everyone in the high school knew that Billy was sick of her. "Bored the shit out of me," he told Daryl Mosely.

As she opened her locker after school, Billy, surrounded by senior boys, called to her from his own locker across the hall,

"Bring the letter sweater and class ring when you come to school tomorrow. They weren't a present, in case that's what you were thinking. Just a loan."

Laughing, he loped away to baseball practice, boys trailing in his wake, hooting and punching each other.

July 1949

They'd been swimming at Sioux Woman Lake, and afterward, Beverly rode her bike into town with Sally to pick up a couple of pairs of nylons that Lundeen's had put aside for Rose.

Laurence Lundeen was leaving the store as Beverly and Sally entered. Holding the screen door for them and noting their still-damp hair, he observed, "You look like a pair of naiads."

"What's nides?" Beverly asked when he was out of earshot.

Sally shrugged.

Alice Penny found Roses's stockings and charged them to the Hanson's account. "Say hello to your mother," she told Beverly as the girls were leaving.

"Used to be nobody gave my ma the time of day, but now Rose's got some money." Beverly hmmphed. "Want to have a Coke at Eggers'?"

When old Mr. Nichols died the previous year, Mr. Eggers purchased the tiny shoe-repair shop next to the drugstore. Knocking a connecting doorway through the wall, Eggers installed a jukebox and booths. But Sally still preferred the soda fountain with its high swivel stools, mahogany face, brass footrest, and marble counter.

Climbing onto a stool, she ordered a root-beer float. Beverly wanted Coke. Behind the counter, Estelle Preuss, who was twenty-five and still living at home, took their order.

When her back was turned, Beverly leaned close to Sally. "I hear she's gotta marry some gandy dancer from over by Worthington." Beverly rolled her eyes as if to say, "Aren't you glad it isn't you?" She had nothing against gandy dancers. It was the possibility of Sally getting knocked up like Estelle Preuss that worried her.

At the end of the fountain, where it curved, Laurence Lundeen sat drinking iced tea and working the crossword in the *Minneapolis Morning Tribune.*

He wore a sky blue shirt, beige linen-blend trousers, and a blue and cream patterned tie. His gold cuff links were probably real gold, Sally thought, and the tie bar as well. Recently she'd read an article about pastel colored dress shirts being the latest thing for men. They hadn't made an impact on Harvester yet, but of course Laurence Lundeen was not the typical Harvester businessman.

"Sally," he called to her now, "have you seen Olivier's *Hamlet*? I hope I've talked Angus Belling into a one-night showing."

Although the movie had won Best Picture and Best Actor Academy Awards, Mr. Belling would not schedule it for a normal run at the Majestic, for fear of losing money.

As always, Sally was flattered by Lundeen's attention. She hoped he was not drawn to her in the same way he might be to a painting or an antique. Or a pastel dress shirt.

"I haven't seen *Hamlet* but I want to," she told him. "My grandma said it played in Mankato. Her literary study group went. I've only seen Laurence Olivier in *Wuthering Heights*. I thought he was, well, heartbreaking." Was *heartbreaking* too dramatic a word? Did she sound affected?

"Heartbreaking," Mr. Lundeen repeated. "He certainly was. In *Hamlet*, too, but in a different way."

Sally's cheeks burned red with the warmth of this confirmation. Beside her, Beverly was finishing her Coke and saying, "I gotta get back to the farm."

Sally slid off the stool. "It was nice to see you, Mr. Lundeen. Thanks for asking Mr. Belling to run *Hamlet*." She turned to leave, but swung back again, feeling giddy and a little glamorous. "You're the only person I know who'd have taken the trouble."

Outside the drugstore the two girls made plans for Beverly to stay overnight on Saturday for Harvester Days, then waved their good-byes as Beverly pedaled off. Since Donald's late-summer football scrimmages often lasted past post office closing, Sally stopped to check the box and found a notice to pick up a package at the window.

After hanging the damp swimsuit on the clothesline, she carried the parcel into the house, setting it on the kitchen table. Someone named Eunice Parsons had mailed it from Rochester, Minnesota, addressing it to "The Wheeler Family."

The note inside bore no salutation but began:

My name is Eunice Parsons and I was Stella Wheeler's room-mate at the St. Peter hospital.

I have recently been released for the second time. The first time I came home, I had the box I'm sending you among my possessions. I don't know how that happened, just some mix-up. Anyway, I had to go back, and when I came home again, I found the box in a closet and discovered that it belonged to Stella.

I debated what to do and finally decided it legally belonged to you. You may not want it but I have to send it.

Stella and I were very close when we were at the hospital. She was sweet and beautiful and I loved her. I will never forget her.

Sincerely,
Eunice Parsons

Beneath this note, the box was stuffed with correspondence. Sally scrabbled through it, examining envelope after envelope. Letters from Donald, from the grandparents, from Sally, hundreds of letters, all addressed to Stella. None opened.

Letting herself down onto a chair, Sally stared past the box. Long minutes passed while she sat, holding the meaning of the box away from her.

After five minutes she went to the junk drawer and, jerking it open, extracted a red grease pencil. Across one of her own letters to Stella she scrawled "I hate you!" and tossed it back into the box.

Dragging a stepladder from the basement to the second-floor hall, she climbed to the attic trapdoor and slammed it aside. Demons of heat flew out. Hoisting the carton up into the dim attic, she shoved it hard and heard it whisper across the rough, unfinished floor into the deep shadows under the eaves.

Hot and grimy, Donald arrived home from football practice about half past five. Noting that Sally's door was closed, he went ahead and showered and changed, then searched the icebox for dinner, discovering a bowl of leftover potato salad and half a quart of milk.

When he'd opened a can of tuna and sliced the tomatoes Desiree Navarin had sent home, he called up the stairs to Sally. Seating himself at the table by the open window, he rose again to look for an onion, which, it appeared, they did not have. He'd left a note on the counter asking Sally to pick up onions, meat, and bread. The note was still there.

"Sally," he called again, this time with impatience.

A minute passed, a bedroom door opened, and she hollered down in a faraway voice, "I'm not hungry."

"Well, would you please come down anyway?" Sally was hardly overburdened with chores. She did little enough. The least he could expect was that she'd stop at Truska's and pick up a few groceries. Turning on his heel, he tramped back to the kitchen.

From the icebox he grabbed a pitcher of iced tea *he'd* made and slammed it down on the table.

The late sun beat angrily on his cheek and neck as he ate.

Perspiration gathered under his arms and between his shoulders. He pulled the shade down, casting the room into a muted sulphur glow and cutting off whatever small breeze might otherwise find him.

"Yes?" Sally stood in the doorway, wrapped in a heavy robe, despite the heat.

"What the hell are you wearing that thing for?"

She blinked. "What?"

"Never mind. Why didn't you go to Truska's? We're out of bread and meat. And a slice of onion would have been nice with the tuna."

"I forgot. I'm sorry." She did not sound sorry. Her voice carried a dull wonderment that anything as trivial as a slice of onion should concern him.

"You may think these are unimportant matters, young lady, but if this house isn't going to fall apart, you've got to shoulder your responsibility. You're not a little kid any more. I can't do everything."

"I said I was sorry. What the hell do you want me to do, rupture my appendix?"

Donald's jaw snapped shut as quickly as it had snapped open.

Sally groaned, spinning away, back upstairs, slamming the bedroom door so hard the entire second floor rattled.

The bedroom had grown shadowy, the air oppressive. Although she was soaked in sweat, Sally took no notice.

She could hide the unopened letters in the attic, but she couldn't rid herself of them. Stretched out on the bed, she felt them hanging over her.

Drifting into a troubled, suffocating sleep, she woke after an hour, feeling trapped in the house. Trapped with the letters. Pulling on the clothes she'd earlier discarded, she flew down the stairs and out the backdoor.

A few months back, after long soul-searching, Donald had decided to postpone a master's degree in history until Sally was out of high school. Coaching baseball, assistant-coaching a couple of other sports, chaperoning dances and trips, he had little enough time for her as it was.

He loved history. He loved the process of unraveling it, the connections, progressions, backtrackings, mysteries, and lapses, the detection of lies and misdirections. Gumshoeing was what it was.

And he liked the library, the peace and escape. Like church, but with books.

Encouraged by Desiree Navarin, he went on studying. She tracked down syllabi, reading lists, and texts. She wrote letters, tracing original and secondary sources. She brought him baskets of tomatoes and cucumbers and carrots.

Donald read and took notes and, along the way, grew confident that he could hold his own in classes with other graduate students.

Some time ago, however, while tracking down land-grant statistics, conscience had made him unwilling to take further advantage of Desiree.

"I'll write the letters," he'd told her when she suggested where the information might be found.

"I'm a librarian," she'd said, a tetchy note in her voice. "This is what librarians do."

"No, this isn't what librarians do. You don't do this for anyone else."

"No one else has asked me," she said, giving her head an impatient, oblique twist.

"You're busy enough already."

"Let me do this!" She sounded like his mother when he was a kid and Irmgard was out of patience with him.

Now, gathering up papers, books, and notebooks from a library table, he saw that it was nearly closing time. Desiree was too indulgent with him, made him feel too much at home.

He watched her move with unhurried grace from room to room, closing windows, sliding chairs into place, turning out lights, and collecting books left lying about. She touched fingertips to oak as she passed reading tables, caressed shelves of novels with a passionate eye. Chatelaine of the Stacks, Donald thought.

"A letter came from Dr. Brekken," she told him, returning to the high desk to riffle through the correspondence in a wire basket. "He has some source suggestions." She pulled a typewritten letter and an appended list from an envelope, unfolded them, and laid them on the desktop in front of Donald.

Heads bent close over the pages, Donald murmured suggestions while Desiree took notes.

Slamming open the door from the street, Sally burst in.

The two heads at the desk shot up, traces of a symbiotic tenderness still clinging to them.

Sally hesitated in the doorway, looked from one face to the other, and stammered, "I . . . I . . . ."

Behind her eyes something leapt, as to a conclusion.

Sally's gaze was feverish as she raised a hand to shade her eyes against the fiery sunset haloing buildings along the west side of Main Street.

The weather was hot and tropical, as if, she thought, a storm lay crouched just beyond the western horizon, gathering itself to descend with unimaginable violence, cracking a whip of wind, shattering the Ferris wheel and merry-go-round and kiddie cars, washing them away with the rest of the broken refuse that moments earlier had been the Harvester Days celebration.

Despite the humidity, however, the sky was a wan diaphane, flowered with pale moon and paler stars.

Up and down the avenues peripheral to Main Street, beat-up old Fords with rumble seats and shiny new Buick Roadmasters with chromium smiles drifted again and again, as though swimming laps in a pool of warm water. High-school and college boys from Red Berry and St. Bridget and who-knew-where-else leaned out car windows, whistling at local girls and calling "Hubba hubba."

"Hubba hubba, ding, ding, Baby, you've got everything. Hubba hubba, dong dong, You won't have it very long" was too much to yell out before the next girl came into view.

When dusk congealed enough for headlights to be turned on, the boys pulled the cars to the curb, and wearing twill trousers

and white shirts with rolled-up sleeves, they insinuated themselves into the throng of locals.

Hanging together in threes and fours, they sidled in and out
of the flow of celebrants, now riding the tilt-a-whirl, later collecting in shapeless clots on the sideline, scheming, speculating,
laying odds.

"There's some cute guys from Red Berry over there," Beverly
indicated, casting a sideways glance in the direction of three
scrubbed looking young men hanging around the Knights of
Columbus' wheel of fortune.

"You think so?" Sally said, dismissing them without a second
glance.

"What's the matter with them?"

Waiting in line to buy a ticket for the Ferris wheel, Sally
nudged her friend forward. "They look like they're on their way
to Sunday school," she said coldly.

"So what?"

"I don't like boys who look so, well, clean."

"You want 'em with dirt in their ears?"

"Don't be dumb." Sally fished change from a small, white
patent-leather purse. "But they should look a little more
dangerous."

"Oh, brother," Beverly groaned. "Just remember, some guys
who look dangerous *are.*"

Behind them, one of a pair of St. Bridget boys thrust a rather
knowing face between the two girls. Addressing Sally, he
asked, "Don't suppose you'd care to treat a couple of strangers
to a ride on the Ferris wheel?"

"You do look strange," Sally told him. "But, no, we don't care
to." She looked askance at Beverly as if to say, "Now *he's* more
like it."

The two boys, soon to be high-school seniors, followed the
girls onto the Ferris wheel, riding in the gondola behind them.
The more knowing of the two craned his head up, laughing a

mocking, insinuating laugh and calling, "How about the tilt-a-whirl, then? Wanta give us a ride on the tilt-a-whirl?"

When Sally and Beverly rode the merry-go-round, the boys followed, grabbing the galloping steeds behind them from Reverend Gordon's two little kids who were too meek to protest.

"You take candy from babies too?" Beverly called.

"Depends on the candy," the bolder of the two yelled back, above the groan and wheeze of the calliope.

Later, as the girls stood in line at the American Legion booth to order hot dogs, that same boy offered, "Let me," and handed change to Sonny Steen to pay for the food.

Beverly was not comfortable with this, but Sally, flushed and feeling almost drunk, said, "What can it hurt?"

The girls wandered along Main Street, pausing to note the hemlines of the fall dresses displayed in Lundeen's Dry Goods. "If they get any longer, they're going to be down to the floor," Beverly said, disapproving.

The boy who'd paid for the hot dogs appeared from nowhere and, confident Sally wouldn't make a scene in front of a crowd, grabbed her hand, pulling her through the crowd toward the Ferris wheel.

"What do you think you're doing?"

She tried to sound angry but a terrifying electricity raced up her arm from their joined hands, and she couldn't hear her own voice for the roar in her ears.

With tickets already purchased, he yanked her along in his rough wake, running to catch the last gondola.

"What's your name?" he asked as they threw themselves, breathless, into the swaying seat.

"Sally."

"That all?"

"Wheeler."

"Sally Wheeler," he said, testing it to see whether it would do.

"'I wonder what's become of Sally,'" he sang, looking at her invasively.

She struggled for breath. "What's your name?"

"Colman."

"Coalman?" she laughed. The picture of Mr. Steuben, who delivered coal, came to mind, Mr. Steuben with his blackened hands and face and coveralls.

Sally's laughter was a hat pin pricking the boy's ego. Had she reacted differently, he might have romanced her for the night, tested how far she'd let him go, said he'd call, and then forgotten her. She was a looker, but she wasn't a C-cup, and she wasn't flirty, the way Luanne Knoppler was.

"It's spelled C-o-l-m-a-n," he said, as if she were the intellectual equal of an earthworm. "My mother named me after Ronald Colman," he explained with a mixture of embarrassment and bravura. Plenty of girls had told him he looked like Ronald Colman, though he knew he looked more like Errol Flynn. "People call me Cole. Do they call you Sal?"

"No." Feeling boneless and faint and slightly sick, Sally squared her shoulders with a sangfroid that was all pretense and gazed off over the rooftops of the little two-story Main Street.

"My last name is Barnstable," the boy in the Ferris wheel gondola told her, although she hadn't asked. "I've got relations here. Neddy Barnstable, d'ya know him? My folks own Barnstable's Department Store in St. Bridget. You must have been in there."

She nodded, her hands on the safety-bar stiff and cold.

The chick was a snob, Cole concluded, maybe one of the brainy, National Honor Society types. He rocked the gondola.

Sally was afraid of heights. She forced herself to ride the Ferris wheel because she did not want to be teased, but she never rocked the seat, leaned forward, or looked too closely into the works. Now this boy was rocking back and forth, as boys did. Her heart fluttered with fear. To any other boy she would have said "Stop it" in an angry and imperative tone, but to this one she could not.

Sensing her terror, he slid his right arm around her shoulders and rocked the gondola with his left hand.

Sally was paralyzed.

Cole Barnstable was pleased. When the Ferris wheel stopped to let them step down, Sally's knees gave way as she alighted. The attendant reached to grab her, but Cole put an arm around her waist and, holding her close to his side, led her away. Landing this little trout wasn't going to be hard, he thought.

Sally searched for Beverly in the crowd but didn't see her.

"What's your friend's name?" she asked the boy.

"Dave."

"Do you see him anywhere?"

"No."

Cole wasn't concerned, nor was he looking for Dave. "Maybe they went for a walk. We can get my car and drive around looking for them."

His car was his mother's Futuramic Oldsmobile convertible with Hydra-Matic Drive and windows that rolled up and down with the press of a button.

"What's the big deal if we don't find them?" he asked when they'd explored all the streets within a four-block radius of downtown. "We'll ride around for a while, then come back and look some more."

Sally had never been in a convertible. In Minnesota they were considered impractical, and few people could afford an impractical car. Generally, those who could were too practical to buy one.

The night was perfect for driving with the top down. They passed Katherine Albers' house, and inexplicably, Sally wanted to call out, "Look at me, Mr. Albers. It's Sally Wheeler, and I'm riding around in a 'boat.'"

Now and then she sneaked sidelong glances at Cole Barnstable. He resembled Neddy, but his hair was darker, his nose longer, his shoulders heavier. And something in his posture seemed to gather itself, to impend, like an avalanche.

Below Sally's brain, where these thoughts floated like fila-
ments of cottonwood fluff; below her heart, where brutal blood
pounded its way in and out of straining chambers; below her
stomach, even, where unaccountable hunger made her feel in-
substantial and close to death, a hot, coiled pain gripped her.
When Cole Barnstable reached out to run his fingers along the
side of her neck, the pain curled tighter.

He navigated in ever wider circles until they were on the first
ring of country roads surrounding Harvester. As they drove the
road behind Bacal's Hill and the football field, Cole turned onto
a rutty little lane leading to a grassy plot where people parked
their cars when they came sledding. He steered the convertible
off the lane and alongside a stand of Russian olives whose tor-
tured arms flung up the cheap silver of moonlit leaves.

"We shouldn't stop," Sally told him without meaning it.

He turned off the engine and lights, pushed the seat back,
and sat with his left shoulder against the driver's side door,
looking at her. He knew that she'd expected him to grab her.
Since he hadn't, she was confused, relieved, and disappointed.
In a few minutes she'd begin wondering what was wrong with
her that he didn't want to kiss her.

He held out a hand, palm up, like a salver. She lay her hand
on it. For fifteen minutes they sat like this, Sally exhausted by
desire.

Just when she'd concluded that he wasn't attracted to her,
he pulled her toward him, brushing her lips in the barest hint of
a kiss. In the same manner, he kissed her closed eyes. She
sighed as though at the end of a great labor and bent her head to
run her tongue along the base of his neck. His skin tasted like
cinnamon.

He told no lies, whispered no endearments, not even as he
drove through her hymen, nailing her to the dusty grass where
dry olive leaves crackled like fire beneath her. He did not tell
her that she was beautiful. If he had, she might have found the

strength to resist him. She had not had to despise his flattery nor see through a clumsy pretense of affection.

In the tall grass at the base of the trees, crickets knitted with their knees; a quarter of a mile away a dog barked three times and fell silent; and across a mile of village streets and the vastness of the past half hour, faint calliope music gasped.

Beverly sat cross-legged on Sally's bed, sputtering, "You didn't!"

"Yes, I did," Sally told her, wanting to sound unruffled and indifferent.

"Godsakes."

"If you're going to bawl me out, forget it." Sally unzipped her cotton dress, yanking it off over her head. She pulled a hanger from the closet, scrutinized the dress more closely, then tossed the garment in the laundry heap on the floor.

"The evidence is on the back of your slip," Beverly told her.

Sally tugged the slip around to find a burnt-sienna half-moon stain near the hem. "I didn't pull it up far enough, I guess."

"The backs of your legs are all scratched too."

"You're mad at me, aren't you?"

"Not *mad*. Disappointed."

"You sound like Sister Mary Clair."

"No I don't. I sound like your friend."

"I'm not the first girl to lose her virginity, not even the first girl in our class, I bet."

"I don't care about you losing it, but did you have to lose it to . . . to . . . Cole Barnstable! That Dave wasn't any prize, either, so I came home."

"I'm sorry. We really did look for you." Sally stepped out of her slip and grabbed a nightgown from the back of the closet door. Dropping it over her head, she sank down on the edge of the bed. "I had to do it."

Beverly grunted. "Cole Barnstable can't keep his pants on.

263

He got some girl from Red Berry in trouble last year when he was a *junior,* for Godsakes, and his dad paid her dad a lot of money."

"How do you know?"

"Ronald Oster."

"He told you that tonight? What were you doing, talking about me?"

"I stopped to buy an Orange Crush before I came back here. He was buying a Coke, and he asked if that was Cole Barnstable you'd been riding with on the Ferris wheel."

"And then he just happened to tell you about this girl from Red Berry, as if I was naturally going to let Cole go all the way."

"I guess he had it right, didn't he?"

"MotherofGod, it'll be all over town tomorrow that I'm p.g. Well, I'm not. He wore a safe."

"Cheaper than paying off your dad."

Sally headed toward the bathroom.

"What would your dad think if he knew?" Beverly asked.

Sally paused in the doorway without turning around. "I don't give a damn what he'd think."

Donald had heard the girls come home, Beverly first, around ten-thirty, letting herself in the backdoor, then a couple of hours later, Sally, getting out of a car and calling a soft good-night to someone. Who? She'd missed her midnight curfew.

When he heard Beverly's "You didn't!" he'd gotten out of bed and quietly closed his door. Whatever it was, he didn't want to know. He was still trying to sort out what had happened at the library last night when Sally'd run out as though she'd seen a ghost.

Maybe he should have confronted her when he got home. Maybe he should have said, "What is it you think you saw?" But he believed that most problems solved themselves if you didn't make an issue of them.

Much escaped him, he knew. Around the time of Stella's

death, something had changed between Sally and him, something he'd thought he would come to understand but hadn't.

Throwing back the sheet, he got up and padded to the west windows, one on either side of the bed, to check whether they were raised all the way. The curtains fluttered, but the air was hot. Moving on to the windows overlooking Third Avenue, he examined them as well, though they were south-facing and rarely caught a breeze.

Stella used to sit in the rocker here, looking out. What had she looked at? No houses faced onto Third Avenue, only side yards and garages. Letting himself down onto the rocker in a careful, ponderous way, he sat staring across the street while Beverly's disbelieving voice washed back on a new tide of misgiving. "You didn't!"

Atop the McNaughton's garage, a white glass ball skewered on a lightning rod reflected the glow of a street lamp and, like a single appraising eye, glowered reproachfully at Donald.

He closed his eyes against its judgment and lay his head against the rocker.

The following week's *Standard Ledger* featured the two teachers who would be new to Harvester Public School when classes commenced in September: Miss Emily Podraz, incoming third-grade teacher, a recent graduate of St. Cloud State Teachers College, and Mr. Drew Davis, instructor of speech and twelfth-grade English, who had taught for five years in California, spent a similar number of years in sales, and was now returning to his "first love" in his home state where "winter is winter and not a damp chill off the Pacific."

Miss Emily Podraz' photo, doubtless her college graduation picture, showed a mild-featured young woman in a Peter Pan collar and pale plastic-rimmed glasses, stiff smile both determined and hopeful; Mr. Davis's portrait was an expensive "study," chin lowered, head turned a quarter to the left, eyes pensive.

Noting the slight puckering of Mr. Davis's brows, which probably connoted suffering, Sally was glad she'd signed up for speech. The alternatives had been trigonometry, advanced home ec, bookkeeping, or chemistry. Not a choice, really.

She studied the grainy picture of the speech instructor, feature by feature: strong chin; generous mouth; deep-set eyes; freckles; and a shock of wiry, tightly curled hair, which was probably red. A Jimmy Cagney look. Sally knew that she was going to like the man.

Dressed in jeans and one of Donald's shirts, she sat on the front stoop riffling through the local paper and waiting for Cole Barnstable to take her swimming, the third time since Harvester Days that he had called and driven over from St. Bridget.

On each occasion they'd gone all the way. Twice each time. It still hurt but not as much. And one way or another, she'd managed to have an orgasm. She supposed that he continued to date her because she let him go all the way. She didn't care.

Cole pulled up in front of the house and honked. Sally waved, tossed the paper inside the screen door, and grabbed up a towel-wrapped swimsuit and a rolled-up blanket. "I'm leaving now," she called to Irmgard Wheeler, who was spending the week.

This afternoon Cole drove a blue Chevrolet with *Barnstables* painted in script on the front doors. Next year, when he graduated, his parents were giving him a car for college, but until then, he drove whatever was available. The day before yesterday he'd shown up in a delivery truck. Although he was demanding something red and sporty when he got his own car, he didn't mind what he drove in the meantime. After all, he said, it was he who gave the *car* class, not the other way around.

Cole said things like that without blushing or even grinning. Outrageous things: men were superior to women; Mediterranean Europeans were inferior to northern Europeans; and so forth.

Although Sally disagreed with him about almost everything, she could never be sure when he was serious and when he was teasing or talking to hear himself. If she were to question one of his wild assertions, she knew that he would throw his head back and hoot at her gullibility, so she maintained a dubious and disdainful manner.

Sometimes she laughed at him, lightly, derisively. He liked that. When she laughed in that way, he often cast her a gaze so wanton it frightened her. But his glance struck directly to a part of herself that was dark and unheeding. With Billy Rabel, she had been in control. With Cole, she was not.

His right hand lay on her thigh as they drove to the lake. Because she'd let him go all the way, he had a sense of ownership, and ownership carried privileges, like putting his hand on her thigh.

Cole drew the Chevrolet to the shoulder behind a considerable line of other cars. With only a handful of days remaining until school opened, the beach parking lot was full.

Kicking gravel out of her sandals, Sally breathed the dog-days smell of the lake: algae; dead fish; and warmish water, which was rank but not unpleasant. When they'd changed into swimsuits, they smoothed the blanket out on dry, beaten-down grass beneath cottonwoods and birches.

The gentle rise near the water was already covered with towels and blankets, one of them shared by Neddy Barnstable and Katherine Albers. Sally noted this with a fleeting pang of annoyance, which could not be jealousy since she had turned down Neddy's invitations.

Katherine was wearing a turquoise swimsuit that showed off her pale hair. Sally wished that Katherine wouldn't hunch her shoulders. It made her look ashamed of having breasts.

"Ned!" Cole called to his cousin. "How in hell are you?"

Neddy rose, said something to Katherine, then pulled her to her feet with one hand. Together they strolled over to Sally's blanket. They were a handsome couple, both blond, although Neddy's hair was not so buttery and his skin was more deeply tanned.

Neddy stood just off the blanket, his weight on one foot, and cast a long, reflective look at Sally. *He knew.* He looked unforgiving. A flush crept up Sally's face.

Cole lay his hand on the back of her neck, his fingers gripping her lightly. "You want to play golf next week?" he asked Neddy. "I can come get you."

Would Cole discuss her with Neddy? Sally wondered. Had

he already? Would he brag about what he'd taught her, things he'd learned from a Washington Avenue whore in Minneapolis when he was a sophomore? She heard herself saying, "I love your swimsuit, Katherine."

"Would you like to walk along the beach?" Katherine asked.

Sally started to scramble to her feet, but Cole handed her the bottle of Johnson's Baby Oil. Unscrewing the cap, she poured oil onto his shoulders, massaging it across the broad expanse of brown back, and up the muscular isthmus of neck. Recapping the bottle, she told him, "I won't be gone long."

As they waded shin-deep in water, threading a path amongst toddlers playing in the shallows, Sally asked, "Do you like Neddy?"

"He's nice."

The answer depressed Sally as she felt that Taking Into Account a Person's Niceness probably characterized sensible romances, romances that "went somewhere." Not that she was looking for a romance that was going somewhere, but doubtless life unfolded more smoothly and reasonably for people who were deliberative and judicious.

"Do you like Cole?" Katherine asked with genuine interest.

Sally was touched by her gravity and thought for several moments before telling her, "I don't think I like him, but maybe I love him. Please, don't tell *anyone* I said that."

"I won't."

When Cole was around, Sally felt that she couldn't breathe, that her head was being held under water.

"Have you ever met someone that you thought you'd known before you were born?" she asked.

Katherine shook her head.

"I feel like I've known Cole since Day One of the Universe, like we came from the same lump of clay."

When I put my hand on his arm, she thought, it's as if two parts of me that got separated a million years ago are back together.

She grabbed up a wishbone-shaped box-elder seed floating past.

"Will you marry him, do you think?"

Marry him? Sally felt she might sink down in the shallows and drown. "No. We'll never get married." She tore the seed in two and tossed it aside. "I might kill him, though," she said and laughed.

Katherine stumbled and, when she recovered herself, walked a couple of paces ahead of Sally.

"It's scary," Sally observed of her feelings. But she couldn't get the conversation going again. Katherine had withdrawn into a brown study.

Neddy and Cole had gone off with Ronald Oster and a couple of other boys to play a rough, silly game with a beach ball in four feet of water. About fifty yards up the shore, out of the way of smaller children, they raised hell, yelling and shoving each other's heads under.

Returning to Sally's blanket, the girls lay drowsing. More than half asleep, Sally thought she saw Mr. Albers standing by the bathhouse, his suit jacket slung over one shoulder, hooked on his index finger. Her eyelids were so heavy, she couldn't open them again to make certain.

Sally woke to find she was sweaty, headachy, and alone. Heaving herself up slowly, she trudged through the hot sand down to the water where she stood stirring the green surface with a toe and wondering if she should have said the things she had about Cole and herself. Wading out to the end of the dock, she scooped up water, splashing it on her face, then turned to scan the beach for Katherine.

Well, Katherine must have gone swimming. But she wasn't in the water anywhere along this stretch of beach, nor was she around the raft. Cole and Neddy still played their exhausting game. Sally surveyed the lake, raking the gray water in wide swaths.

Out in the middle, someone was swimming, headed toward the far shore. Fatigued, the swimmer's arms barely broke the surface of the water, the legs not at all. The head was held at a painful angle, cocked too high for a long-distance swim.

"What the hell's she doing?"

Sally hauled the Knights of Columbus rowboat down to the water and climbed in. Taking up the oars, she fitted them into the oarlocks and began rowing. At water-safety lessons she'd learned how to dip and pull to get the greatest speed. Even so, the boat felt like a boxcar.

She tried not to think of Katherine. When she did, her arms panicked and grew clumsy, and the oars skidded on top of the water. Instead, she recalled Lark telling her about the day she'd learned to swim, right here at this beach, during the Knights of Columbus Memorial Day Picnic. Beverly had taught her, and Lark had got so cocky and overconfident, she'd set out for the raft, which, though not far away, was too far for a first-time swimmer. She'd nearly drowned. In fact, she'd made an Act of Contrition and just about prayed her way through the rosary by the time Beverly hauled her up onto the raft.

Remembering Lark, Sally regretted not writing to her for — how long? Two years? Longer. The last time she'd written was when Stella died. And the last time she'd heard from her friend, Lark was living with her grandparents in Blue Lake.

Mrs. Erhardt was in California with her sister, Betty, and Mr. Erhardt had left Harvester for parts unknown. Sally didn't know how any of this had come to be, and she never would if she didn't stay in touch.

Tonight she'd start a letter. Maybe Lark could visit at Christmas. Although Blue Lake was only sixty-five miles away, it was part of a different athletic conference, so the girls never met at football and basketball games.

"Katherine! Katherine! For God's sake, grab the oar!"

Katherine could not have swum another twenty yards, but

she continued to struggle, swallowing water with each tiny wavelet. Down to the last ounce of strength and ready to slip under, she still resisted.

"Take this oar or I'll hit you over the head with it!" Sally screamed at her. "I'll knock you out and drag you in!"

Katherine was alongside now, and Sally handed her a life buoy. "Put that over your head. Here, hang on. Hang onto it, for Christ's sake!"

Ten minutes later, when Katherine had rested a little, clinging to the anchor rope Sally had thrown over, Sally let herself down into the water on the opposite side of the boat in order to balance it while Katherine dragged herself up over the strake.

Katherine lay in a heap on the bottom of the boat. Sally pulled up anchor and rowed as fast as she could. Were it the weekend, half a dozen fishermen with outboard motors on their boats would be within hailing distance, but not today.

"What the hell did you think you were doing, Katherine? You aren't that good a swimmer." All the way to shore, Sally rattled at the girl. "I'm a better swimmer than you are, and I wouldn't try to swim across. This is just . . . crazy, for God's sake. I can hardly believe you did this. You must have sunstroke. Normally you're so sensible." She didn't know what she was saying and never recalled it afterward.

Nor did she recall much about saving Katherine. What stuck in her memory was the tiny, lone figure in the center of a gray expanse, cut off and unnoted.

September — October 1949

Donald's mother and father visited over the Labor Day weekend, and after Harry left, Irmgard remained for a week, sewing
curtains for the bedrooms and cleaning out Donald's closet.
While she was with them, Donald invited Drew Davis, the new
speech and English teacher to dinner.

"Have you met anyone yet?" Sally asked him. "Miss Bailey,
the second-grade teacher, is too old for you, I suppose, but she's
really nice. She'd make a good friend."

"Sally." Irmgard directed a sharp glance across the table.

"Mr. Davis might like to choose his own friends," Donald
told her.

"Delicious pork roast, Mrs. Wheeler," Davis said.

Lovely manners, Irmgard observed. He'd been raised properly. Son of a history professor at Macalester College, hadn't he
said? Nice for Donald to have a colleague who might share his
interest in history, someone besides that librarian.

"Have you met Mrs. Navarin?" Irmgard asked. Desiree
Navarin needed a new friend to mother.

"Met her first thing. Prevailed on her to put books on reserve
for my classes."

"She's, um, a helpful person," Irmgard observed. Passing the
peas, she asked, "What took you to California? The war?"

He put the napkin to his lips, touching the corners of his
mouth, then smoothed the linen over his lap again. Clearing his

throat, he told her, "Sorry to say, I wasn't able to serve. Actually, I hoped to find work in the movies. I hesitate to tell people that. They usually laugh." He smiled at them, sharing his embarrassment.

The embarrassment was genuine, Donald thought, as was the refinement. Life in Harvester would not be smooth sledding for Drew Davis. His athletic pastimes, he'd revealed when pressed by basketball coach Jack Vargo, were tennis and fencing. Tennis and golf might have passed, just barely, but tennis and fencing would put people off. Davis could have fudged the answer, but he hadn't. Donald admired that.

Sally stared at Mr. Davis. He wasn't handsome. He was magnetic. His eyes, the pale blue of flax flowers, simply *gripped* you. His hair was not so dark as auburn, nor so light as carrot. Brickish, it was. And his voice was as rich as Walter Pidgeon's. "You studied acting in college?"

"I had a double major, theater and English," he told her. "A theater major is more than acting, though, it's theater history, stagecraft, directing, literature of the theater, and so forth. Were you thinking of a theater major?"

Sally was flattered but flustered. She knew nothing about theater or theater majors. "I've never even been in a play."

"You were the narrator in that Christmas Program," her grandmother reminded her.

"In the second grade!" Sally laughed, covering her face with the napkin and looking out from behind it with coy discomfort.

"Well, you were very good."

"Oh, Grandma, please. How do you know if I was any good?"

"I've seen a movie or two in my life." Irmgard rose and began gathering up plates. "And I wish I'd seen Mr. Davis in one of them. I bet he'd have been a regular Randolph Scott."

Drew Davis laughed hard at this, throwing his head to one side as if looking askance at something. When the laughter died, lines around his eyes and mouth fell into somber self-mockery.

While her grandmother visited, Sally felt that she was being watched by an all-seeing eye. Paring potatoes, she would turn to find Irmgard studying her with a grave, absorbed look. When she came to breakfast after being out with Cole, her grandmother was pleasant but full of probing little questions and worried glances.

Irmgard *was* worried. Cole Barnstable brought Sally home past her curfew, her clothes wrinkled and grass-stained. In the morning, the child's room smelled of beer or worse. One time he'd sat in the car and honked the horn for Sally to come out, as if she were a carhop delivering curb service. Irmgard had put a stop to that, told Sally she absolutely was not to open the door and run out in answer to the horn. And when Cole came up to the house, Irmgard told him too.

He'd laughed. Not in a way that was so fresh it provided Irmgard with any real ammunition, but slyly so that everybody knew that he knew what was going on. Irmgard saw that he was clever and cocksure of himself where Sally was concerned. She didn't want to think what that meant.

Sally knew that her grandmother worried about her going all the way. She lived in dread that Irmgard would ask her outright. She would have been amazed to learn that Irmgard couldn't bear to ask, for fear Sally would tell her.

Instead, Irmgard went to Mass and prayed that Sally hadn't let Cole Barnstable have his way or, if she had, that she wouldn't get pregnant. When Irmgard returned to Worthington, she felt guilty about leaving Sally and Donald undefended.

But Harry needed her at home. He was neat, but he wasn't clean. He hung his clothes up when he took them off, but didn't remember to throw them in the Maytag. He picked up the newspapers and stacked them on the table in the back hall, but never ran the Hoover. Irmgard sighed, packed her Noxema, hair net, and Daily Missal, and went home to put her own house to rights.

Sally was going to hell in a handbasket, was Beverly's opinion. And Cole Barnstable was to blame. Sally was out drinking and running around to dances, even midweek dances, messing around in the back seat of a car *and* letting her homework slide. When she turned up in class, she looked like the devil, often wearing the previous night's makeup and clothes.

"My mom says she looks like a chippy," Angela Bussey told Sue Ann Meyers.

Beverly was standing in line to use the girls' rest room at halftime during the Harvester-St. Bridget football game and could not help overhearing the conversation.

"Did you see her at the Homecoming Dance?" Sue Ann asked.

"She was half-drunk. I'm amazed she and Cole didn't get kicked out."

"They drink vodka so they won't smell," Angela told her.

"Where do they get vodka? You can't buy vodka in Minnesota."

"Cole knows some salesman from South Dakota who gets it for him, some guy who sells stuff to Barnstable's Department Store," Angela revealed.

"Sally used to be a nice girl," Sue Ann Meyers sniffed. "Even if her mother *was* crazy. But my mom says I can't run around with her anymore, and she's not to be invited to my Christmas party. My mom won't hear of it."

"You're having a Christmas party?" Beverly asked, turning around.

Startled to find Sally's best friend standing in front of her, Sue Ann bent to examine the bells she'd fastened to her shoelaces.

"Where're you gonna have the party?" Beverly pursued. The Meyers' living room, where everything was protected by Mrs. Meyers' hand-crocheted afghans and doilies, was big enough to hold five or six people if they were all sitting down on something afghanned.

"In the basement. In our rec room."

"I didn't know you had a rec room," Beverly exclaimed. "Where in the basement is that?"

"Well, we call it a rec room. There's a card table and games and my phonograph player that I got for my birthday. And my mom put up a curtain so you can't see the furnace."

"Sally's sure gonna be sorry to miss a party down there," Beverly said. "I bet you'll have Coke and potato chips, and if everybody's real good, you'll play your 'Nature Boy' record."

Sue Ann pretended not to understand what was going on. Beverly was still friends with Sally—her only friend, except maybe Katherine Albers, who liked everybody—and Beverly had a wicked mouth. You didn't want to get into a match with her because she'd make mincemeat of you.

"Well, I'm just telling you what my mom said," Sue Ann pointed out. "Sally's wild as they come, and she'll probably be making a trip to Chicago one of these days to visit her sick aunt." Sue Ann tossed her ponytail. "Or maybe her dad'll get a lot of money from Mr. Barnstable."

Sally never skipped Mr. Davis's speech class. Even if she planned to ditch school for the rest of the day, she'd show up for his 11 A.M. class. The room, facing Main Street, was on the third floor, two flights above Miss Bailey's and with a treetop view. Maybe the treetops contributed to her sense of being in a separate little country, removed from Harvester entirely. In any case, she felt safe there.

An exotic place it was too. Mr. Davis had tacked up quotations; copies of wonderful paintings; reviews of plays running in New York and the Cities; reviews of books; interviews with famous and not-so-famous people; and a striking fragment of tapestry, which he forbore to explain.

From Hapgood's Second Hand, down by the railroad tracks, he had bought a bookcase, filling the shelves with novels, Samuel French editions of plays, *Theater Arts, The Saturday Review of Literature, The Atlantic Monthly,* and *The New Yorker.*

The first day of class, Mr. Davis spoke at some length about the way that a speech class ought to conduct itself—members showing respect and kindness toward one another. He hoped that everyone would eventually be so comfortable that speaking in front of the group would be no more daunting than chatting at the dinner table.

The course began with twelve students. One or two had signed up because they'd heard that speech was a cinch grade.

After all, any fool could talk. Sure, it might be embarrassing to stand up and do it in front of classmates, but any fool *could*.

On the second day, however, when the assignment was to speak for two minutes on "Something I Bet You Didn't Know About Me" and Mr. Davis called on Angela Bussey, not first, but fourth or fifth, she burst into tears.

Was she frightened to stand up? Mr. Davis asked. Angela shook her head yes. Would she, this one time, like to say her speech sitting down? No. Well, would she like to go last? Again, no. What did she feel was the solution? At this point Angela ran from the room, sobbing, and Mr. Davis asked Beverly to find her and, if possible, bring her back.

By supper time, thanks to Ronald Oster and one or two others, half the people in Harvester had heard that Mr. Davis had made Angela Bussey cry. Of course, some people were skeptical. Angela had been crying with regularity since kindergarten. Angela prided herself on her tender sensibilities.

The following day she transferred to bookkeeping, and no further crying occurred in speech class. But the rumor of Mr. Davis making a girl cry was an unfortunate beginning for him.

One day early in the fall, with the principal's permission, Drew Davis took the class on a walk around Harvester, admonishing them to *look* at the town, to observe it like strangers, experience it, and contemplate it—trees, grass, buildings, people, animals, whatever came into view, struck the ear, touched the skin, was savored by the nose or tasted on the tongue. The next day's assignment was to tell the class "What I Never Noticed About Harvester Before."

"Process the world, don't ignore it," he told them again and again. "Think!"

Sally was enchanted. While it was true that giving a speech made a person nervous, if you managed to stammer your way through a little presentation, Mr. Davis clapped and congratulated you. When a pupil concluded a speech that had shown original thinking, the teacher sprang from his chair at the back of the room and dashed to the front, clapping, bravoing, and extolling lavishly.

The first time this happened, Ronald Oster sniggered aloud, as if Mr. Davis were the most bizarre abnormality he'd witnessed since the Steiners' three-legged calf. For a moment, an expression of sadness or betrayal blanched Davis's face beneath his freckles. But the moment was fleeting, and no one was later certain they'd seen it.

Mr. Davis went right on clapping and bravoing good speeches. His joy in original thinking felt to Sally like the sun on a bitter day, shining fully and intensely on your face. She scoured the crannies of her mind to come up with inventive, entertaining ways to present assignments.

One day early in October the assignment was a how-to speech. Katherine Albers, using Sue Ann Meyers as a model, showed the class how to French braid hair. Neddy Barnstable taught them how to get a dog to swallow a pill.

"I'm going to demonstrate how not to sell tickets to the St. Boniface Fall Bazaar," Sally told the class when her turn came. Her lips stuck to her teeth, and her whole body trembled, yet a strange feeling of exhilaration possessed her. For a few minutes she was in control.

"When I was small I had to sell tickets to the bazaar for a couple of years. This is how I did it."

Assuming the posture of a seven-year-old, Sally stood before an imaginary door and raised her fist to knock. But before her hand struck the door, she recalled something and began rummaging desperately in the imaginary pockets of an imaginary jacket for misplaced bazaar tickets. Finding them and gripping them tightly in one hand, with the other she hitched her skirt and scratched her leg.

Again raising her hand to knock, she noticed something on her wrist and, upon examining it closely, discovered it to be frosting, which ought to be licked off.

Not only was Mr. Davis at the back of the room laughing, but so were the others.

When at last she knocked and the lady of the house answered, Sally launched into a presentation beginning "Mrs. Bensinger, my name is Sally Wheeler," which brought a laugh since everyone knew the Bensingers were next-door neighbors of the Wheelers. "And I'm selling tickets to St. Boniface's Fall Bazaar, which you might not want to go to because you are Baptist, and I think Baptists don't believe in games of chance, which is one of the things they're going to have at the bazaar, besides beautiful hand-sewn items made by the sodality ladies, which you might want to buy because they would make your house pretty . . . although your house is already pretty pretty, I mean, it's very pretty, well, it's okay, and you might want to buy some of the homemade baked goods although you *do* bake of course, but these are delicious, I mean, I'm not saying *yours* aren't delicious . . ."

Sally was soaring, light and powerful. Again and again Mr. Davis burst into laughter, but so, too, did Neddy Barnstable and Beverly and Sue Ann Meyers, who did not even like Sally.

Reluctantly, Sally came to the end of her presentation. Gazing up at an invisible Mrs. Bensinger and shoving the imaginary bazaar tickets back into the pocket of the make-believe jacket she said, "I'm sorry you have a million things to do, Mrs. Bensinger and the flies are getting in the house and you've already bought tickets from Russell Steuben and Mr. Bensinger will soon be home for supper and my nose is running—it is? and my shoe is unbuckled? . . ." Here Sally bent to fasten an imaginary buckle and when she rose, found the Bensinger door had been closed. "Mrs. Bensinger? Mrs. Bensinger? . . . Thank you, Mrs. Bensinger."

As Sally floated back to her seat, hot and trembling, not quite hearing or seeing, Neddy Barnstable leaned forward and whispered, "Terrific speech." Mr. Davis at the front of the room was singing out, "Imagination! Thinking, thinking, thinking!" and other pleasant words.

Sally's presentation anticipated assignments that Mr. Davis had in mind: preparing short scenes, rehearsing them, and performing them in class. If several of sufficient quality could be pulled together into a twenty- or thirty-minute program, the class might "take them on the road," presenting them to English classes or whoever would sit still.

Gradually, over the weeks, a little company of performers calling themselves the Harvest Moon Motleys emerged from speech class, writing and performing sketches for other classes, for businessmen's luncheons, P.T.A. meetings, and other convivial assemblages.

Hitherto unrecognized talents were let loose on the world: Neddy Barnstable was found to have a gift for satiric monologue, an audience favorite being one about serious crime in Harvester. Katherine Albers could be depended upon when beauty and a clear, sweet soprano were required, which was not infrequently. Sylvia Donaldson was a fair tap dancer, and Beverly could pull together the wittiest suggestion of a costume from fabric scraps and cast-off trumpery.

Mr. Davis was pleased. Public speaking and theatrical presentation were, in his opinion, two parts of the same discipline, and his Motleys would be better public speakers for their experience in the troupe.

The social set of which Mr. Davis became a part was amused and pleased by the whole idea of the Motleys, suggesting themes and venues for them.

This set was comprised of Miss Bailey, Mr. Lundeen, the Navarins, Whites, and the Barnstables. Traditionally, socializing between schoolteachers and the community was frowned upon, a chief consideration being that the peccadillos of each would become known to the other and the information be dangerous or, at least, burdensome. But Miss Bailey, who had taken Drew Davis under her wing, was a long-standing friend of Mr. Lundeen, so Davis was welcomed into the Lundeen crowd.

They gave small dinner parties where wine was served with the meal, a practice nearly unheard of in Harvester. Books, phonograph records, and recipes were shared, the latter including French and Italian dishes.

Laurence Lundeen grew basil, thyme, and other cooking herbs. When Mr. Hardesty at the *Standard Ledger* learned of this, he wrote an article, accompanying it with a photograph of the sunny spot in Lundeen's backyard where the herbs grew. Along with the article and photo ran one of Laurence's recipes, a simple *poulet sauté* calling for basil and thyme.

Dagney Bensinger, reading the piece, exclaimed, "La-de-da. Talk about your airs."

Acute chagrin narrowed her eyes and pursed her lips, as if the article had been written expressly to cast doubt on the merit of the way *she* lived, the way *she* cooked. The reaction lingered. Long after the next edition of the *Standard Ledger* was lining the bottom of Petey's birdcage, her breast constricted whenever she though of *poulet sauté* .

From that day forward, when she spied Laurence Lundeen or one of his friends at the library or in Truska's, she felt the sharp prick of rejection. Her chin shot up and sparks flew from a fire whose source had transmogrified from *poulet sauté* to "that Lundeen crowd." They were riding for a fall, that bunch.

"My stars! I've got a two opener!" Irmgard Wheeler warbled.

The day after Thanksgiving, Edna and Herb Elway, Donald and his mother played bridge in the dining room.

In the kitchen, Sally and Neddy Barnstable worked together at the table, sketching out a ten-minute skit for the Motleys to perform during intermission at the Christmas Dance.

The general idea was that Santa had decided too many folks in Harvester had been naughty this year and he was going to bypass the town on his Christmas Eve run. A town meeting was called in the gymnasium to discover who had done what to upset Santa. A brouhaha ensued as men, women, and children pointed fingers and argued over each other's wrongdoing. Teeth were knocked out, noses bloodied, hair pulled, clothes torn. At the height of the melee, Santa burst upon them with a great bag of treasures, crying, "There's been a terrible mistake! St. Bridget's the town too naughty for presents!"

Clapping eyes on the bloody spectacle, however, he shook his head sadly, turned on his heel, and called:

> On your knees, say your prayers.
> No more books or teddy bears.
> You want presents? My advice:
> One whole year of being nice.

Together, Neddy and Sally had worked on the rhyme, but neither was satisfied. "It hasn't any punch," Sally moaned.

"We can punch it up later."

Neddy had asked Katherine Albers to the Christmas Dance for which he and Sally were penning the skit. With Sally, he was distant but polite. Now and then she wondered how he was with Katherine, who was scrupulously proper, at any rate in public. Did Katherine let Neddy put his hands under her blouse when they were alone? When Sally's imagination ran in this direction, a thrill of discomfort seized her.

Around four-thirty, they completed the outline. "Should we show it to Mr. Davis before we write the dialogue?" Sally asked.

Neddy telephoned Davis, and ten minutes later they stood outside the door of the speech teacher's apartment above Eggers' Drug Store. Sally knocked, hoping he would invite them in so that she could see where he lived.

"*Entré,*" Davis said, ushering them into a long narrow hallway where he had hung framed costume designs rendered in watercolor.

"Did you do these?" Sally asked.

"Yes. For a costume class. They're not very good."

"I think they're wonderful."

"This way," he said, leading them to the left and into his living room, which overlooked Main Street.

"Gosh, we're interrupting you," Sally said when she saw Mr. Lundeen sitting in an armchair in front of a low table where a chess set was in play.

"Nonsense. Sit down. Toss your coats there," he told them, indicating a chair by the door to the hall.

"Was all this furniture here?" Sally asked.

"Just the stove, refrigerator, and bedroom set. Larry let me use Lundeen's truck to haul the rest from the family attic in St. Paul."

Larry. Sally had never heard Laurence Lundeen called that.

"May I get you a Coke?" Davis asked them.

"Thanks," Sally replied before Neddy could decline. Because fraternizing between high-school students and faculty was disapproved of, rarely did a student visit a teacher's apartment. "I like the way you've fixed things up," she called to Davis, who had disappeared to fetch Cokes.

On all the side tables little groupings of photographs were arranged, people unknown to Sally. She would like to be someone whose picture could be found amongst these, someone thought valuable or interesting enough to be included.

Above the sofa hung an oil painting in a deep, ornately carved gilt frame, the subject a vaguely familiar landscape. Crescent Ridge State Park, maybe? Adorning other walls were theater posters and programs. The entire effect, to Sally's way of thinking, was worldly and stylish.

"Where are you going to college next year?" Laurence Lundeen asked, adding, "*each* of you." Leaning forward in his chair, he returned a pawn he'd been holding to the collection of "captured" pieces beside the chessboard.

"I don't know if I'm going," Sally told him.

"Why is that?"

"I don't know what I want to be."

"Don't let that stop you. Even if you get married immediately afterward, you must go to college. You must, *especially* if you're planning to get married. You'll want something besides your husband to contemplate year after year."

Sally laughed, and Lundeen laughed at her laughter, pleased.

"What about you?" he asked Neddy.

"I think I'm going to Princeton. Grandpa Shelborne went there, and it's kind of expected."

"Do you want to?"

Neddy considered. "Yeah, I think so. I've never been back East. I'd like to see what it's like." He smiled. "And Grandpa's paying for it. Mom says don't look a gift horse in the mouth, especially an expensive one."

Once again, Lundeen laughed.

Sally and Neddy reviewed with Davis the outline they'd prepared for the skit. As he listened, he lit a cigarette from a handsome copper-clad table lighter.

Laurence Lundeen rose, heading toward the kitchen. A couple of minutes later Sally heard water running, then the sharp crack of ice cubes being loosened in a metal freezer tray. Reappearing, he carried two highball glasses and handed one to Drew Davis.

"Can you have the dialogue ready by Monday?" Davis was asking.

Sally, who was amazed that the teacher would smoke and drink in front of students, told him she thought they could. "My dad's got mimeograph paper at home. I'll have a master for you to run off Monday morning."

Back on Main Street, standing in front of the drugstore, she looked at Neddy.

"He trusts us," Neddy explained.

December 17, 1949

Leaning over the bathroom sink, peering at herself in the mirror, Beverly wanted to know, "Green or blue eye shadow?"

"With the coral dress? Green."

Both girls were in their slips, Sally sitting on the toilet, waiting to use the mirror.

"Are you gonna use eyeliner?" Beverly asked.

"Of course. Anyway, I'll need it for the skit. If you don't use liner, your eyes absolutely disappear when you're performing."

Holding one of her eyelids down, Beverly drew a line along the row of pale lashes. She was in the "crowd scene" of the skit, after all.

The Christmas Dance started at eight, and Leroy Mosely rang the Wheelers' bell at ten minutes before the hour. Donald answered.

"Beverly here, Coach?"

"Come on in. You'd better have a seat. Hard telling how long it'll be."

But Beverly, dressed in a dark coral velvet dress, came prancing down the stairs in her black suede baby doll heels at eight, carrying Rose's small black bag and wearing Sally's rhinestone earrings.

Leroy whistled and stood up.

"I hope you parked right at the end of the walk," Beverly told him. "'cuz I don't wanna ruin these shoes."

At eight-thirty Sally came down. Cole had not arrived. "Are the roads icy?"

"I shouldn't think so," Donald said.

Donald wanted to tell Sally that she looked nice, but the truth was he thought the tight black faille sheath with deep vee neck too daring and mature for a high-school girl. Although she wore several strands of pearls, the cleavage of her small breasts was evident. And the sheer black stockings did nothing to alter an impression of brazenness.

His silence was frank.

Sally had known that Donald would not like the dress. Even so, his reaction oppressed her. She would have been more upset, however, if he had liked it. The point of the dress was to let people know she didn't give a damn.

She glanced at her watch. Eight forty-five. Cole was frequently late, and ordinarily she didn't much care, but tonight she was performing with the Motleys at the ten-o'clock intermission. If he didn't show up soon, they'd have almost no time to dance before she had to change into costume.

Sally was embarrassed, cooling her heels in front of her father. "I think I'll wear my silver bracelet," she said, running back upstairs and taking refuge in her room.

When Cole had not arrived at nine-thirty, she came down again. "I know he's had car trouble," she said, although she was certain he hadn't. "Could you give me a ride to school? I've got to change into my costume."

In the girls' shower room, stepping into frumpish Cuban heels for her role, Sally said, "Now I *am* worried. It's almost ten."

Beverly snorted. "Save your energy for the skit."

"He's never been this late before."

"He's a bad penny," Beverly assured her.

Once Sally uttered the first line of her role as a trouble-making busybody whom she'd patterned after Dagney Bensinger, she forgot about Cole. Wearing a flowered rayon dress with a listing hem and a wickedly prim toque wrapped 'round with tatty netting, she accused and incited, left and right, swinging her purse with calculated abandon.

Although the skit was only ten minutes or so in length, Sally was swept up to a crest from which the view was endless. Then, when Neddy had delivered the last line and the crowd was done clapping and whistling, she trailed back down to the real world of failed Christmas dances.

At five minutes to eleven Cole wandered in, drifting around the edges, detached, as if the dance were a curiosity he'd gone a little out of his way to observe. Indeed, he had not dressed for a semiformal occasion, but wore khakis and a plaid shirt under an outer jacket he didn't remove.

A Ladies' Choice was announced, and Sally whispered to Katherine Albers, "Would you mind if I asked Neddy?"

Katherine shook her head.

Not a word was exchanged during the dance. When the song ended, he asked, "You want me to take you to Cole?"

"No. Walk me to the punch table, please."

She poured herself a cup of Kool-Aid and carried it with her as she wove in and out of the fringe of couples standing at the edge of the dance floor. Working her way toward Beverly and Leroy, she smiled ruefully at her friend. Beverly shot her a "What'd I tell you?" look.

Chin lowered, Cole crossed the gymnasium, looking hard at Sally. Unblinking, she returned the stare.

Bending, he spoke in her ear, "Get your coat."

She moved away and peered into his face, unsmiling.

"Get your coat," he repeated.

"Why?"

"Because I don't want to hang around here."

"Why?"

"Not in the mood." His hands were thrust deep into the pockets of his trousers, and his shoulders, inside the heavy jacket, were slumped, giving him a concave, withdrawn look.

"I'll see you later," Sally told Beverly. Without a word to Cole or a glance in his direction, she headed toward the coatroom, as he slouched after her.

The blue Chevie with *Barnstables* on the doors was parked half a block from school. "Where're we going?" she asked when he slid in, ramming the key into the ignition and slamming the car into gear.

The car whined away from the curb and minutes later was hurtling down the highway toward St. Bridget, Cole's foot lying heavy on the accelerator. The speedometer needle reached ninety and hovered there.

Sally did not worry about the speed. Cole was a good driver, fluid and natural, and although he'd been drinking, he was not drunk nor close to it.

In a night pure and clear and crackling, the stars stood out from the black sky, hanging in the foreground of space on invisible threads.

"You missed the Motleys," she said.

He didn't answer.

"We were good. Everybody liked the skit."

He expelled his breath contemptuously but said nothing.

They met no other cars until the rhinestones scattered along the horizon became St. Bridget. He turned the Chevrolet down residential streets unfamiliar to Sally and then, out beyond the country club, into winding lanes of new homes. The absence of mature trees gave the neighborhood a cold, naked look.

At the antipodes of a cul-de-sac, teetering on the black rim of prairie, Cole pulled into the wide driveway of a sprawling white brick "ranch" house, the sort everyone had started building at the end of the war.

A dim light burned behind draperies. Cole climbed out of the car and Sally followed. Only their crunching footsteps broke the silence.

Cole led the way to a wide brick veranda covered by a long gentle sweep of roof extending from the house and supported along its front edge by a series of rugged posts. The door and windows facing on the veranda were bracketed by black shutters whose cross braces had script B's sawed through them.

Inside, the house smelled of newness: paint and varnish, carpeting and wood. The cotton-batting hush peculiar to houses with wall-to-wall carpet and heavy, voluminous drapes made Sally feel claustrophobic.

Cole pulled off his jacket and tossed it down on a bench. Sally did likewise.

"Nobody home?" she asked.

Cole headed down the hall toward the back of the house, growling something indistinct. To Sally's right, and two shallow steps down, lay the living room where a single table lamp burned before an expanse of draperied windows. Connecting the living room and hall and perhaps all the rooms in the house was the thick beige shag carpeting whose long loops reached out to snag Sally's high heels. She slipped out of them, slinging them beneath the bench where the coats were heaped.

At the far end of the living room, lights extinguished, a monolithic Christmas tree, thickly encrusted with artificial snow, reached to the ceiling, claiming the broad space within a bay window. The hundreds of glass balls were silver, and Sally surmised that the lights, when lit, were white.

Scattered beneath the bottom branches were a dozen or so boxes wrapped in silver paper and tied with silver ribbon, metallic surfaces twinkling in the pale light from the table lamp fifteen feet away.

Somewhere far off, Cole was calling, but Sally stepped down into the living room, circumnavigating its beigeness — walls, carpet, drapes, upholstery. A great deal of blonde wood gleamed dully. No photos were clustered on tables. Here and there, several large unframed mirrors broke the pale reaches of plaster. Sally supposed Mrs. Barnstable must find all this restful. An untrammeled stretch of Sahara, astonishingly cold at night.

Sally hunkered to read the gift tags. Every box was for Cole.

"Creepy, isn't it?" He stood in the doorway shaking the ice cubes in a glass with an inch of brown liquid in it.

"Where're your folks?"

"Fort Lauderdale."

"How come you're here?"

"I don't like Florida, and I especially don't like it at Christmas."

"So you're staying here alone? They let you do that?"

Turning back in the direction from which he'd come, he called, "C'mon back here. It's not quite so spooky."

"Well, it *is* kinda spooky," he laughed as she found her way into the den. He had set a match to a fire laid in the grate of a stone hearth the size of a barn door.

Hunt prints were arranged on walls paneled with pecan wood. Sofa and chairs upholstered in caramel colored leather and trimmed with brass nailheads, were scattered across the ubiquitous beige shag carpeting. To the left of the door, a butler's stand held liquor in matching decanters with little necklaces identifying the contents as scotch, bourbon, or gin.

On a kneehole desk to the right of the door, Sally finally spied a couple of framed family photos: one of a tanned, handsome couple sitting in a fishing boat, holding up a string of what looked to be northerns; the other, Cole at eleven or twelve. Kneeling at the end of a dock, empty lake behind him, his arms clasped the ruff of a big dog of indeterminate color and doubtful breed.

Sally picked up the picture. "Your dog?"

Cole nodded.

"What's his name?"

"His name was Rex."

"Did he get killed?"

"You might say. He was put down when we moved in here."

"Why?"

"He'd ruin the carpet." His voice was caustic.

He handed Sally a glass of bourbon and Coke; slogged through the shag to the sofa; and plopped down facing the fire, legs extended.

"Your folks are going to miss you at Christmas," she assured him, curling up at the opposite end of the sofa.

"Like a headache."

"Will you be alone?"

"Ned's parents asked me to Christmas."

"I can't believe your parents left you."

He looked at her as if her head rattled with loose screws, then stared into the crackling fire. An hour passed without words. The fire burned low, throbbing and hissing. Sally dozed.

"I should go home," she told him, rousing.

Getting to his feet, he pulled her up, leading her by the hand through the house, past kitchen and dining room, around into a bedroom wing.

His room was at the very back, facing a rear yard of thin young trees and, beyond that, a field of corn stubble thrusting up through snow. Undressing by cold moonlight, they slid between icy sheets, reaching out for each other's warmth.

Sally woke first. "Cole! It's five o'clock!" The moon had fallen down in the west, though the sky was still black.

He stirred, rolling over languidly.

"Cole, my dad'll have the sheriff out looking for me!"

He laughed a kind of humming laugh, his mouth nuzzling her ear. He was testing his power. No, he was testing her commitment. Whatever sort of test it was, it was important to him. His mouth tasted of scotch and Camels.

Donald sat in one of the shabby green wing chairs, an empty coffee cup and a half-full ashtray on the table beside him. He'd been through Panic, Anger, and What Have I Done to Deserve This, reaching the ashy plains of Burned Out and Numb.

When he heard tires grinding the scree of ice and snow at the front curb, he rose, pulled the bathrobe sash tight, and raked both hands back through thinning hair. Six-thirty. Still dark, but just barely. The paperboy had slipped the *Minneapolis Sunday Tribune* inside the storm door an hour ago.

Sally carried it in with her, had it in her hands when she looked up and saw Donald. "Daddy, I'm sorry. I know you must have been worried. We fell asleep in Cole's car. We were talking, and we just fell asleep." She pressed the furled newspaper to her breast.

"I don't believe you," he told her calmly, a little surprised by the steadiness of his voice.

He sat down.

"When you left here tonight, you were wearing makeup, plenty of it. Your face is washed clean. That doesn't happen while people are asleep in cars. You spent the night with that boy, but not in a car."

"Daddy . . ."

"Take off your coat and sit down."

His calm frightened Sally. Hanging her coat in the closet,

she sat opposite him in the other green chair, tugging the tight black sheath down over her knees. Why hadn't it occurred to her when washing her face in Cole's bathroom to reapply makeup? She jerked her shoulders impatiently and lifted her chin.

"We should have had this talk before," Donald said, lowering himself again into the chair, running his hands along the threadbare arms. "I'm to blame." He studied the liver spots that had begun to appear on the back of his hands. "Too many topics I thought were 'women's talk,' things a mother discusses with her daughter. I guess I hoped that you'd learn from your friends how a young woman ought to conduct herself."

He felt foolish. *How a young woman ought to conduct herself?* The words were right out of one of those instructional films the kids laughed at in class. "Party Manners for Teens" or something like that.

"To put it simply, a seventeen-year-old-girl does not come home from a dance at six-thirty in the morning. There is nothing to do until that hour that is . . . acceptable."

Sally said nothing.

"Well," he told her, leaning forward, "to get down to cases, what you're doing is dangerous. Immorality I won't go into. You're a practical girl. I'll appeal to your practicality. What will you do if you get pregnant?"

"I'm not going to get pregnant. It's not even a possibility, so forget about that."

"The world has heard that before. You know what I tell my baseball players? I tell 'em safes don't always work. If you don't want to marry the girl *now*, don't sleep with her. If you want to go to college, if you want to see the world, don't sleep with her."

He leaned back, again running hands along the chair arms. "You're my daughter, and I love you and I want the best for you. I don't want you sleeping with Cole Barnstable. And I sure as hell don't want you marrying him."

"You don't even know him. Anyway, Cole isn't going to ask me to marry him."

"Then don't stay out with him till six-thirty in the morning. And I don't mean it would be all right to stay out until six-thirty if he *were* going to marry you."

Maybe because he was exhausted or because so much was at stake, tears stung his eyes. Sally stiffened and looked away, appalled.

"You don't know the possibilities you've got locked inside you, Sally. If you make a mistake now, you'll never know." He dug in the pocket of his robe for a handkerchief.

She stirred in the chair. She must be wondering how long he would go on. "If this boy cares about you, he won't want to ruin things for you."

"Oh, please."

She was right. Seventeen- or eighteen-year-old boys didn't think that way. Or damned few did.

His mind was gummy from lack of sleep. He was bungling it. Not remembering the things he'd wanted to say. One thing he did remember. "Do you love Cole Barnstable?"

Sally didn't answer at once. If she said no, she was a slut for staying out all night with him. If she said yes . . .

"I don't want to talk about that," she said.

"Don't you think you owe me an answer?"

"I don't know."

He struck the chair arm with his fist, not in anger but in finality. "You're not to see Cole Barnstable for a month. Make that until the first of February."

She said nothing.

He sank his chin into his hand. If he'd thought for a minute that confrontation would open her up, he'd been wrong.

"Go to bed."

The eastern sky was graying when Sally crawled into bed beside a soundly sleeping Beverly. Eyes wide, she lay huddled against her friend's warm back, weighted with the thousand unspoken words piled up heavy as stones inside her.

Beverly got up around ten the next morning and Sally, although she was still exhausted, rose too, answering briefly Beverly's question: "What happened last night?"

Digging her everyday clothes out of a satchel she'd brought with her, Beverly breathed "Godsakes." Well, one good thing, Sally wouldn't be seeing Cole Barnstable for a month and a half.

Disloyal was how Beverly felt, accepting an invitation to Sue Ann Meyers' Christmas party in the Meyers' rec room, but Rose had told her, "This is your last year of high school. You go to all the parties you get invited to. Enjoy yourself." As a compromise, Beverly was sleeping over with the Wheelers after the party so she could report to Sally everything that happened.

Officially, Christmas vacation began on the nineteenth, the Monday following the Christmas Dance, and that was the night Sue Ann had scheduled her party. "Because it's so interesting, isn't it, having a party on *Monday*, practically wicked."

"Well," Beverly said, returning from the bathroom, wiping a drib of Pepsodent from the corner of her mouth, "at least the guys are dancing at these dumb parties now."

"But what did they say about me?" Sally had been waiting to hear. Hearing it from Beverly would be easier than hearing it from Angela Bussey.

"Not much."

"You're lying. If you don't tell me, I'll ask Angela. She'll tell me every mean thing and more."

"Well, Sue Ann knew that you didn't get home till morning Saturday night," Beverly told her, scraping a hairbrush back along her scalp and through her hair as she'd read in a magazine to do. After years of being no color with a name, her hair was becoming ash blonde, and she'd begun to take care of it.

"Mrs. Bensinger probably told Sue Ann's mother," Sally noted. "They're in sewing club together. She probably called everyone in sewing club to tell them."

"The wages of sin," Beverly snickered.

"Did Katherine Albers say anything?"

"She never does," Beverly observed, pulling her hair back tight from her face and regarding the effect in the bureau mirror. "She'll probably be the first American saint."

"She's Methodist."

"Methodists don't get to have saints?"

Sally shook her head.

"Damned shame. I wouldn't mind praying to St. Katherine of Harvester to intercede for me. You got any bobby pins?"

"Top right-hand drawer. So what else should I know about the party?"

Beverly began stabbing bobby pins into her hair in back.

"Tell me."

"Well, Cole Barnstable was there." Like Sally's grandmother, Beverly always called him by both names, distancing him with the formality.

"What was he doing there?" Sally demanded. "And why didn't you tell me right away? And if I'm a slut for staying out all night with him, how come he isn't a . . . a lecher? How come he's welcome at parties where I'm not?" Only this afternoon she'd called him to say she couldn't see him until February, and already he was out catting around.

"He wasn't invited. He came with Neddy and Katherine," Beverly explained. "He probably came because he thought you'd be there."

"Who did he dance with?"

"Well, who was he *gonna* dance with? Katherine and Angela and Sylvia, people like that."

"Who did he talk to?"

"Look, I don't make a study of Cole Barnstable."

It was going to be a long six weeks.

December 22 — 25, 1949

In early November, Beverly had gone to Mrs. Stillman, asking
for knitting lessons. As soon as she'd got the hang of knit-and-
purl, she'd begun making scarves for Charlie and Baby Delores
for Christmas.

When Sally saw the red scarf with black fringe Beverly had
whipped up for Charlie, she demanded to learn the secret and,
racing to Lundeen's for needles and yarn, started throwing soft
brown stitches onto a big pair of needles in order to complete
one for Cole by December twenty-fifth.

A week before Christmas she had unraveled the scarf so
many times, correcting dropped stitches, it had the look of
something passed along from one abusive owner to another
through a succession of savage wearers.

Christmas wasn't until Sunday, and the Elways wouldn't arrive until early Saturday, but Harry Wheeler had retired from
his courthouse job the first week in December so he and
Irmgard drove over from Worthington on Thursday.

After dinner, while Harry and Donald walked downtown
to buy cigarettes, Irmgard fetched a copy of *Good Housekeeping*
from her grip and settled down in the living room to read a
new two-part novel.

Sally, fingers cramped, shoulders aching, was bunched in a
corner of the sofa, knitting needles clicking as irregularly as
cheap dentures, every row of knitting punctuated by sighs and
curses.

"I don't want to hear another 'damn,'" Irmgard told her, looking up from the magazine.

"Look at this," Sally cried, holding up the scarf. "Can I give it to someone for a present?" Despite the scorn in her voice, Sally hoped her grandmother would say, "Anyone would be tickled to get that scarf."

Irmgard heard the wretchedness in Sally's voice, but the knitting was dreadful. Laying aside her magazine, she rose and took the scarf to examine.

The yarn had been split by the needles in hundreds of places, stitches were missing or unaccountably increased. One row was loose, the next crabbed. A knot the size of a marble showed where a fresh skein began.

"Please, Grandma, can you help me?"

"Don't you have something else you could give the person? Then you could take your time with the scarf and give it to them later."

"I don't *want* to give them something else!"

"Is this for Cole Barnstable?" Irmgard asked.

"Yes." Sally lunged for the scarf, but Irmgard swung 'round, out of reach.

She knew from her son that Sally was in trouble over the boy, though Bub hadn't explained why. Despite her misgivings, however, she sat with the scarf for an hour, catching up dropped stitches, removing the enormous knot, passing along knitting tips. And early Saturday morning when the thing was still shy by a foot of the required length, she took up the yarn and needles herself and finished it.

Together she and Sally knotted the black fringe to the ends of the scarf and blocked it on the ironing board, using wet towels, pins, and the flatiron.

At a quarter past eight Christmas morning, while the rest of the family was sipping second cups of coffee around the dining-room table, Sally ducked out, with Cole's present under her arm.

The temperature was in the twenties, the sky cloudless and intense, like thick blue glass. The crust of the snow, delicate and crisp as a Communion wafer, glinted blindingly. Bearing left onto Fourth, Sally slowed, hugging herself.

She crossed Second Street. Who would answer the door? Probably not Cole. Neddy? If it were Neddy, what would he think? That she was chasing after his cousin. She didn't care.

What if the person who answered tried to take the package from her without calling Cole to the door? What if it were the formidable Mabel Barnstable, Neddy's grandmother, and she looked down her nose?

Sally didn't care. She wasn't going to leave until she delivered the present to Cole.

Reaching Catalpa Street, she halted, took several deep breaths, and veering right, crossed catty-corner, plunging north. The houses here were big and set well back on wide yards.

She felt everyone in Harvester watching through lace curtains as she trudged up the long, ascending drive, the grinding of gravel beneath her boots loud enough to crack icicles off of eaves.

The doorbell rang with an old-fashioned brrrrrnnng. At length, she heard footsteps and turned to see a man's shape behind the curtains. The door swung in.

"Cole."

"Sally?" He looked sidelong at her.

She held out the green and gold-wrapped package. "I made it," she said. "It isn't very good, but well, I made it."

"Wait," he told her and turned back into the foyer. After a minute he reappeared holding out a pretty white box embossed to resemble damask.

"Cole, for pity's sake, close the door," implored his Great-aunt Mabel. "There's a terrible draft in here."

"I have to go," Sally said. "I sneaked out." She reached a gloved hand, laying her fingers on his arm.

Raising the package she'd given him in a salute, he backed into the foyer. "Thanks."

Sally turned to leave. Descending the steps, she glanced back. The door was still open several inches, and within the narrowing gap, she glimpsed his unmindful, reckless smile.

December 25, 1949

Sally tore open the box before she reached the corner. Inside was a sterling silver identification bracelet with *Sally* engraved on the front and *Cole 12/25/49* on the back. Hanging from one of the links of the bracelet was a tiny silver heart.

All the way home her thoughts were like high puffy clouds that break up and coalesce again and again as they are blown across the sky. Fanciful thoughts. Touching upon miracles and Kismet.

Then, helping Grandma Wheeler with dinner preparations while Grandma and Grandpa Elway drove off to services with the Methodists, her head was heavy with tenderness as she executed a slow glissade around the dining-room table, laying out best china and silver. Passing around again, she smoothed folded linen napkins into place with hands drooping and languid as swans. On her wrist the bracelet glided up and down with the movements, each time sending a message of connection.

The rest of the family was gratified and relieved by Sally's sweet mood, and although they noted the bracelet and surmised that it had come from Cole, they failed to connect her cheerfulness with it.

On Christmas night, Sally and Beverly closeted themselves in Sally's room, to compare Christmas swag. In the dining room, amidst the lingering redolence of roast turkey and sage dressing, card-table conversation flowed on a stream of contentment and delusion.

"I haven't seen her this happy since she was a tot," Edna observed, trumping Harry Wheeler's king of diamonds with her deuce of clubs, pulling in the trick, and leading with the jack of spades to finesse the king on board.

"She's getting past the 'terrible teens,'" observed Irmgard who was sitting out this rubber. "They say thirteen to sixteen are the worst years . . . for girls, anyway."

"She seems to be trying to please," Donald noted.

"Well, I never saw much wrong with her to begin with," Herb Elway insisted.

"No, nor me, neither," Harry Wheeler added, leading the trey of hearts to the board, which had a void, and trumping it with a small club.

"Well, what would anybody expect from a *grandfather?*" Edna sighed.

Irmgard wanted to say, "I think she's finally recovering from Stella," but of course you wouldn't say a hurtful thing like that in front of Edna and Herb. Instead, she observed, "She's not wearing as much makeup as she was at Thanksgiving."

On the dining-room windowsills, rolled-up tea towels absorbed the condensation running down the glass as a result of the day's prodigious cooking.

Holding her cards against her breast, Edna Elway stared at the darkened windows, momentarily holding up play. "Maybe she's getting over . . . Stella." With a convulsive little twist of her shoulders, she glanced down at her cards, saying, "Harry, I'm afraid Donald and I are going to set you in your contract." Casting Harry a smile at once impish and rueful, she picked idly amongst the bridge mix for a peanut.

Wednesday afternoon, Beverly drove Elwood and Rose's new green Plymouth to town and picked up Sally.

Although she'd taken driver's training in the tenth grade and had her licence, Sally didn't often drive Donald's ten-year-old Dodge, now frail and reluctant in its declining years. Donald was talking of trading it, come spring, for something newer, although still secondhand, but meanwhile, Sally infrequently felt the need of a car.

When the Elways visited, Grandpa sometimes handed her the keys to the Fleetwood. Someday, Sally thought, she wanted a convertible like Cole's mother's. But these days she did not mind walking and didn't really understand the mystique attached to driving up and down the same old streets, tooting the horn at your friends, rolling down the window and calling to them, or pulling to the curb for conversation of no consequence.

Beverly, on the other hand, had an affinity for cars and trucks and tractors. She was not so much given to driving fifty times around town as to heading for the highway and "opening it up." This Sally understood better. Speed made you feel both powerful and free, and driving through the countryside with Beverly, Sally often felt released. By flying fast enough, you could outrun yourself.

"What time d'ya have to be back?" Beverly asked.

"In time to make supper."

Beverly chose the highway to St. Bridget to "open it up," and they sped west at eighty-five miles an hour on a road clear, dry, and nearly empty of traffic.

"D'ya want to drive past Cole's house? D'ya know where it's at?"

"I kind of know, but I don't think we should."

"Good." Beverly looked askance at her friend.

Since Cole had given her the bracelet, which she wore night and day on her left wrist, Sally wanted to adhere to the conditions Donald had set down, not to please Donald, but to be worthy of the bracelet.

As they came in sight of the St. Bridget water tower, Beverly slowed to the speed limit. In town she guided the Plymouth toward the business district around courthouse square and, when she'd turned into the square, asked, "Want to stop for a Coke?"

"Sure."

"The hotel okay?"

"Fine."

The St. Bridget Hotel dining room was considered the most sophisticated within several counties' range. On the upper walls, which were papered with regimental stripes of green and ivory, hung gilt-framed paintings of plump, robust fruit, gleaming decanters of wines and oils, fresh-killed game and fresh-caught fish, all flung casually down on damasked boards.

Below the regimental stripes, oak wainscotting, dark and burnished, paneled the walls, and beneath one's feet, deep brown velvety carpet hushed the clatter of crockery. The tables were linen clothed, the chairs cushioned with green velour.

In the afternoon, wives of local businessmen often gathered in the dining room for committee meetings or impromptu bridge games. Retired businessmen hung about long after lunch to read the newspaper or smoke a cigar.

Finding a little table near the low-silled windows overlooking the square, Sally and Beverly ordered Cokes. Shrugging out of her coat, Beverly said, "Isn't that Mr. Davis?" She pointed toward Barnstable's Department Store, across the square.

Sally looked back over her left shoulder. "Looks like him. Same kind of coat," she observed of the tan, belted camel hair emerging from the store. She'd assumed that the speech teacher would go home to St. Paul for Christmas. Well, maybe he had and was back.

"There's Mr. Lundeen." she noted, "coming out of the tobacco store. Looks like they're going to run into each other."

"Dummy." Beverly rolled her eyes. "They're *together.*"

"Oh. I suppose you're right."

"You ever been in Mr. Lundeen's house?"

Sally shook her head. "You?"

"When I used to do odd jobs and deliveries for Mr. Eggers."

With her straw Sally prodded the ice in the tall glass.

"The house was different than I thought it'd be."

"He showed you around?"

Beverly scooped a piece of ice from her glass with a long spoon and cracked it between her molars.

"You shouldn't do that," Sally told her. "You could break a tooth."

"Yeah, I know."

"So, how come he showed you around?"

"I guess I was gawking like I'd never been indoors before, and he thought I might like seeing the place. Also, I made a fuss about this painting he had in the front hall, so he asked me if I'd like to see some others."

"What was it like . . . the house?"

"Not real big. About the size of yours, I guess, only it's got a front hall instead of just an entryway."

"And?"

"The thing I remember most was all the paintings. Everywhere, even the kitchen."

"What kind of furniture?"

"I thought it'd all be with little skinny legs, but it wasn't. There were different kinds. He said, 'I've got a horse from every barn.' Anyway, it was nice. Comfortable but classy."

"Did he show you any of *his* paintings?"

"There were a couple in a hallway. Landscapes. Places around Harvester. They were pretty good. Impressionist.

"He could see I was interested in all the paintings. He asked if I sketched and I told him I did, so he showed me his studio and talked about studying and places where I could do that if I was still interested when I got out of school. Whenever I see him, he asks about my sketching. And if he's seen a Motleys' costume that I did, we talk about that."

Beyond the window, the two men were crossing the snowy square, conversing with bold gestures. Once or twice they paused in their tracks, each wheeling to face the other, waving his parcels, as if a heated argument were being waged. Then they would laugh.

Plodding on, through calf-deep snow, they reached Mr. Lundeen's Chrysler, tossed their purchases into the back seat, and burst into laughter again as they climbed in and drove off.

"His folks went down on the *Lusitania,* you know."

Sally nodded.

"He's got a picture of them in his living room. Before they went to Europe."

"What'd they look like?"

"Good looking, I guess. Old-fashioned. His mother's dress was down to here," Beverly said, indicating her own ankles. "His dad was wearing one of those light colored suits like Mr. Lundeen wears in the summer and holding a panama hat." She paused, running a finger around the base of the glass. "What're you thinking?"

"I don't know. Nothing. Ready to leave?"

The early setting sun threw scarves of peach and mauve across the white fields and cast a shell pink glow down the west-facing walls of farmhouses.

As the Plymouth crested a gentle rise where the road swung in a generous arc down through a little dale, Sally watched four crows—they must be ravens, they were so big—fling themselves upward from the trees and, with an arrogant indolence, slew slowly across the woods to roost again in the same stand of cottonwoods.

Davis's apartment for approval before she typed it on ditto masters.

"If you can read this today and write your suggestions on the back, I'll pick it up tomorrow."

He nodded, then recalled as she was turning away, "I've decided on *Our Town* for the senior-class play. Thornton Wilder."

The next day, handing back her script, Davis told Sally, "We'll do this for the Valentine Dance. I want you to direct it. Neddy's directing a five-minute sketch of his called 'The Basketball Lunatic.' They'll make a nice pairing."

Sally had climbed the wooden steps, each with its grooved black rubber mat, and was standing on a larger mat at the speech teacher's door.

"Did you get a copy of *Our Town* out of the library?" he asked. He liked this girl. She was a girl he would trust, although he couldn't have said why. Bright, strong-willed, defensive, she drank bourbon and had gone all the way according to senior girls he'd overheard.

"Yes," she said. "Kind of soppy, but . . ." The tip of her tongue explored the corner of her lips, searching for the word. ". . . sly." She gazed down the cold stairway at the murky transom above the lower door. "My Grandpa Elway talks about people who throw a clever strike . . . they get one past you before you've even had a chance to stare at them. Isn't that *Our Town*?"

"What d'ya mean you're trying out for the class play?" Cole asked, his voice in the darkness of the panel truck muzzy and low, so that Sally had to strain to hear.

"I want to be in *Our Town* . . . that's the play."

In the back of the van, Cole had spread the thick quilted mats Barnstable deliverymen used to protect furniture and appliances. On these he and Sally had lain down for the first time since Donald had forbidden them to see each other.

Cole had pulled the van into Crescent Ridge State Park, halfway between St. Bridget and Harvester. Because the park was several miles off the main highway, lovers rarely used it in winter for fear of getting stuck or having a battery go dead.

When Cole drove them to places like this, and he'd driven them to many, Sally couldn't help reasoning that he'd brought other girls to them. In the beginning that hadn't bothered her. But something had changed.

If Cole had told her she kissed better than the others, that he'd never felt about any of them the way he did about her . . .

But he wouldn't. If she couldn't take him on faith, she was out of luck. But his appetite for being taken on faith seemed insatiable. He ate up acquiescences, always requiring further proofs of how serious she was.

Even so, Sally was like a tightrope walker who must stand forever at midpoint on the wire, halfway between complete submission, which would prove her love, and complete refusal, which would prove her worth.

He played with a tiny lock of her hair, murmuring, "I don't want you to be in the play."

"Why?"

"I just don't."

He wouldn't say, "I'm jealous of it" or "I need your time more than they do." He had to make a deal as Spartan as possible so that when she gave in, if she did, it could only be out of love for him.

Girls, Cole had concluded, were better at giving in than guys. Because she was a girl, what he was asking wouldn't be so hard. And he would have that ecstatic moment of knowing how much he meant to her before his disillusionment set in.

He made a sound in his throat of absolute disgust and frustration, squeezing his eyelids so tightly they felt as if they might turn inside out. Of all the girls he'd known, she was the best.

"But I have to," she said, ". . . be in the play."

"Why?" His voice wasn't angry or injured, but soft and childlike.

What could she say? She had to be in the play because —
"Because I can die and come back as somebody else." She couldn't think of anything more satisfying, necessary, impossible to explain, or impossible for someone else to understand, than that.

She could barely make out his face in the darkness, but she felt it nod. Did he understand?

Cole did understand wanting to be someone else.

"Can't you try to understand?" she asked.

"I do," he said with more vehemence and more sarcasm than he'd intended. The thing was, if it was a choice between what she wanted and what he wanted, he had to get his way, he had to know. Oh, God, he hated this.

He put both hands into her long hair. He couldn't bring himself to say, "Do you see what a mess I am?" In the child's tone again, which didn't sound as plaintive in his ear as it did in hers, he said, "Please." The word was as much as he could concede and more than he ever had. But, please *what?* Please give in or please don't?

"First, your dad won't let you see me for six weeks," he went on, "and now, you're going to tie yourself up with a play?"

He pulled his arm roughly from beneath Sally's shoulder, sat up, and began buttoning his shirt.

Feeling cut loose and frightened, Sally, too, sat up and silently began to dress. Something more was going to be said, wasn't it? She shivered. Her fingers were cold, and she had trouble with the buttons on her blouse.

Well, wasn't it?

Sally did not fall asleep until four-thirty. When the alarm rang at seven, she crawled out of bed, eyes hot and tender from staring at the ceiling. Her hands shook, and she dropped the bathroom glass in the sink and broke it, then cut her hand cleaning up the pieces.

She could have pleaded flu and stayed home from school, but what was the point? If she dozed in class, what difference? She was getting C's in everything but the two classes from Mr. Davis, anyway.

The following day, Beverly told her, "You look like the frayed end of a rope."

Sally turned away, too tired for anger.

She failed a current events' test in social studies, fell asleep in study hall and was given half an hour of detention by Miss Burns, the study-hall monitor.

The basketball team was playing its Friday night game at St. Bridget. As an assistant coach, Donald had left with the team on the bus late in the afternoon.

Around six Beverly called.

"You want to go see *The Heiress*?"

"I don't think so."

"You break up with Cole?"

"No. Who told you that?"

"Nobody. But the past couple of days you looked like you might've."

"Well, I didn't."

"Simmer down. I was just askin'. If you change your mind about the movie, meet me at the Majestic for the first show. And don't forget about Motleys rehearsal tomorrow afternoon."

Sally brewed a cup of tea and carried it to the living room, settling on the sofa with Dorothy Parker's *Enough Rope*, but the pages swam in front of her.

Seven o'clock came and went. Eight; nine. At ten, she rinsed the teacup and climbed the stairs. Lying awake, she listened to cars munching along the ice and snow of Second Street. When she thought that one of them had stopped in front of the house, she leapt from bed, but it was only Lester Bensinger dropping his mother off next door.

"Dumb cluck," she hissed at herself the second time she jumped out of bed.

The next morning Donald asked, "Have you lost weight?"

She shrugged.

"You're looking thin." And blue half-moons stained the skin beneath her eyes.

All Saturday she Hoovered, dusted, scrubbed, and polished. When she had finished the second floor, she gathered up the laundry, stuffing it into the clothes chute in the bathroom. Dusting and vacuuming the stairs as she went, she carried the cleaning gear to the first floor and set to work on it.

Donald had agreed to play bridge at Superintendent Engel's, filling in for Harv Franie, the high school principal, who was away at a regional meeting of principals. Tonight was the fourth or fifth time during his years of teaching that he'd been asked to fill in. He was never quite at ease playing cards with the boss and wasn't altogether sure why.

Declining to substitute at bridge would have been impolitic

however, and besides, Donald felt sorry for the Engels and Franies, who were even more isolated from the community than the faculty was. Girding his loins on each occasion, he showed up with a box of mixed nuts or after-dinner mints, prepared for an evening of weak bidding (except for Alice Engel who bid angrily); gingerale; and later, coffee and lemon bars, which disagreed with his stomach.

When her father had driven off at seven twenty-five in his new three-year-old black Dodge, Sally paced the living room, chain-smoking half a dozen Pall Malls. Later, she sat at the dining-room table laying out a game of solitaire. Tonight, tea made her stomach feel shriveled and her tongue styptic. Tossing the cards aside, she picked up Dorothy Parker again, but it was no use. Dragging upstairs, she slipped off her robe, dropping it on the floor of her room.

The second time the doorbell rang, she heard it. Snatching the bedroom curtain aside, she peered into the street. The panel truck. Plucking up the robe, she swept out of the room and down the stairs.

"Were you in bed?" Wearing his tan jacket and the scarf she had knit him, he stood on the stoop, hands thrust deep into his pockets.

"About to be." She stepped aside and held the door.

"You want to get dressed and go out?"

"I guess."

Outside, heavy flakes had begun drifting down, concealing the dinge of old snow. Cole drove north out of town and turned onto the road to Red Berry, ten miles away.

At the easternmost edge of the village the Dakota Ballroom squatted, a neon Grain Belt sign buzzing and flickering above the door. Except for this and the single light standard in the washboard parking lot, the Dakota was as black and monolithic as a worn-down mesa. The ballroom windows were covered by featureless shutters through which no glimmer escaped.

Cole threaded the car through the crowded parking lot and around to the stygian back of the building before finding an empty space. Reaching across Sally, he pulled a brown paper bag from the glove compartment.

Smoke, din, and the reek of spilled 3.2 beer filled the vastness of the ballroom, along one side of which lay row upon row of rude wooden booths. A waitress hurrying from booth to booth with a tray of setups and beers spied Cole and Sally and pointed to an unoccupied booth.

"Be right with you," she mouthed, not attempting to make herself heard above Marvin Mink and the Uptown Eight, playing "Bonaparte's Retreat."

On a post between booths were hooks for coats, and Sally hung her jacket there. Pulling off her boots, she slid them under the bench and sat down opposite Cole.

Laying the brown bag on the seat beside him, Cole ordered two Coke setups. With the garnet stone of his class ring, he sat tapping the brown painted linoleum surface of the table, which was worn to a pentimento of emerging mustard yellow and the faint black lines of tarpaper backing.

When the setups arrived, Cole held them one at a time under the table, mixing vodka into each from the bottle in the bag — the convention if you were under twenty-one.

The band finished "Bonaparte's Retreat," cleaned out mouthpieces, mopped brows, and launched into "On a Slow Boat to China." Cole nodded toward the floor, and Sally led the way.

He was a graceful, unselfconscious dancer, easy to follow, never reticent to twirl her or to dip. Sally enjoyed the notice others took of them.

Remaining on the floor for the next number, they lindied to "The Old Master Painter." Like a matador's cape, Sally's red ballerina skirt flung out and around each time Cole spun her. As the song ended, he dipped her until her black hair brushed the talcumed oak.

Back in the booth, they drank what remained of the Coke and vodkas, and Cole ordered fresh setups. Sally fished a Kleenex from her bag, blotting her face.

"You look good," he told her and touched the back of his fingers to her red cheeks.

In the six months she'd known him, this was Cole's first compliment. "Thank you," she said, wiping the tabletop with the Kleenex to cover her confusion.

At ten past eleven the Uptown Eight began Cole Porter's "So In Love," and Cole took her hand. They danced close, her arms around his neck, his around her waist. As the song ended, he looked at her, she nodded, and they collected their coats from the booth.

He made love to her, whispering words very particularly for her, not just the paltry currency of passion, spilled carelessly in the flood of climax.

Cole left Sally at quarter past one and began the drive back to St. Bridget. The night was clear and still now, although thin drifts of snow, like twisted white ribbons, were flicked across the surface of the road.

Halfway home he felt himself falling down the other side of the evening, the other side of love, which was sickening contempt for himself and Sally and a thrusting away of intimate memories.

He'd nearly told her that he loved her. *Jesus*. Worse, he was certain she'd come close to saying she loved him. A cold sweat broke on his brow. His gut burned and convulsed.

At the next mile-road crossing, he swung off the highway, slamming on the brakes and leaping from the car. In the drifts beside the road he knelt, retching and washing his mouth with snow.

Back in the panel truck, he sat gripping the wheel as shudders ran through him. Minutes passed and stretched into half an hour. At length he backed the car onto the highway, heading toward St. Bridget.

From eyes screwed deep into their sockets tears oozed, and through the tears, the lights of St. Bridget looked like the foamy scum of dirty wash water.

In her bed, Sally sighed and thought, *A perfect night. The only perfect night of my life.*

The Valentine Dance followed the home game with Worthington. Sally had told Cole about the dance, told him the Motleys were performing at intermission.

In dim balconies along either side of the gym, parents (mostly Motleys' parents) and a few townspeople had gathered to watch the intermission performance. Donald had said he would be there. Probably Miss Bailey and Mr. Lundeen would.

Half an hour before intermission, Sally scanned the faces ranged around the gymnasium, then headed backstage to the girls' dressing room to begin applying the elaborate Columbine makeup. She had relied on Beverly's ideas for the costume. Beverly had a knack for coming up with oddly felicitous touches.

"You have to wear your red ballerina skirt," Beverly had insisted. "Pantomime is like a dance. Besides, the skirt's red . . . ta da! . . . like a valentine."

She'd rummaged through Sally's closet, emerging with a white peasant blouse with drawstring neck and short, gathered sleeves. "This on top," she announced, holding it up. "I'll applique a red heart here," she said, indicating a spot that would lie over Sally's left breast. "You've got plain black ballet slippers?"

Now, as Sally sat before the dressing-room mirror, Beverly fastened a length of one-inch black velvet ribbon around her friend's neck. "*Très* chic! And for the final touch . . ."

"What's that?"

Beverly held another, shorter length of black velvet ribbon, a red cloth rose attached. "Hold out your right hand. This goes around your wrist."

"How come?"

"Hands are important in pantomime, dummy. The rose draws attention to them." She studied Sally in the mirror. "Don't forget the beauty mark."

When Beverly had finished with her, Sally drifted out of the dressing room and into the shadowy area behind the back curtains. She liked to be alone, to get into her part and prime herself, before going on stage. Pacing slowly in the dim reaches of backstage, she ran through the valentine pantomime, movement, and music (Stravinsky's Concerto in D Major for violin and orchestra, which Drew Davis had put on reel-to-reel and spliced to fit the story).

Then Mr. Davis was at the microphone quieting the crowd and introducing the Motleys. From offstage the brassy, tape-recorded music of the "Harvester Fight Song" swelled to a deafening crescendo and subsided, ushering on "The Basketball Lunatic."

Beneath the sound, Sally heard the click-click as light-board levers were flipped, the slip-slip as rope was tugged through pulleys, hand over hand, drawing apart the heavy velvet curtains to reveal a stage where Leroy Mosely as the lunatic basketball player sat at a table center stage. Out in the gymnasium, students clapped and hooted at Leroy's opening business involving a plate of pancakes.

A knot of concentration lay in Sally's midsection, like a wound-up spring waiting to be released. She glided back and forth, catching bits of onstage dialogue between Leroy and Katherine, interrupted by ripples of laughter. At length she heard the hard beat of a basketball, dribbling across the stage, signaling the end of the skit. Amidst clapping and whistling, the curtains whooshed together.

Sally breathed deeply three times, sucking air into the bottom of her lungs, then exhaled completely, purging her lungs and relaxing her diaphragm.

Strains of Stravinsky leapt into the air, and she grabbed up the valentine box from the prop table, hurried onstage, and took her place on the wooden riser representing a front porch.

The fill-lights above the stage dimmed, the curtains parted, and the travel spots came on, supplemented by dimmed-down footlights. Sally felt the spotlight on her face the way a sailor feels the wind direction, without thinking about it.

Everyone played his part perfectly, she thought, including the audience, which laughed at the proper places — for instance, when the suitors each in turn made grandiose and silly ceremonies of delivering their valentines into the box.

The casts of the two sketches took their curtain calls together, and linking hands with Katherine and Leroy Mosely, Sally searched the ranks of faces in the gym for Cole's.

In the dressing room she slathered Alboline cream on her face and neck, tissuing away the character of Columbine. Wearing jeans and a shirt once more, she folded the costume into a brown paper bag and slipped out of the building.

"Home already?" Donald asked. He had arrived minutes earlier and was standing at the open refrigerator. "You were good. Quite an actress." He closed the refrigerator, forgetting for a moment what he'd been fetching, remembering instead a long-ago day on Bacal's Hill, just after Stella'd been committed: Sally on the Flexible Flyer sailing down the hill, a princess without a care in the world

Cole did not call that weekend. Tryouts for the senior class production of *Our Town* were in Mr. Davis's room Monday after school.

Sally read, but not well. Katherine, who was also reading for the part of Emily, did much better, and Sally was fairly certain Katherine would get the part. The cast would be posted on Friday.

Leaving tryouts early, Sally went home and, without undressing, crawled into bed. The house felt cold, the bed icy. Crawling out again, she pulled an extra quilt from the hall closet. Beneath the added layer, she rubbed her feet together and wrapped her arms around her middle.

At seven, Donald brought up a bowl of tomato soup.

"I'm not hungry, Daddy."

He set the bowl on the bureau and lay a hand on her forehead. "Coming down with something?"

"I don't think so."

"Did you try out for the play?" he asked, sitting at the edge of the bed.

She nodded.

"How did it go?"

"Bad." She turned toward him. "But that's not why I'm in bed. I'm tired. That's why."

"Well, get some sleep," he said, picking up the bowl of soup. "I'll put this in the refrigerator in case you want it later."

She rolled back on her side and closed her eyes.

Thursday, at the end of speech class, Mr. Davis asked Sally to come in after school.

When she showed up at three-ten, he motioned her to take a seat in the front row near his desk. He perched on the corner of the desk, arms crossed, leaning a bit forward, peering closely with his flax-flower eyes. "Are you all right?"

"I'm fine," she said warily.

"During tryouts Monday you seemed . . . preoccupied . . . as if you weren't really there."

Sally said nothing.

"You've lost weight."

Sally looked out the window into the gray, attenuated elm branches.

"I don't have any business asking, I suppose, but is something going wrong in your life right now?"

She looked at him and for the first time wished that she *could* talk.

He shifted. "You're talented. But you know that. Don't you?"

She nodded.

He walked to the bank of windows, leaning an elbow on a sill, and turned toward her. "I wish I had a talent like yours."

"Isn't teaching a talent?"

"If I have a talent, it's teaching." His voice was tentative.

"Don't you like teaching?"

"Oh, yes, I like it."

"Well, then?"

He crossed back to the desk and sat down on his chair, playing with pencils and other paraphernalia, rearranging them absently. "You're my best actress, and I want you to play Emily. This is between you and me."

"But, Katherine . . ."

"Katherine reads well, but you're an actress."

Sally considered. "You sure this isn't some kind of therapy?" She twisted in the seat, embarrassed by the idea.

"I'm casting you as Emily because you'll do the best job."

She wouldn't have accepted the part if she'd thought it was *only* therapy. He really seemed to believe that she'd do the best job.

Outside, in the bitter February afternoon where the snow and the sky were the same coal-smoke gray, Sally stood for a moment, staring down Main Street, her breathing shallow and erratic. *What about Cole?*

After the night at the Dakota Ballroom, Cole waited two weeks to call Sally.

"So, what've you been up to?" he asked.

"Nothing much. School. You?"

"The usual."

"I read *The Way of All Flesh.*"

"Oh, yeah?"

"Mr. Lundeen was reading it in Eggers' Drug Store, and I asked him about it, so he loaned it to me."

"Any good?"

"It's about a guy named Theobald Pontifex who has these terrible, unloving parents. They practically ruin his life. It takes him years to recover from them."

"What'd they do, beat him?"

"No. They were always telling him he ought to do things for his own good when they really meant for *their* own good. They were incredible hypocrites, very religious and cruel."

"Who's it by?"

"Samuel Butler. Sometimes I think religion makes people hypocrites. They can't measure up to the rules, and they're afraid other people are noticing, so they pretend. Sometimes they pretend so hard, they actually believe they're good, and then they start worrying about *other* people being good, you know?"

"What, uh, happened about the class play?" He'd hoped she would bring it up, but she wasn't going to.

"I tried out. I got the part I wanted."

"Yeah, well, I gotta go. Dave n' I're going to *Battleground* at the Lyceum." He hung up. *Jesus. She didn't care enough about him to give up the class play!*

Slamming the door of his room, he grabbed the putter standing in the corner and smashed the mirror over the bureau. Though the glass shattered with the first blow, scattering over the Danish modern bureau top and onto the beige shag carpet, he kept swinging, battering the thin wooden backing until it, too, fell in splintered pieces.

327

Saturday evening, February 25, two days before rehearsals for *Our Town* would begin, the Motleys piled into the school station wagon, and Mr. Davis drove them to the St. Bridget Country Club where they were performing for the Founders Day Dance.

Since the end of the war in 1945, St. Bridget had pushed beyond the country club into what was now referred to as West St. Bridget where Cole and his family lived on a cul-de-sac named Prairie Circle. There, ranch houses marched in lock step up and down nearly treeless streets where scrawny, fast-growing poplars were planted in windrows across backyards as interim shade, shelter, and charm until newly planted maple, oak, and ash could rise up to replace the old trees felled by the developers.

But the country club, originally an automobile club, retained some of the idiosyncratic charm of an earlier era. Recumbent upon the gentle curve between two small, spruce-grown hills, the club house lay like a dowager upon a fainting couch. Built in a modified Queen Anne design, its cedar-shingle siding was weathered to a soft gray, and its many impractical, yet agreeable, French doors opened onto stone terraces.

A number of the younger set were speaking openly of the need for something more modern, less drafty. Even here on the prairie, where towns were by the measure of history very young, the commitment to graceful monuments, a virtue of the recent past, was already giving way to expediency and boxy functionalism. Schools were no longer constructed with belfries, nor county courthouses with clock towers. Verandas found no place on hotels, nor locally quarried stone a role in building.

But between these two small spruce-grown hills this aging doyenne, with her airs and crotchets, remained a testament to the idea of institutional responsibility to beauty or, at the very least, commitment to a well-meaning dignity.

From Country Club Road the gravel drive wound up between tall pines to a broad, hedged parking area to the left of the building. Just before 9 P.M., Mr. Davis pulled the Ford station wagon into the lot, and the Motleys tumbled out.

Carrying the big tape player, Davis led the way to the back entrance, which opened into the kitchen. As he reached the door he turned to shush them. "Very professional, now, all right?"

The Motleys followed Davis through the kitchen, where several middle-aged women in white uniforms were washing dishes and cleaning up after a banquet, and into a hallway off which were doors to the Help restrooms. In these the cast changed into costume and applied makeup while Davis went ahead to check on the makeshift stage, an area near the bandstand where Slim Shane and the Sweet Notes were playing.

When everyone was costumed and made up and Mr. Davis had arranged the necessary small table and two chairs on the stage for the "Basketball Lunatic," the Motleys gathered quietly in the shadowed mouth of the passage leading to the ballroom and studied the country-club crowd till it was time to go on.

"They must've cornered the market on organza," Beverly whispered to Sally, noting the women's cocktail dresses.

Sally peered around the big room. The band stand was wedged into the far left-hand corner, the stage to the right of it or almost in the middle of the far wall. Along the right- and left-hand walls, linen-draped tables for eight were scattered, and in the center of the room lay the open dance floor.

The bar was snugged up against the short wall immediately to the right of the passage where the Motleys waited, and to the left, a wide archway led to the foyer. Sally liked having a sense of the house they were playing to, both in terms of its size and the makeup of the crowd. This crowd she judged to be the "Oh, aren't they cute!" sort.

As her gaze swung round the room, she spotted Brenda and Ed Barnstable, Neddy's parents. She'd forgotten that they were members. The couple to Brenda's left must be Cole's parents. For one thing, the man, although fortyish and thickening in waist and jaw, bore a striking resemblance to Cole.

The band concluded "Ain't Misbehavin'," paused to let dancers straggle back to their tables, then struck up a fanfare. Neddy, emcee for this performance, made his way to the band-leader's microphone and began his introduction, which in-cluded some of his "Serious Crime in Harvester" monologue, adapted to a "Serious Crime in St. Bridget" routine.

While Neddy performed, Sally's glance strayed to the Barnstable table. Cole's mother, or the woman Sally assumed to be his mother, wore a slim black cocktail dress, with long, cling-ing sleeves and a low, square neckline. Her dark hair was scraped back in a sophisticated chignon. Far and away the most soigné presence in the room, she sat surveying the other tables as though born to the role of grand duchess and *arbiter elegantiae*. Her circulating glance embraced or dismissed with a detachment altogether lacking in self-consciousness.

As Neddy reached the end of his introduction, the cast of "The Basketball Lunatic" made its way along the right-hand wall. As it crept past the Barnstable table, Brenda waved to Katherine Albers and smiled a proprietary smile.

The audience applauded, and the "St. Bridget Fight Song" boomed forth from the tape recorder, covering both Neddy's exit and the cast's entrance. To Sally, it seemed that the sketch

330

had barely got underway when it was over, and it was time for her to carry the valentine box and tiptoe along the right-hand wall toward the stage.

From the corner of her eye, she saw Brenda bend her head toward Cole's mother, whisper something, and nod toward Sally. Trembling with nerves as she had not done since second grade, Sally concentrated on Stravinsky and felt Miss Bailey's hands grasp her shoulders, heard Miss Bailey's voice tell her, "Take a deep breath . . . make them forget that the car wouldn't start this morning and the dog died last Saturday. . . ."

Placing each foot daintily, Sally carried the valentine box out onto the "porch," set it down with a pretty, doll-like smile, and willed the audience to surrender. For the moment, the Barnstable women, no less than the others, deserved to be entertained, made to forget that the car wouldn't start this morning.

And then it was over and people were clapping and the cast was taking a bow and Sally was exploring the audience as she always did during bows, looking into the eyes of as many individuals as she could so that they knew she appreciated them singly as well as collectively. Denise Barnstable returned her glance, adding Sally up and, Sally felt, dismissing the total.

At the back, in the foyer where the light was dim, Cole stood leaning against a wall. He stared directly at her. And she stared back.

When she straightened from the next bow, he was gone.

March 1950

Monday night Mr. Davis and the cast began blocking *Our Town*. By the end of the week they had completed all three acts. As the seniors with the most acting experience, the Motleys, not surprisingly, were cast in most of the major roles, a circumstance resented by one or two of their classmates.

Angela Bussey and Sue Ann Meyers had each set her heart on playing Emily. When Angela was asked to head up the props crew, and Sue Ann to play Mrs. Soames, a tiny stream of vinegary resentment trickled out into the village.

Most people shrugged. Some recalled having themselves been rejected. But a few, grievances still stuck in their hearts like thorns, said, "The Methodists and Romans think they run things, don't they?"

Or they said, "I heard he plays favorites with those whatcha-call-'ems, Mottles."

Or they said, "If you don't play contract bridge with the swells in this town, you get high-hatted."

And Mrs. Bensinger, on her way home from her daughter-in-law Evangeline's, where she'd found mouse droppings in the dish cupboard, said to Sally, who was on her way home from Rabel's Meat Market with a pound and a half of round steak, "I wouldn't let a daughter of mine act in a play at the high school. No offense intended, but the theatrical crowd up there's getting a bad name."

Sally's face burned. "What's being said, and who's saying it?"

Deeply offended that Sally would ask, Dagney Bensinger snipped, "I hear that certain people are putting themselves forward, trying to be Somebody." She drew her arms up inside her coat sleeves and tight across her waist. "I'm getting chilled to the bone," she said as if Sally had waylaid her.

To put oneself forward and try to be Somebody was unwomanly.

Sally did not hear from Cole during the first two weeks of rehearsal while the cast memorized act 1.

Several times she picked up the phone but replaced the receiver when the operator said, "Number, please."

Leaving school one night after rehearsal, she paused to admire the full moon hanging over the Water and Power Company. A blue Chevrolet like the one with *Barnstables* on the side was parked down past the Water and Power Company and the public library. However, when Sally bore left toward home, the driver didn't start up the engine to follow.

Another night as she hung at the bedroom window, she saw a pale blue Chevrolet pass beneath the light a block away at the corner of Third Avenue and Third Street, but it did not turn down Third Avenue toward the Wheeler house. For twenty minutes she remained at the window without seeing it again.

On a Wednesday morning nearly halfway through the weeks of rehearsal, Sally fell asleep during French class, and Miss Burns assigned her half an hour of detention. At three-fifteen, she made her way to the detention study hall and fell asleep again. Mr. Thompson, who was monitoring detention that day, sent her to Principal Franie's office.

"If class play rehearsals are too much for you," he told her, "Mr. Davis will have to replace you. Studies have to come first."

"Rehearsals aren't too much, Mr. Franie."

"Well, what is it, then?"

"I . . . I don't know."

Elbows resting on the arms of the oak desk chair, he eyed her closely, studying her through the steeple he'd built of his long fingers.

"Miss Burns says your French grades are borderline," he told her.

Sally nodded. What could she say? It was true.

At length Principal Franie cleared his throat and sat forward. "You'll have to spend an hour in detention tomorrow." He watched her leave, shaking his head. A strange girl. Wild, they said. A shame for Don Wheeler.

"Third act lines by Monday," Mr. Davis reminded the cast as they bundled out into the cheerless late March Saturday after-noon. "Sally, would you stick around a minute?"

He roamed the nearly bare stage picking up after the cast. No matter how many times you admonished them, they always left something behind: a blue scarf, a chemistry text, a lipstick.

When a straggling Leroy Mosely finally let the gym door slam behind him, Drew Davis heaped the gleanings in a little pile on the floor beside one of the set's straight-back chairs and sat down.

"Harv Franie says you're having problems," he told Sally, who was standing beside the arched trellis outside the Gibbs' "house."

"Sylvia Donaldson is understudying me, isn't she?"

He nodded.

"I think I should quit the play." Sally stared at the dusty wooden floor, pitted and stained. She ran the toe of her shoe across a scar left by a set cleat. Yes. She should quit.

Davis shifted, saying nothing. Elbows on his knees, he stud-ied his loafers, at length glancing over at her. "This doesn't have anything to do with your studies, really, does it?"

She shook her head.

"Can you talk about it?"

Again she shook her head.

"I can't keep you from leaving the cast, especially since Miss Burns has complained about your French grades." He scanned her face for some clue, but she was closed up hard and tight as a walnut shell. Larry had told him a little about her mother. He'd like to ask Sally about that. Naturally he wouldn't unless she brought it up first.

"Have a seat," he said, pointing to another of the straight-back chairs. "Have you thought any more about what you want to do after high school?"

She shook her head.

"Still don't want to go to college?"

Sally shrugged. "I don't think so."

"What about a drama major?"

She considered this and shrugged again.

"You *do* like acting, don't you?"

"Oh, yes."

"Is your family opposed?"

"No . . . No, they're not. I mean, I've never talked to them about it."

"You could light out for New York after graduation and look for an acting coach. I could provide you with names. Or you could audition for the American Academy. Think about it. We'll talk about it when we're done with *Our Town.*"

"All right."

"I'd never advise anyone to choose it unless they were . . . exceptional, unless they had a *passion* for it. It's exhausting and demanding. And chances are, it won't make them any money." He smiled.

"Is your teaching like that? . . . something you have to do no matter what?"

Rather abruptly he bent and began gathering up the pile of flotsam.

"Mr. Davis?"

He ran a trembling hand across the face of the chemistry

335

book. Her question was casual. . . . *Something you have to do no matter what? Did you serve in the war, Mr. Davis?* That, too, was a casual question.

"I never imagined teaching could get a hold on me the way it has." He heard the tremor in his voice and rose, glancing at the big mesh-enclosed clock. "Look at the time. I've got an appointment."

Sally found her coat backstage and pulled it on. "See you Monday, Mr. Davis," she called as she crossed the gym to the doors at the far end.

At the light board, Davis began pulling levers, extinguishing footlights and work lights, spots and overhead fills. By pulling the master switch he could have doused them all, but in his consternation that did not occur to him.

Late March — Early April 1950

Sunday afternoon, when she had studied lines for two hours, Sally tossed the script aside and stood at the window watching doomed snowflakes fall, melting as they lit. She drummed her fingers on the sill, paced for a few minutes, bureau to window, window to bureau, looked in the mirror without seeing herself, and fled downstairs, grabbing a coat from the entry closet.

Main Street on Sunday was dead except for the Majestic Theater, Anderson's Candy and Ice Cream, and the Loon Cafe. A covey of cars huddled in that vicinity.

The snow had stopped, and the wetness on the sidewalk and street had been wicked up by a wind that rattled signs and set them keening and clattering, like the Rabel's Meat Market sign swinging on its standard.

Climbing Mrs. Stillman's stairs, Sally knocked on the battered storm door, not yet replaced by the screen door of spring, a season one could not take for granted before May.

"Come in!" Helen Stillman held the inner door as Sally hurried in out of the gust. "Give me your coat, dear. Gracious, you came away without gloves or a scarf, and it's raw out there. I'll put this in the bedroom." Noting how haggard the girl had grown, she turned away, calling over her shoulder, "Make yourself at home."

Sally sat down on the perilously yielding sofa.

"Mrs. Stillman," she called as the older woman set the kettle on the stove, "I've decided that when I'm making money, I'm going to buy a convertible and drive to Harvester to take you for a ride. Do you think you'd like to ride in a convertible?"

Helen Stillman came to the kitchen door. "In the summer? I'd feel like a queen."

While the water heated, Mrs. Stillman returned to the living room and sat in the rocker. "How is the play coming?"

"Pretty well."

Helen Stillman cocked her head. "Anything wrong?"

Sally didn't answer at once, but sat tracing the flowers on the cretonne. "I'm thinking about quitting."

"Why is that?"

"It's too complicated to explain."

"I hope you won't quit. If you're going to be an actress, it's important to be in as many plays as possible." She pressed her prim black shoes to the floor and set the rocker gently in motion. "I'll never forget when you were a first or second grader, and you narrated that little play at Christmas." She rose to check on the teakettle.

Carrying the tray in, she said, "Your mother told me once that she'd always wanted to be a nurse. I thought it was a shame that she didn't get to do that." She set the tray on the table beside the rocker.

"I always wanted to be a teacher," she went on. "Wasn't it fortunate I was able to?" Pouring pale tea into the cups, she added milk to Sally's and held it out to her.

"So many times I thanked God for teaching," she said, passing the cookies. "I could get so wrapped up in it, I'd forget my troubles for hours on end. What if I hadn't had a, I don't know what you'd call it . . . an obsession? . . . like that? Well, I don't even want to think about it."

The old woman leaned back against the green wicker.

"Everyone's born with an obsession, I've always thought, but so many get sidetracked. Then they hunger all their lives and never know what ails them. Men beat their wives and women

338

turn slovenly, all because they wanted to fix cars or be mission-aries in China." She rocked in companionable silence.

Sally lay her head against the back of the sofa, closing her eyes, recalling the Sunday after Hilly's suicide when Lark had run away from Mass because the bishop wouldn't allow Hilly to be buried from the Catholic church.

Mr. Erhardt had stormed out of St. Boniface and gone searching for her with the truck, punishment on his mind. Lark had reached this apartment, and here she'd been kept until the next day when Mrs. Erhardt had calmed her husband down.

Mrs. Stillman saw that Sally had fallen asleep. Fetching the shawl, she spread it across the girl's shoulders, then phoned Donald to let him know where the child was.

That night Cole telephoned.

"Have you quit the play?"

"No, but listen, Cole. I need to explain."

"Forget it."

Dress rehearsal, Thursday April 6, was a shambles. Actors went up in their lines; Ronald Oster missed several light cues; Katherine tore her first-act costume on a nail; Leroy, who'd been nursing a cold, lost his voice; and the main curtain wouldn't close.

When Neddy, who played the Stage Manager, had delivered the last line of the play, cast and crews assembled onstage, groaning.

"What the hell happened to the curtain?" Neddy wanted to know.

"Sorry about that light cue at the beginning of act 3," Ronald Oster said.

"I haven't forgotten a first-act line since the second week of rehearsal," Delmore Preuss told them. "Tonight I forgot half of 'em."

"We're falling apart," Beverly said.

Carrying a clipboard, Drew Davis strolled onstage and sat hind-side-to on one of the straight-back chairs. He ran down the notes he'd made during rehearsal, including a couple for Ronald Oster on lights; one for Sylvia Donaldson, the prompter; and a reminder to Beverly, who was both acting the part of Mrs. Gibbs and serving as costume mistress.

"We'll need Katherine's costume mended by tomorrow afternoon." Laying the clipboard aside, he told the actors, "You were lousy tonight. But better lousy at dress rehearsal than at opening night. Go home. Get some rest. I'll see you here in makeup and costume at one o'clock tomorrow."

The next afternoon the cast performed *Our Town* for grades one through twelve, a boisterous, shuffling, chair-scraping crowd, smaller children down front, junior high toward the back, and in the balconies along either side of the gym, senior high students, sniggering now and again at something romantic or sad. During the third act, girls sniffled and dug Kleenex from their pockets. Backstage, the performance was chalked up a success.

They gave two performances for the town, one that night and another Saturday night. The Elway grandparents arrived about eleven Saturday morning, looking tanned and jaunty, Edna in a pair of navy slacks and a red sweater with nautical brass buttons down the front.

Since Herb's retirement on January first, they'd been playing golf and bridge in Ft. Lauderdale. Once more voluble and opinionated, Edna had got back her old sense of style as well. No more runners in the nylons, no more forgetting salon appointments. Yet now and then a chill passed through her, like an icy little breeze running through the house on a hot afternoon, slamming doors and raising gooseflesh.

The Wheeler grandparents pulled to the curb just after 2 P.M., bearing jars of last summer's canning: tomatoes and peaches and watermelon pickles and even a couple of mason jars of home-preserved chicken.

"It'll soon be time to do it all over again," Irmgard explained, "so I have to get rid of these." Some such assurance always accompanied the giving away of things, as if the recipient were helping her no end by accepting the goods.

"There's coffee in the electric percolator," Edna said.

Irmgard, who was stowing jars of food in the cupboard, would have liked to know if Sally was still seeing Cole Barnstable. The child was emaciated. Still, she was calm and pleasant enough. Best not to rile things up.

Edna, slicing a pound cake she'd picked up at Madsen's new supermarket in Mankato, paused, gazing up at Irmgard, who stood on a kitchen chair putting away jars of food, a homemade white cotton slip showing as her dress rode up. How nettled she used to get at Irmgard and her boxes of homegrown, home-canned food. They seemed an affront. Now she had difficulty recalling why.

She shrugged and set a plate of sliced pound cake on the table, shoving it toward Harry Wheeler. She and Irmgard were becoming the women they ought to have been at thirty, women it had seemed impossible to be at thirty: loving without owning; knowing that you were not responsible for everything, that some things would succeed or fail, fall apart or heal entirely on their own; that mistakes were just that, mistakes, not wickedness; and that what other people thought didn't matter nearly as much as you'd been told.

Tears of relief and forbearance sprang to Edna's eyes, and she turned quickly toward the refrigerator, opening the door and withdrawing the cream bottle.

Irmgard, glancing down from her perch on the chair, saw the mistiness in Edna's eyes and climbed down, crossing to her, taking the cream from her, and setting it on the cupboard. Clasping the other woman in a seemingly casual hug, albeit the first she'd ever given her, Irmgard told her, "I'm thinking about getting a pair of slacks." Now where had *that* come from? she wondered. "Yours are something like I had in mind. I don't have your figure, of course. Do you think I could get away with slacks?" She was rattling on, making things up as she went along, but it felt right.

Studying her grandparents, Sally felt an ardent tolerance. They weren't young. In fact they were quite old. In their seventies. Sagging and wrinkling and worrying about dying must be awful. Nothing could compensate a person for that. Considering how awful it must be, her grandparents were remarkably cheerful. No doubt they often pretended, which was brave of them.

"Pound cake?" Grandpa Elway was asking, holding out the plate.

"No, thanks, Grandpa. I have to go upstairs and run through my lines." Kissing each one on the cheek, she said, "I love you. Please live a long time."

They stared after her, dumbfounded.

April 1950

The act 2 ending was spectacular. Wearing a wedding gown, Sally linked her arm through Leroy's and marched to the strains of Mendelssohn back up the aisle of the minimal stage setting, down the steps leading into the gymnasium, and down the long "church" aisle between the folding chairs where her grandparents and Donald were sitting.

The audience clapped, and two or three people even bravoed, although in Harvester *bravo* was still considered foreign and a bit affected. People who were Trying to Be Somebody shouted "Bravo!"

Sally and Leroy scurried around the corner of the school, in through a side door, and down a first-floor hall to the sloping, linoleumed hallway leading backstage.

There Sally left Leroy and headed for the girls' dressing room to change into her third-act costume. She had plenty of time for costume and makeup changes during the long intermission while members of Future Homemakers of America set up a punch table at one side of the gym and carried platters of cookies from the home ec room.

Dressed in the simple white frock of the third act, Sally sneaked onstage to the tiny hole in the main curtain through which actors peeked at the audience. Although Mr. Davis had said that this was unprofessional, Sally figured actors had been peeking at audiences for as long as stage curtains had existed.

Her grandparents and Donald were holding paper cups of punch and standing along the east wall talking with Mrs. Stillman. Future Homemakers scurried about importantly. Sometimes boyfriends accompanied them, stealing kisses or feels in the nearly darkened hallways between the gym and the home ec kitchen.

Up the long linoleumed passage from the gym to the main hallway of the high school they flurried, past the darkened, pebbly glass panel of the door stenciled *Superintendent.* Turning right, whispering and giggling, they fluttered down the dim hall to the end where a brightly lit home ec door stood open.

"Lemme look now," Beverly said, nudging Sally aside.

Sally retreated to the furthermost corner to run over act 3 lines, among them her important "goodbye, world" speech. Three or four minutes later, Ronald Oster flipped the tape recorder on, and "Blessed Be the Tie That Binds" filtered quietly out into the auditorium. Mr. Davis gathered the cast on stage, and Ronald began slowly lowering the houselights, a signal for the audience to return to their seats.

As the cast stood clustered around the director, he told them, "This is it, then, our last act together." He swallowed and for a second lowered his head. "You're the best thing that's happened to me in a long time." He clasped his hands above his head. "Get out there and break one more leg."

Sally waited for the umbrella-carrying mourners to sing "Blessed Be the Tie That Binds," her cue to emerge from among them and converse with the "dead" who were sitting on straight-back chairs onstage. For any person in the audience not familiar with the story, it was a small gasp of a moment, discovering that the young woman they'd seen married minutes earlier was now dead and wandering among the dead of the cemetery.

Sally was immersed in the scene. More than that, she was absorbed into it, molecule by molecule, until the boundaries between her and Emily disappeared. She and the other characters and Grover's Corners, New Hampshire, and the gymnasium and all the people in it comprised a distinct little universe, removed from Harvester, St. Bridget County, Minnesota, and the United States.

And then, Neddy as the Stage Manager was saying "Eleven o'clock in Grovers's Corners . . . Goodnight," and they all spun back into the solar system and into Harvester, landing with a soft thud in the theater/gymnasium where people sitting on folding chairs began clapping and blowing their noses and wiping their eyes, and actors onstage bowed and smiled and felt shaken and very giddy. The people on the folding chairs went on clapping and clapping.

Suddenly the intercom system hummed to life, clicked on by someone in the superintendent's office way up the long linoleumed passage, in the main hall. A disembodied male voice issued out of the two speakers high on the wall at either side of the proscenium. "Attention. Attention."

Onstage, the cast stood motionless, still holding hands in a curtain call. In the gymnasium, people who had begun reaching for coats from the back of chairs halted, cocking their heads to give their good ear to the intercom speakers. What was this now, a reminder about the upcoming May Day celebration or the gymkhana at St. Bridget High School?

"Attention, ladies and gentlemen." The voice was slightly fuzzy but nevertheless perfectly audible. "Before you leave, you should know that the director of tonight's performance, Mr. Drew Davis, is a fairy." Pause. "A homosexual, if you prefer. Mr. Davis was dismissed by the school board of Clarkston, California, in 1944 for his perversion. Thank you for your attention and goodnight." Click.

Backstage someone had the presence of mind to close the curtain. The cast stood rooted, still clasping hands. Offstage, Sylvia Donaldson began weeping.

"For Christ's sake," Neddy finally swore, "what's going on?"

"Goddamn," Beverly hissed.

Sally sank down on a straight-back chair from the "ceme-tery." Actors and crews drifted about the stage, cursing, mutter-ing, asking questions no one answered. What did it mean? What was going on? Who'd been on the intercom?

"A fairy?" Katherine Albers asked, "what does that mean?" She looked from one to another of them. "Tell me. What's going on? Are they going to fire Mr. Davis?" Her face seemed to melt as silent tears spilled over the rim of her eyes.

Beverly, who had strayed offstage, now wandered back car-rying the bouquet of red roses the cast had bought for Drew Davis. "Where's Mr. Davis?"

Donald pushed aside the curtain and glanced about, search-ing for Sally. Crossing the stage, he took her arm. "Let's go home."

Standing around the living room as if it were a lobby, the family waited, Edna asking anyone who would listen, "How did some-thing like this happen? Doesn't the school board check a teacher's background?"

"Well, I don't know anything about it," Irmgard told her, "but Mr. Davis was here, in this very house, to dinner, and you'd never meet a nicer man."

Herb Elway suggested, "This is just some crackpot kid stunt. Some fellow who got a bad grade from Davis. It's a damned shame."

Sally hung up her coat and climbed the stairs.

"Who did it?" Irmgard asked. "And how did they get into the office?"

"It wouldn't be hard getting into the office," Donald told his mother. "It's on the first floor. The janitors started taking the storm windows off this week. Any decent-size kid could climb in if a window was left unlocked."

"Well, this has taken the wind out of me," Edna said, dropping onto a wing chair. "I feel . . . a little sick. Can you imagine someone like that teaching young boys?"

Irmgard recalled Mr. Davis the night he'd come to dinner. When she'd asked whether the war had taken him to California, he'd replied, "No. Sorry to say, I wasn't able to serve."

"Dear me," she said suddenly. "Dear me."

Sally closed the door and, in the dark, crept onto the bed.

If she'd dropped out of the play, this—this would never have happened. Although Cole had muffled his voice, she had recognized it.

Where had Mr. Davis disappeared? Had he gone to his apartment? To Mr. Lundeen's house?

Was Mr. Davis a homosexual?

If he was, had Mr. Lundeen known? Was he . . . ?

How many people were going to be hurt because she hadn't dropped out of the play?

She would like to crawl into a box and lock the lid after herself.

Seeing no light beneath Sally's door, Donald and the grandparents each in turn used the bathroom and went along to bed, without saying good-night. Ruefully, each recalled forgetting to tell her how wonderfully she'd played her part.

Sally woke at five, after two hours of sleep. She rose and sloughed off the *Our Town* costume. Shivering, she yanked on a pair of jeans and a sweater and stepped into loafers. With a dishrag she scrubbed makeup off at the kitchen sink, scouring her skin raw, then tossed the rag aside and grabbed a jacket from the hooks beside the backdoor.

Outside, the sky had begun to pale in the east. Where snow had fled, leaving the world nude and fragile, a thin silvery rime frosted the faded grass. Along either side of the street, wisps of chimney smoke spiraled upward like escaping souls.

Hugging the jacket close, Sally tramped aimlessly in the thirty-degree morning, at one point standing atop Bacal's Hill and looking down at Harvester. She thought about Grover's Corners, New Hampshire, where Simon Stimson, the choirmaster, had been a drunk.

In Grover's Corners the problem of someone being homosexual hadn't come up. Did that mean Grover's Corners had no homosexual? If one had lived there, what would have happened to him?

When she'd first heard about homosexuals—from Beverly?—the idea had been repellent, upsetting, the way learning about sex between men and women had been or, before that, learning about French-kissing.

Every new thing she'd learned about sex had disgusted her, but eventually she'd come to see, or feel, the unextraordinariness of most of it.

She was certain, without knowing why, that she would never want to kiss another girl in *that* way, but she could half imagine that some girls in the world might. What was the difference between her and them? What was the difference between, say, Mr. Navarin and Mr. Davis? If Mr. Davis was a homosexual. If he was, the world knew it now.

Thanks to her.

At seven o'clock Sunday morning Drew Davis delivered a letter of resignation to Superintendent Engel. Although the superintendent was relieved, he was sorry for the man. Closing the front door after the speech teacher, he spent the morning staring into the maw of a scrubbed-out living room fireplace.

After delivering the letter, Davis and Laurence Lundeen packed Davis's things. Laurence drove the truck belonging to Lundeen's Dry Goods up to the curb in front of Eggers' Drug Store and together the two men loaded it.

Trudging back down Bacal's Hill, Sally wandered past St. Boniface where folks were chanting, "Kyrie eleison." She stood for a moment listening.

"Lord, have mercy. Christ have mercy," the voices murmured.

Soon after, she found herself in front of the school. Sitting down on one of the icy stone steps, she wrapped her arms around her legs, hugging them to her.

Down there, to the left, on the east side of Main Street, Lundeen's truck was parked in the cold gray of early morning, Mr. Lundeen and Mr. Davis loading it.

Nothing moved except the two men and the sparrows in the gutter in front of the Majestic, pecking for popcorn. Half a dozen grackles flew down from their perch atop the front of the drugstore, routing the sparrows and strutting along the curb.

Now Mrs. Stillman appeared from around the corner of

Rabel's Meat Market, wearing a dun colored felt cloche and navy blue coat, on her way to nine o'clock Mass. But, no. First she was coming up the street toward the truck, calling to Mr. Lundeen and Mr. Davis as she drew near them.

Sally could not hear. The three were too far away, and the truck stood between her and the conversation. Then Mrs. Stillman made her way back in the direction from which she'd come, definitely off to Mass this time.

What should *she* do? Sally wondered. She must say good-bye to Mr. Davis. Then again, maybe he wanted to be left alone, to put Harvester behind him without the pain or humiliation of good-byes. Maybe she should write to him.

At noon, when Mr. Davis and Laurence Lundeen broke off their work to head toward Mrs. Stillman's, Sally rose from the steps and ran down the sidewalk. Reaching the street, she called, "Wait!"

But the Elway Cadillac drew up in front of her, and Edna jumped out of the passenger side.

"We've been sick with worry," she said. "Look at you . . . no scarf or gloves! You'll have pneumonia. Get in the car."

A block away, Drew Davis and Laurence Lundeen turned the corner out of sight.

Drew Davis left town that day, after having lunch with Mr. Lundeen at Mrs. Stillman's apartment. Mr. Davis and Laurence Lundeen carted Mr. Davis's belongings to St. Paul where they placed them in storage.

On Friday, Sally left school immediately after her last class, hurrying directly home as she had each day that week.

At a quarter past four Beverly called. She was crying, which alarmed Sally.

"Have you heard about Mr. Davis?" she wept.

"Heard what?"

"He's dead. Ran his folks' car into the Mississippi River."

Late the night before, Laurence Lundeen had received a long-distance call from Drew Davis's sister in St. Paul. Davis had been drinking at a bar in Mendota, and, on the way home in his parents' Studebaker, had missed a curve on the serpentine East Mississippi River Road, flying over an embankment and into the river.

Laurence moved among townspeople heedless of gossip or animus. He tended his garden, read his books, and played bridge with that tight little clasp of friends who could afford the association: Dr. and Mrs. White, whose innocence was so sophisticated, or their sophistication so innocent that maliciousness found no toehold in their lives; Ed Barnstable who cared so little for public opinion that no one in the village ever thought of taking Rex or Toby to St. Bridget to another vet—what was the point of punishing someone who took no note?—and the Navarins. Every town, after all, needed a good mechanic and a free librarian.

Although she did not play bridge, Helen Stillman was invited often to Laurence's house, sometimes for lunch, sometimes to sit on the screened back porch, drinking iced tea and enjoying the view of the garden.

On the Friday following Mr. Davis's death, when the speech class straggled in, the classroom looked as it had that afternoon before the final performance of *Our Town*, like a house whose owner has died suddenly, leaving a novel on the side table open to page 12, a coffee cup unwashed in the sink, and a letter stamped and addressed on the hall table.

The girls, except Sally, shuffled around, weeping, running reverent fingers over the piece of French tapestry; gazing long and unseeing at the review of *All About Eve* tacked to the bulletin board; staring out the same window from which Mr. Davis had stared down at Main Street as he searched for an errant thought. The boys slouched at their desks, scowling.

Mrs. Wall had been called in to substitute.

Sally sat with clasped hands resting on the desk, looking neither to right nor left, head high and expression horrified, as though she were looking over a wall at a scene of devastation.

After class, Beverly waylaid her to talk about Mr. Davis. Sally turned and raced away.

Every afternoon after school and all day on the weekends, Sally worked at home, scrubbing and dusting and vacuuming. She cleaned out closets, cupboards, and drawers.

"What's this about?" Donald asked.

She did not seem to understand the question but went on her way, dragging the ladder from the basement and washing the kitchen walls with Soilex.

The Senior Prom came and went with Sally nearly unaware. Graduation rehearsals began.

"You'll want a new dress, won't you? Don't girls usually buy a new dress for graduation?" Donald asked. Sitting at the kitchen table, bent over the morning paper, he noticed a Dayton's ad for girls' summer dresses.

Sally was scouring the sink. "I don't think so."

Donald would call Edna Elway. She knew about things like graduation dresses.

He recognized that Drew Davis's death had knocked the stuffing out of Sally. She wouldn't discuss college. She was making no plans. "What are you going to do?" he'd asked a couple of weeks back. She'd shrugged. He'd come close to yelling, "Get hold of yourself. People die. People even commit suicide, if that's what you think happened."

No clues emerged as to the identity of the person on the intercom, although speculation galloped up and down the streets: the names of a number of high school boys were bandied, as well as various unidentified strangers, no two answering the same description.

However intense, the theorizing was impersonal—what was the death of a fairy, after all? Surmisal was the pastime of those not close to Mr. Davis.

"Well, it was something, about that Davis person, wasn't it?" the Wheelers' neighbor Dagney Bensinger exclaimed as she stood at the fabric counter in Lundeen's, waiting for Alice Penny to wrap up a piece of blue cambric.

"Yes." Miss Penny tore a length of shiny brown paper from the wide roll, lay the cambric on it, and began folding the paper over the little parcel of fabric. From the tall spindle of string she drew what she needed and whipped it around the package this way, then that, with balletic grace and economy of motion.

"Don't knot the string, just tie a bow," Mrs. Bensinger told her. "I save it, and I don't want to have to cut it." String-saving, as a virtue, ranked somewhat above faith and hope.

"Can you figure that Engel, hiring a fairy? Think of it!"

Miss Penny, having written up the purchase and sent the sales slip and cash up the cable to the office, slid her pencil into her neat coif and stood waiting for the receipt and change. She did not like speaking ill of the dead, was in fact quite superstitious about it. In addition to that, Mr. Lundeen would not tolerate gossip in the store.

"I don't know much about it, I'm sure," she said, glancing out the window.

Sally, who had entered Lundeen's minutes earlier, looking to buy a half-slip, stood an aisle away, her rigid back turned to the conversation.

"From the start I didn't care for Davis," Dagney Bensinger continued, insensible to Miss Penny's discomfort. "That whole . . . whatcha-call 'em . . . Motleys business just hit me wrong. Maybe I'm odd, but I don't like people putting on airs and thinking they're movie stars. The Wheeler girl was one of 'em. Trying to be Somebody."

At mention of Sally Wheeler, Alice Penny was suddenly struck by a scene she remembered in Ready-to-Wear when Stella Wheeler had wept while her little girl inched away, hiding behind a table of boys' summer togs.

Now, forty-five and as neat and well-turned out as she'd been eleven years before, Alice Penny drew herself up and gazed along her nose at Dagney Bensinger.

"I've never understood what was wrong with a person trying to be Somebody," she said.

Dagney Bensinger's chin shot up and her eyes narrowed. "'Pride goeth before a fall,'" she said, adding with meaning, "I'd say the Wheeler girl and the rest of them fell quite a ways from their movie-star days, wouldn't you?"

June 1 — 2, 1950

"What do you mean, you're not going to college?" Edna Elway pressed, trying to keep impatience out of her voice.

Thursday evening, the first of June, she sat on the bed in Sally's room, pinning seams, taking them in, as her granddaughter tried on the yellow organdy dress brought from Mankato, an elegantly simple frock with a flaring gored skirt, smooth little cap sleeves, scoop neck, and a fitted bodice with tiny ball-shaped buttons marching down the front to a narrow, belted waist.

She'd brought plain low-heeled white kid pumps as well. Sally was really too tall for high heels.

"How tall are you now, dear?"

"Five feet nine."

Well, it was perhaps a little too tall, but the child was nonetheless beautiful.

"You must *think* about college," Edna went on. "You may not be in the mood just now, but really, you must think about it. Granddad would buy you a little car to drive back and forth if you wanted to go to Gustavus Adolphus where your mother and father went and live with Granddad and me in Mankato. Of course, you could live in a dormitory, too, if you preferred. I'm sure Granddad would still buy you the car so you could come visit on weekends."

Edna wanted to have Sally at Gustavus Adolphus in St. Peter.

St. Peter held unhappy memories of course, but it was close, and Edna couldn't bear the idea of Sally going off to Northwestern or Stanford or some place like that.

"Why do I have to think about going to college if I'm not *going* to college?" Sally unbuckled the little cloth belt, pulled down the zipper in the side seam, and began easing the dress up over her head.

"Careful of the pins. Don't scratch yourself. I'll press it later so it'll be ready for tomorrow night," Edna told her, rising to take the dress from Sally and fetch the padded satin hanger. "Well, because you're going to change your mind later when everybody else leaves for college, and you're left behind in this little whistle-stop."

"Thank you for the dress, Grandma. It's beautiful," Sally said without enthusiasm, handing over the garment. Despite the warmth of the evening, she reached for the old blue chenille robe.

"You know Graddad will pay your way to school. Donald won't be hard up if you go, so don't worry about that. And we could have good times in Mankato, you and I. You could learn to play golf . . ." She was running out of arguments and on the verge of weepiness. Well, she wouldn't let that happen. "I'd be tickled pink if you were close. You'd be my little girlfriend." She laughed. "Well, not my *little* girlfriend. My tall girlfriend." She was beginning to sound absolutely dizzy, she knew, but she was desperate. "Would you like to make fudge later?"

"Thank you, Grandma, but I'm really tired tonight. I think I'll go to bed early."

"Well, that's probably best. Tomorrow night will be late." Forgetting about the pins, she arranged the yellow dress on the hanger, crushing it to her as if it were Sally herself.

Sally and Stella were different in many ways, but oh, dear God, weren't they alike too?

"I don't see what's so bad about Sally not going to college this fall," Irmgard Wheeler said, passing cards during a game of pinocle. "She could work for a year and then go to college, couldn't she?"

"Why waste a year working?" Edna demanded. "And you know as well as I do that young people who say they're going to work for a year end up never going to college. I've seen it happen too many times."

"Well, there's still time for her to change her mind."

But Edna felt thwarted and half hysterical with the need to see Sally in college in St. Peter.

Upstairs, Sally sat beside the open window. How many nights had she hovered here, scanning the street below for a vehicle with *Barnstable's* written on the side?

She had been as addicted to Cole as people were said to be to dope. She'd felt a constant physical wanting. Never again. Look where it had led.

The night grew cool, and she closed the window. In bed, she studied the dark concavity of sky as, one by one, pin pricks of light appeared in it. Off there to the left, they formed a connect-the-dots portrait: short, straight nose, brows arched with irony, a thatch of coarse hair, mouth wry, eyes sad.

Mr. Davis.

Their flowery summer skirts and lightweight trousers wet with perspiration and glued to metal folding chairs, the audience in the gymnasium awaited the strains of "Pomp and Circumstance," fanning pink faces with graduation programs and remarking that they couldn't recall a warmer June 2.

When the graduating seniors had taken their places in rows of chairs on the stage where the temperature had climbed to ninety-five or six, Reverend Gordon offered the invocation.

The guest speaker, a professor of history from Augustana

College in Sioux Falls, South Dakota, intoned grave words about the Brave New World and the United Nations and television, which challenged people to shoulder the responsibility of World Citizenship as it brought them images from the four corners of the globe. Few in Harvester, aside from the Alberses and Laurence Lundeen, had a television set, so the rest could only surmise how a TV would challenge them to shoulder the responsibility of World Citizenship.

Katherine Albers gave the valedictory speech, a poignant farewell to childhood that left Sally pondering whether Katherine had ever known a real childhood.

Then Neddy, salutatorian, was speaking of tolerance and broadening the inner horizon. In closing, he mentioned the loss he felt at the death of a special teacher, Drew Davis, who had taught him to look at learning as both a treasure-house of personal pleasure and a doorway to charity and understanding.

When they'd returned the black robes and mortarboards to boxes in the home ec room, the graduates joined family and friends in the gymnasium where next year's senior boys were wisking away the folding chairs, returning them, collapsed, to the long racks that had been rolled out of the equipment room.

Hairdos and best summer dresses wilting, next year's senior girls tied fancy little ruffled aprons around each other's waists, set out punch bowls and platters of cookies, and began to serve refreshments.

In Harvester, no rite was observed, no event validated, without "refreshments," be they as humble as Kool-Aid and Fig Newtons. Refreshments were something you could do with your hands besides jingle the change in your pockets or clasp and unclasp the catch on your purse. And refreshments were connected, however dilutedly, to the corn, rye, and wheat fields lapping at the village walls. Farmers grew refreshments, that was the sense people had.

Grasping a paper cup of punch and an arrowroot cookie, Sally threaded her way toward Donald and the grandparents who were standing near the open double doors looking expectantly toward the park across the street, as if a breeze had been promised from that quarter.

With his Speed Graphic, Mr. Hardesty from the *Standard Ledger* lolloped along among the throng, aiming his lens and snapping "informal moments" for next week's edition. Although this was the twenty-sixth Harvester High graduation he'd covered, he regaled folks with the same tired jokes in the same corny, overwrought delivery as the first time, in 1924. People laughed or smiled at the hoary silliness of the stories, and Mr. Hardesty snapped their picture. The camera didn't care why you smiled.

He swooped down on Sally and her family. "All right, now, folks, say 'cheese, please, fleas, or sneeze.' As you can plainly see, there ain't no 'breeze.'" A click and a flash and he was gone.

Donald and the grandparents hugged and congratulated Sally. Grandma Elway wiped Sally's wet brow with her hankie, and Grandma Wheeler said it was a pity in this weather that she had to wear nylons.

Katherine Albers floated across the gymnasium, asking Sally as she drew near, "You're coming to my house, aren't you?"

Sally glanced at her family, feeling trapped. She had not planned to go to the party at Katherine's, but now the grandmothers would worry and fuss if she didn't.

"Yes," she told Katherine, handing her diploma and tassel to Donald.

"Run along and have a good time," Grandma Elway said.

"You're only young once," Grandma Wheeler called after her.

The impressive three-car garage behind Katherine's house, so scrubbed it looked new, was strung with crepe paper and nosegays of balloons. At one end, a picnic table groaned with soda pop, hot dogs and hamburgers, potato chips, potato salad, homemade peanut-butter cookies, and a bakery cake splashed with mortarboards and tassels of icing and the word *Congratulations!* On a portable phonograph, Nat "King" Cole's "Mona Lisa" was playing.

Mr. and Mrs. Albers stood by the table with Neddy's parents, greeting guests as they arrived. Pale, thin, and elegant as a new moon, wearing a two-piece dress of soft, shimmery ice blue fabric, Velia Albers smiled her closedmouth smile and looked through her guests' heads to what Sally thought must be a glacial landscape.

Hearty and proud, Reggie Albers stood beside Katherine, now and then whispering something in her ear and laughing his jackhammer laugh.

"Number One," he bellowed, squeezing her. "Carleton snapped her up like she was Miss Einstein. Could've gone anywhere, written her own ticket, but I said, 'Honey, your old man's gonna be mighty lonesome if you go all the way out to Stanford or Sarah Lawrence.'"

Katherine smiled dutifully.

Brenda Barnstable, already tanned from spring golf, fondled her genuine gold charm bracelet and searched the room for someone to whom she could recount her afternoon on the fairway. Glancing at her watch, she calculated how soon she could reasonably plead a headache and ask Ed to take her home. She'd like a seven-and-seven, but of course it wouldn't be right for a chaperone in front of the kids, although she knew very well that half of them drank.

Maybe when they went into the house and left the kids alone, Reg would serve drinks, although Reg's drinks, except the ones he mixed for himself, were so weak they tasted like mistakes. Well, all she really wanted was something cool. She had to be up early tomorrow and ready to tee off with Denise at eight. What would she do without Denise and Hal?

Brenda's eyes swept around the Albers' garage as she recalled her own graduation party at the Minikahda Club, that sweet old country club perched above Lake Calhoun in Minneapolis. How had she ended up in this one-horse dump?

Where *was* Ed? There, talking to that strange Wheeler girl. What in God's name did he find to talk to her about? She was perversely detached and almost never smiled. A watcher. Made you nervous. The eyes just watched their way right into you. She had good posture, you had to give her that. Most girls as tall as that would be stoop-shouldered. Obviously she had a good opinion of herself, the way she held her head.

Brenda was thankful that Neddy had never gotten really interested in her. When they were little, she'd been concerned. He'd seemed worshipful. But in high school he'd had the good sense to date Katherine. Katherine was odd enough, but at least there wasn't insanity in the family.

Across the room, Ed Barnstable had asked Sally what her plans were.

"I haven't any," she said.

He laughed. "At least you're honest."

"College would be a waste of money."

He looked sideways.

"I don't want to be a teacher or a nurse. If I want to read books, I can go to the library."

"Isn't there something you like to do, something that makes you happy?"

He noticed the patches of shadow beneath her eyes, the weariness in her glance, the effort she seemed to expend responding to his interest.

"You were excellent in *Our Town*," he told her.

Our Town. Mr. Barnstable hadn't recognized Cole's voice on the intercom, that was obvious.

Minutes later Neddy appeared at Sally's elbow. "Dance?"

The song was nearly ended. After spinning her away, Neddy pulled her close to him. "Sally?"

Her breast heaved with dread.

"We have to talk about Mr. Davis," he said.

"No!" Letting go his hand, she ran and didn't stop till she was halfway home.

The grandparents left Monday morning without further discussion of Sally and college. Herb Elway had warned his wife that if she went on about school, she'd only set Sally against it for good. It galled Edna to leave with things up in the air. She hadn't even extracted a promise from Sally to spend the month of July in Mankato.

Beverly, who was going to the University of Minnesota in the fall, had agreed to work for Mr. Eggers again, and Neddy, who would be off to Princeton in September, was helping his dad in the veterinary office. Sally labored at home.

But Donald insisted that she help him celebrate his June 14 birthday by having dinner at the hotel in St. Bridget, then seeing *Born Yesterday* with Judy Holiday at the Lyceum. He wore his best blue summer slacks, a blue and white seersucker jacket, and a white shirt.

"Want to find some music on the radio?" he asked. He'd had a car radio installed a while back, thinking it might please Sally. But she rarely drove.

"No, I don't think so," she said, rolling her window down another three or four inches, letting the rushing air cool her face and tangle the tiny loose curls that gathered around her brow.

The sun still blazed above the horizon as they left the Dodge on the square and crossed the street to the St. Bridget Hotel.

The hotel air-conditioning made Donald feel prosperous and not quite himself, and he rebuttoned the top button of his shirt, adjusted his tie, and ordered a manhattan while he waited for the chicken Kiev.

"Is that a Grandma Elway special?" he asked, referring to the sundress Sally was wearing.

She nodded. "Grandma thinks I'll break out in a rash if I don't have the latest 'frock.'"

Although Donald did most of the talking during dinner, Sally responded with nods and little skewed smiles. Over dessert she gave him his present, Samuel Flagg Bemis's *John Quincy Adams and the Foundations of Foreign Policy*, which he had two or three times mentioned.

As they emerged into the heat of the sunset, Donald was relieved: the opportunities in a darkened movie theater for the occasion to be spoiled were surely limited.

Sally laughed several times during the movie, and Donald was looking forward to talking about it on the ride back to Harvester. Then, as the crowd poured out into the lobby, someone hailed Sally.

She spun around, stopping so abruptly that the couple behind them nearly ran her down.

Twenty feet away Cole Barnstable stood by a "Coming Attractions" board.

Sally stood perfectly still for long seconds, her face devoid of expression or recognition. Finally, Donald took her arm and led her out to the street.

She woke at four-thirty unable to remember anything after Cole's calling her name in the lobby of the Lyceum. The drive home and what came after that were a blank. She looked to see what she was wearing. A plissé nightgown.

At five she got up and began again to clean.

In the twilight that evening she emptied wastebaskets into the trash barrel by the garage and set a match to the refuse.

Standing back, she watched the smoke rise as the papers caught. Cleaning out and burning the leavings and clutter were part of scraping life down to a pure, cold, smooth bone.

When the fire was leaping, she threw Cole's note into it:

Dear Sally, Thank you for the scarf. I like it and wear it every day. It looks great with my tan jacket. Old Bob who lives next door said, 'You can trust a girl who knits for you.' Is that true???? Thirty-three more days. Cole.

The edges of the paper turned brown, shrank, shriveled, then writhed and burst into flame. Sparks like diamond chips rose up the lavender sky.

The wallet-sized picture went next, and finally, reaching into the pocket of her skirt, she pulled out the silver identification bracelet with the heart charm. She looked at it lying in a glittery little heap in her palm, at last tossing it into the fiery barrel.

With long arms flung across her chest, she threw her head back and rocked on her heels, wringing out a kind of strangled keen.

The day came when Sally could find nothing more to clean, so she mowed the lawn, trimmed hedges, and weeded what was left of long-neglected perennial beds. Then she asked Donald to buy paint so that she could begin work on the siding, a job they'd put off until the house was shabby and gray.

Rising early, she and Donald scraped, sanded, and primed the clapboard and trim until the sun was high and hot. Then, while he put the tools away in the garage and soaked the brushes in turpentine, Sally made lunch.

During the hot afternoons when her father would not allow her to paint clapboard, Sally began to clean again, finding new tasks—airing mattresses and washing and ironing curtains.

The little Royal portable typewriter Grandma and Grandpa Wheeler had given her for graduation remained in its case, unused, the satin bow and card still tied to the handle.

On June 25 an army from Communist North Korea invaded South Korea, and within a few weeks, American boys were being drafted to fight for the United Nations in South Korea. Delmore Preuss enlisted, but two or three young men from the graduating class, who would otherwise have gone to work on farms or under the grease rack at the Chevrolet garage, opted for college to stay out of the draft.

Around the time of the North Korean invasion, Katherine Albers and her mother left unexpectedly on an extended trip to Europe, renting a house in Dorset after spending three weeks on the Continent. "Well, they can afford it" was what most people said, and "Katherine's been working hard on her studies. Valedictorian, she was, after all." The trip occasioned more than the usual talk, simply because no one from Harvester, except soldiers, had been to Europe since before World War II.

Although Katherine wrote many postcards to her friends from Dorset, the cards were not overly newsy, and no one really knew what Mrs. Albers and Katherine were *doing* there. Why would you plunk down in England to do something you could as well be doing at home?

Sally received a card showing a quaint village with flower-filled front gardens. "Our village looks like this," the card read. And "I'm reading P.G. Wodehouse. Mother's choice. She says I'm too serious."

Another card, this of seaside cliffs, said, "Have you seen the ocean, Sally? It's wide and gray and rough. Like life, right? Haha." Sally stuck this one in the frame of her bureau mirror.

One day soon after Katherine had left for Europe, Beverly pulled into the Wheeler's drive when she got off work at Eggers'. Slamming the door of the '46 Chevie Elwood and Rose had given her for graduation, she bounced up the back walk.

"Hello?" she called through the screen door.

Sally had finished the dishes after an early supper while Donald walked downtown to buy a magazine. "Yes?" she said and turned from the stove where she was wiping around the burners and knobs with the dishrag.

Beverly opened the screen door and flounced in, flopping down at the table. "How the hell are you? Haven't seen you since the night they let us out of prison."

"I'm busy, you know, helping Dad."

"What doing?"

"Lots of stuff." She wiped the counters.

Beverly nodded. "Wanta go to the Dakota Ballroom? Cliff Keyes is playing."

"Not tonight."

"God, woman, you *are* antisocial. This is all mixed up with that shit Cole Barnstable, isn't it?"

Sally said nothing, but wiped down the refrigerator door.

"And Mr. Davis? Is it to do with him, too?"

"Why do you ask that?"

Although she couldn't see Sally's face, Beverly knew from the tone of her voice that she'd struck a nerve. Eyes narrowed, she said, "Tell me."

"It isn't anything to do with him," Sally said with annoyance.

"Look," Beverly told her, still talking to Sally's back, "you can lie till the cows come home, but that won't make it truth." She rose to leave. "We've been friends as long as I can remember, but I'm tired of getting pushed aside and lied to whenever you're down in the dumps. You're like a damned closed-up fist, and everybody's supposed to understand because it's Sally, the One Whose Mother Was Crazy. Well, you know what? We *all* had an unhappy childhood. What makes you so special?" She slammed the door on her way out.

Sally tossed a couple of bedspreads down the clothes chute. When she'd stuffed them into the Maytag along with Oxydol and warm water, she stared around her at the basement.

Hauling the Hoover and its attachments down the stairs, she began sorting through boxes of old clothes, piles of magazines, cans of paint that had turned to stone. Now and then she paused and cocked her head on one side as if listening.

By the shelves of Grandma Wheeler's preserves, beneath boxes of empty mason jars, was Stella's trunk, unopened since she'd left Harvester in the backseat of the Elway car.

Frowning, Sally hefted paint cans and climbed the stairs.

During the next days, she laundered the few rag rugs dotting the basement floor, then scrubbed the floor and walls and the stairs leading up to the kitchen. When she had dry-mopped away the cobwebs from between the joists overhead, she washed all the empty fruit jars and packed them, wrapped in newspaper, in cardboard boxes. With a damp, soapy cloth, she wiped off the shelves of preserves, then the preserve jars themselves, careful not to loosen the labels. The top of Stella's trunk was fussily cleaned and afterward buffed with a dry cloth.

No spot was too obscure or unlikely for Sally's dust cloth and damp rag. The furnace and water heater did not escape. Nor Donald's workbench.

And when the basement shone and smelled of bleach and ammonia, it was time to begin again on the bedrooms . . .

Donald's blood chilled when he recalled the manic cleaning Stella had once done.

Neddy, who was working in his dad's office for the summer, called Sally the morning she began waxing her bedroom furniture.

Donald insisted she take the call.

"I've got a problem," Neddy told her.

Sally said nothing.

"The town council voted to have a program in the park the night before Harvester Days."

When Sally did not respond, he went on, "They're going to have a band concert and some kind of show . . . they don't know what they want, only that they want it. Sylvia Donaldson'll sing 'Bali Ha'i'" he said dryly, "and her sister Marilyn'll twirl her baton. The girls from Martha Beaverton's Tap and Toe'll do their 'Yankee Doodle' number. The usual. They want the Motleys to do something. I told 'em I didn't know if I could get a group together. Katherine's in England; Leroy's uncle died down in Iowa, and he's gone there to farm till the crops are in. That leaves us rag-tag and bobtail." He paused. "Sally? You still there?"

"I can't do it."

"Why?"

"I . . . just can't." Her voice traveled light years to reach him.

"Think about it, Sally. Just think about it for a couple of days. I'll call you on Friday."

"I can't . . ."

"Think about it."

Sally wiped up her bedroom, then found the Johnson's paste wax under the kitchen sink and began rubbing a thin film on the floor with an old sock.

When he called Friday evening, Neddy asked, "Have you thought about the show?"

369

"I can't."

"Why?"

"I'm not going to talk about it. I'm sorry."

At length Neddy asked, "Could you write a sketch? We need new material." He waited for her to respond, and when she didn't, he said, "I'll call you on Monday."

"No."

"I'll talk to you on Monday."

Saturday, Sally waxed and buffed the furniture in Donald's room and the guest room. Sunday, she washed clothes, ironed, and mended.

Rolling back the carpet in Donald's room on Monday morning, she wiped and waxed and buffed the floor there. At one-thirty, when the furniture was in place again and the carpet vacuumed, Sally stood barefoot in the bedroom doorway, mopping perspiration from her forehead with the hem of her blouse.

Downstairs Donald answered the door and called to her, "Neddy's here." When she did not answer or appear, he called peremptorily, "Sally!"

Neddy stood up, trying not to stare. Sally's curly hair stood out from her head like a dirty bush. The hand thrusting it back from her face was red and sore. Her blue jeans were hooked over her hipbones. And the feet protruding were like the feet in an El Greco print Mr. Davis had tacked up on the wall in his class, flesh melted, pale bluish skin stretched over bone.

"Sally."

She hesitated at the bottom of the stairs, a look of tired perplexity on her face.

"Have a chair," he said as though she were the guest.

She sat on the sofa, tucking her feet up beside her.

"I came over to talk about the program for Harvester Days." Now that he saw her, he didn't know what to say. "I know you're really busy. I won't stay long. But maybe you'd like to hear . . . you know, the plans."

He sat down again on the wing chair where Donald had left

him. "I guess I told you there'll be a band concert. I'm trying to come up with a sketch or a couple of sketches for the Motleys, well, those of us who're in town."

"I can't."

"That's okay. Don't worry. I'm pushing a few ideas around on paper. It'll work out."

She seemed to relax.

"Whatever the Motleys do, it'll be dedicated to Mr. Davis."

"Mr. Davis?"

"What d'ya think?"

She nodded.

"Beverly likes the idea, too. We're gonna bust our brains to come up with something special. The problem is being so damned short of personnel. But we'll do it. I'm not worried. If you get any ideas, though, would you let us know?"

Mr. Davis. Again Sally nodded.

After Neddy left, Sally cleaned out the medicine chest and wiped up the bathroom floor. When she had scrubbed the sink and toilet, she ran water in the tub. Shrugging out of her clothes, she dropped them down the laundry chute and climbed into the bath.

Lying back against the rim of the tub, she closed her eyes. Mr. Davis's face emerged in the aqueous gray behind her lids, the flax-flower eyes floating like pale twin moons, gazing unblinkingly into her head.

The next day the temperature at 11 A.M. hovered around ninety-five. Sally cleaned the garage with the same fierceness she'd given the basement.

At 9 P.M., she fell into a slumber so deep, she was buried beneath the sand in the deepest trough of the ocean. There Mr. Davis in a harlequinade costume and makeup led her through dark vastnesses where heavy draperies hung from the sky, and she lost her way and found it again, lost Mr. Davis and found him again.

As a predawn breeze bellied the curtains, she floated up into a dream-empty sleep and woke later without remembering Mr. Davis in harlequinade. But she reached for a notepad from beside the bed and tried to sketch his face. With no facility for sketching, she soon gave it up and lay doodling the odd word or phrase that came to her head.

By four o'clock that afternoon she'd finished the garage, going on to wash and wax the car, Hoovering and dusting the interior, sorting out the glove compartment, and vacuuming the trunk.

When she was returning the scrub pail and rags to the basement, Donald called down, "All right, that's *enough* for today. We're going for a drive in the clean car. No argument."

He drove around town, then turned south into the country on Highway 14, observing, "I'll bet the farmers can hear the corn growing these hot nights."

When they reached the St. Bridget road, he swung left, in the opposite direction and turned again, south, onto a township road. And so they drove, up and down dusty country lanes, past farms sleek with the prosperity of continuing postwar demand.

Headed back toward Harvester, Donald pulled in at Bussey's Corner and parked under the cottonwoods. He knew better than to ask if Sally wanted anything. When he returned to the car, he handed her a bottle of Nesbitt's and strolled through the rough grass to a fence beyond which rows of thigh-high corn waved green pennants.

Sally followed.

"Your mother and I used to stop here for pop when we were first married. I couldn't tell you how many times we sat at that table over there or stood here under the trees, drinking root beer and making plans."

He paused, giving Sally a chance to respond. When she didn't, he went on, "You look so much like her, standing there. She wasn't quite as tall, and her hair was a little straighter, but otherwise the resemblance is remarkable."

He drank from his root beer. "In those days she still laughed a lot. And she could be silly, goofy. And idealistic."

He leaned against a gnarled gray fence post, casting a side-long glance at Sally. "In many ways you're like her. And yet, you're essentially different. You're much tougher, for one thing. Which is meant as a compliment."

Sally sat down in the grass. He wouldn't turn to look at her because he might lose his nerve. Sally could do that to you.

"You live by a very rigid code. I haven't a notion what it is or where you got it. Sometimes I think you made it up, like some absolute monarch. Like the Empress of One Hundred." He grinned. "But you're the Empress of One."

Turning at last, he said, "Just remember, a good monarch is compassionate."

At 2 A.M., Sally padded downstairs and sat in darkness beside the kitchen window. Stillness covered everything: trees did not whisper, no radio played, no cars thrummed along Highway 14, no child cried "Everybody in free!" One ought to be able to hear the war, Sally thought.

The screen door creaked as she pushed it open and crept outside. At the bottom of the back steps she stood staring at the sky. Yes, it was there. Mr. Davis's face, looking down, sad and expectant.

Closing her bedroom door again, she flicked on the lamp. Reaching for the notepad, she lay doodling as she had on the previous night.

"Sense. Nonsense. Sensible. Making Sense. Kingdom of Making Sense. Empress of Making Sense. Kingdom of Making Sense."

She tore the page from the notebook and lay for minutes, pencil in hand, #2 lead touching blue-lined paper.

The pencil moved as if by itself, although of course it could not do that. But it moved. "Clown. Harlequinade costume. Vivid colors. Kings. Dull robes. (What kings?) King of Law. King of Philosophy. King of Science. Peregrina." Where had that name come from?

Sally reached for the dictionary on the lower shelf of the bedside table. "*Peregrine*. Coming from foreign places. Foreign. On a pilgrimage; on one's travels."

A little after four she fell asleep. The pencil rolled off the bed. The notebook slipped to the floor.

At ten she woke with a start, jumping out of bed and snatching on jeans and a shirt. She was going to mow the lawn today and dig up daylilies from the crowded beds. Then she heard the rain at the windows, heard the elms thrashing and creaking.

Now what would she do? The sky was dark and heavy. After pacing for several minutes, she decided to scrub the sofa and wing chairs with frothed-up Ivory flakes and old towels as she'd seen Grandma Wheeler do.

At five, Donald laid out an early supper of hot dogs and potato salad. The rain had moved on, and he opened the breakfast-nook window.

"You have to eat something," he told Sally.

"I'm not hungry, and I can dig lilies while the ground's still wet."

"You can dig lilies when you've eaten something."

With an injured sigh, she threw herself down on a chair, ate a tablespoon of salad, grabbed a hot dog, and slammed out the backdoor. The mosquitoes were savage after the rain, but she paid no attention.

By nine, she'd piled up a bushel basket of lilies to be replanted the next day along the south side of the house. When Donald saw her putting the basket and the spade in the garage, he climbed the stairs and ran a bath for her.

"You're filthy," he told her when she came in. "And wash your hair, too, while you're at it."

Although she seemed to take no note of him, she did close the bathroom door, and minutes later he heard the "swoosh" as she lowered herself into the tub.

She was in bed and asleep by nine-thirty, and awakened at three by the fire whistle. Slipping out of bed, she made her way into Donald's room and peered out the south windows down Third Avenue toward the firehouse to see the truck pull out when the volunteers arrived.

The whistle had blown only two or three shorts, so the fire wasn't anything serious. Still, the sight of the engine and the men answering the alarm always struck a painlike chord in her.

"With all the windows open," Donald said, propping himself up on his elbow, "the alarm sounds like it's next door."

Returning to her room, wide awake now, Sally found the pad and pencil on the floor and took them up again.

Tomorrow she would plant the lilies.

Planting the lilies took much longer than digging them up.
For one thing, the bulbs had to be separated. For another, the
ground along the south side of the house hadn't been spaded for
years and, despite the previous day's soaking rain, was com-
pacted and unyielding.

"Let me help with that digging," Donald offered.

"I'll do it."

"What if I drive out to the nursery and buy straw to mix in?"

She assented to get rid of him. Nearly the entire day she
worked on the lily bed in ninety degree heat, and when she finished the planting, he heard the clicking whir of the mower as
she pushed it back and forth across the yard.

At a quarter past five he carried a glass of iced tea out to the
garage. She was wiping grass from the mower blades and yanking it out of the axle. Perspiration ran down the sides of her face
and dripped from her jaws; her cheeks burned red.

"You'll have a heatstroke," he told her, setting the tea on the
concrete beside her.

She said nothing.

"I'm cooking a ring of bologna and heating sauerkraut.
Desiree Navarin sent home a bag of tomatoes. Come in and get
cleaned up."

At the dinner table she sat with her head propped on the
palm of one hand and started to doze off after a couple of bites
of bologna and sauerkraut.

"Go on up to bed," he told her, and for once, she obeyed. An hour later he called up the stairs, "I'm going to the movies." No response.

Returning at nine-thirty, he found her room dark and Sally asleep beneath the sheet. But at 2 A.M. when he got up to use the bathroom, she wasn't in her bed.

She wasn't in the living room or kitchen, but standing by the kitchen stove, he heard something in the basement and, opening the door, recognized the clicking of a typewriter.

Stella, too, had stayed up nights.

Sally had carried the bedside notebook to the basement, along with the portable typewriter and typing paper from Donald's office. On an old enamel-top table near the washing machine, she typed what she'd written the past several nights.

Again and again she wadded up a page, tossing it aside and inserting fresh paper. At five, when light streamed through windows high on the east wall of the basement, Sally was still bent over the machine, hair flying wildly from her head where she had clutched at it in frustration, face ashy and hollow, eyes bloodshot.

At eight, Donald tiptoed down and found her curled up asleep on a rag rug, a slim stack of typed pages on the table, a note on top.

Neddy—
  Bizarre sketch, maybe too strange for your show.

                        Sally

Later that morning, when she had dressed, Sally stuffed the manuscript into a manila envelope, addressed it to Neddy, and hiked over to Catalpa to drop it into the Barnstables' mailbox.

She spent the afternoon laundering all the table linens in the dining-room buffet. While damask tablecloths and napkins twitched on the clothesline, she dug the Wright's silver cream out of a kitchen drawer and sat at the dining-room table polishing flatware.

Donald had gone off to a planning session of the athletic staff at school, then stopped by the post office to pick up mail. By the time he arrived home, Sally had removed the wash from the line, sprinkled the linens, wrapped them in bath towels, and put them in the refrigerator. She was at the sink paring potatoes.

He tossed an envelope on the table. "From Lark Erhardt." He opened the refrigerator and took out a bottle of milk.

Sally finished paring, cutting up, and tossing the potatoes into a kettle of water before she wiped her hands and sat down at the table.

For several minutes she stared at the envelope without touching it. Picking it up, she held it away from her and turned it over once or twice, at last running a fingernail beneath the flap, and extracting a single-spaced, typewritten sheet.

Dear Sally,

I think it's been at least a year since I wrote you. Some great correspondent, huh? But this summer I haven't been able to get you out of my mind. Maybe that's because we both graduated from high school, and that sort of mile-stone makes a person think of old friends and wonder what their plans are.

What was your graduation like? Ours was freaky, as graduations mostly are. Some boring geezer from Omaha telling us that we were the hope of the future, just like some boring geezer told *him* that *he* was. And what did *his* generation do? Damned near blew us all to hell.

Afterwards, all the hopes of the future went out to the Blue Moon Ballroom and got drunk. That'll teach 'em to keep their hopes to themselves.

I'm working at J. C. Penney this summer, in yard goods and women's lingerie. It's about as exciting as trimming your toe nails, but I like it better than waiting tables at the Highway 64 Cafe which is what I did last summer. I couldn't face one more truck driver or tree trimmer or road construction cowboy who thought "Cry of the Wild Goose" by Frankie Laine was the highest form of the composer's art. They'd punch a whole quarter's worth of "Wild Goose" on the Select-O-Matic at one time, for Christ's sake.

Where are you going to college? I'm going to the U. Don't ask what I'm majoring in, because I don't know. English, I suppose. How about you?

Are you dating anyone in particular? Neddy Barnstable???? Now, why do I ask that, except that I always thought you would.

I told them at Penney's that I wanted a week off in August. Okay, here comes the hard part of this letter. Could I visit you? Some nerve, huh, inviting myself? It was between you and my Great-Aunt Prudence in Devil's Lake, North Dakota who has three yippy Chihuahuas and dropsy, so I thought I'd write you first.

If this isn't possible, I understand, but if it is, could I come the week of August 7? I've got more brass than a Chinese gong, right?

Let me know by yesterday at the latest.

Hi to Beverly, Mrs. Stillman, and your dad.

oxoxoxoxoxoxox,
Miss Lark Ann Browning Erhardt
Sales Clerk

In her bedroom, Sally tossed the letter on the bureau, then stood at the window, pleating and unpleating the dimity curtain. She had no strength for entertaining Lark. Entertaining Lark would be harder than transplanting lilies.

The six o'clock whistle blew as she slammed out the front door. With a wild, abstracted glumness, Sally tramped into the country, north on a graveled lane. Meadowlarks trilled and pitched themselves skyward, mourning doves cozied in along the fences. Sally moaned and huffed and ground her teeth.

"No," she muttered.

When Donald heard her return, he called, "Neddy telephoned. I told him you'd call when you got home."

But Sally didn't call. She ironed table linens.

The next day Sally cleaned the oven, then defrosted and wiped out the refrigerator. She was removing a pan of tepid water from the freezer compartment when Neddy opened the screen door and stuck his head in.

"Sally?" He let himself in.

Sally went about her work, dumping the water into the sink, filling the pan again with hot water from the teakettle, and returning it to the freezer compartment.

"We're going to use your sketch," he said, standing by the door. "It's a strange piece. But it's got possibilities. Now the trick is to find enough people to play the parts."

Sally wiped her hands on a tea towel. "Remember, it's dedicated to Mr. Davis. I mean, if Mr. Hardesty or anybody writes about the program, they should say that it's dedicated to Mr. Davis."

Easing herself between the sheets that night, Sally reached for a pad and pen from the table. With her left hand not knowing what her right hand was doing, she wrote, "Dear Lark . . ."

The next afternoon Neddy telephoned.

"I've got a problem," he told her. "I can't round up enough actors."

Sally said nothing.

"I need you to play Peregrina."

"No."

"If Katherine were here, I'd cast her, but she's not."

"Ask a junior."

"No. It's got to be somebody with experience."

"Ask Beverly."

"She's playing the King of Law."

"Sue Ann Meyers."

"She's the King of Medicine."

"Change the character to Peregrino and cast yourself."

"I've already cast myself as the Clown."

"I'm sorry, Neddy. I can't do it," she said and hung up.

He called back. "I know you're . . . busy. I wouldn't call if I wasn't desperate." He paused. "This is for Mr. Davis."

"Neddy . . . I." Writing the sketch was one thing. Acting would be another. Trying to Be Somebody.

Sally had laundered and mangled the bed linens that morning. They sat in a neat pile on the dining-room table. Stacking them on her arm, she carried them upstairs and slid them into the linen closet.

Walking through the rooms, she reconnoitered. Except for routine dusting, she could find no work. Her long, thin hands ran panicking through her hair.

She lay down on the bed, arms pressed to her sides. What would she think about all day, if not about work?

"I'm off to school," Donald said, standing at Sally's bedroom door.

"What for?"

"Equipment check before scrimmage starts next week." He pulled a slip of paper from his shirt pocket and tossed it on the bed. "We need groceries. Take the car." He turned to leave.

"You can't get them?"

"Can't make it before the store closes," he called over his shoulder.

"... But . . . ."

Sally had not been downtown for nearly two months. It felt small, shabby, and hostile. Unfamiliar. Like a place you might stop for a pack of cigarettes on your way to someplace else. Pulling up in front of Truska's, she sat in the car, willing herself to get out.

When Mr. Schimmel retired from tinsmithing, Truska's bought his small building on First Avenue behind their own and enlarged the grocery store. Now customers pushed carts down narrow aisles, gathering their own purchases.

Sally poked among the cans of Campbell's soup looking for cream of tomato. On the other side of this tall shelving a couple of women were nattering casually as they made their way down the next aisle. The voices were unknown to Sally, and she paid no attention until she caught the word *Lundeen.* Then she strained to hear.

One of the women was saying, "Well, I'm new here, of course, so I'm really not familiar . . ."

"Fred and I drove over from Ula on account of Fred's nephew was something in the show," the second woman confided. "Strange sort of show, no scenery, and the girl dies. But at the end, here comes this message over the loudspeaker, or whatever you call it. Everybody figured it was gonna be, you know, something about the prom or lunch money or something." Sally could not make out the next few sentences, but then a harsh, snorting laugh burst from the woman and the name Lundeen again.

Sally paid for the groceries and fled, Mrs. Truska calling after her, "The boy'll get them."

Backing away from the curb, she nearly crashed into the grille of a pickup, and a moment later she was slamming on the brakes as the Mathers' orange cat tore out from behind a car. The bags of groceries flew, and six of the dozen eggs broke.

Quaking with rage and some sense of failure, of cowardice, of letting down the side, Sally slammed things into the cupboard and refrigerator.

Hurling herself down on the sofa, she pulled her knees up and wrapped her arms around them. For half an hour she sat, picking lint from the upholstery. Twice she got up and started for the kitchen, twice returning. The third time, she reached the phone and lifted the receiver from its cradle.

"Neddy?"

Sally began at once to learn her lines, maniacally, consecrating herself to them, and not just to her own, but to everyone else's in the cast of "The Kingdom of Making Sense."

Although rehearsals would not begin until Monday, she conferred with Neddy almost hourly on a variety of concerns: music cues, prop list, changes in music cues, changes in prop list. Thoughts about costumes.

"How broad do you think we ought to play it?" she asked.

"Plenty. Lots of slapstick. And Peregrina should be like the Columbine character in the valentine sketch. Stylized. A dream figure. She's got to contrast with the Clown, don't you think?"

Saturday morning, climbing onto a stool at the fountain in Eggers' Drug Store, Sally told Beverly, "I need to talk to you about costumes."

Beverly carried a couple of dirty coffee cups to the sink and returned with a rag to wipe off the counter. "You want to order something?"

"Coffee and a doughnut?"

Beverly shrugged and moved along, wiping the counter as she went.

"I'm sorry you're mad at me."

Beverly set the doughnut and cup of coffee in front of Sally and shoved the cream toward her. "Mad? Not exactly. Fed up."

"What's the difference?"

"Mad is when somebody does something stupid and you say, 'Hey, stupid, stop doing that.' Fed up is when somebody's been doing the same stupid thing over and over, and you say, 'Hey, stupid, I've had it. Good-bye.'"

She pulled a box of straws out of a cupboard and refilled the nearly empty jar on the counter, continuing, "There're people who only come around when they're in trouble and want a shoulder to cry on."

Grabbing up a menu, she returned it to the wire holder. "Then, there's you. You only come around when everything's hunky-dory. When they're not, I don't hear from you."

The ceiling fan spun slowly, determinedly, churning buttermilk air. An oscillating table-fan on a shelf behind the fountain played with the tiny strands of Beverly's hair that had worked loose from her ponytail, lifting them, allowing them to fall, lifting them again.

Mr. Rabel came in from the meat market next door, swung onto a stool at the opposite end of the fountain, and ordered a root beer and a Bismarck. When Beverly had served him, she told Sally, "I did some costume drawings for Neddy. You'll have to ask him to show them to you."

Sally nodded. "Lark's coming to visit."

Beverly snatched up a dish towel and dried a couple of tall glasses, returning them to a tray beside the malted-milk machine.

"I'd like to be somebody who comes to you when things are bad, Beverly, if that's what you want, but you were right before, I'm a closed-up fist."

Neddy was directing, and rehearsals were held in the evening in the Barnstables' garage, which, like the Wheelers' in Worthington, had once been a barn.

The sketch ran between fifteen and twenty minutes, fifteen when everyone picked up his cues. Sally was line-perfect from the first night and impatient with anyone who wasn't.

"Sue Ann, for God's sake, you've only got six lines. How can you forget them?"

"Some of us have *jobs*," said Sue Ann, who was working full-time at the Water and Power Company and likely to be twenty years hence.

"Let me worry about the lines," Neddy told Sally.

But Sally couldn't. "I'm happy to run lines with anyone who needs it," she offered.

When she saw Beverly's costume sketches, she wanted to know, "Why is my costume gray? All the kings are in maroon. I should be wearing something brighter. Maybe sapphire blue."

"You're wearing gray to indicate your state of mind and the seriousness of your quest," Beverly told her. "Only the Clown should be in bright colors because he's got the secret of happiness. . . ."

"Well, I absolutely disagree . . ."

Saturday, August fifth, Sally drove Donald's car to the depot to meet the midafternoon train from the west. Parked in the dusty lot, she played nervously with the steering wheel, twisting it, left, right, left, right.

Hearing the train whistle at the crossing a mile west of town, she hit the wheel lightly with her damp palms in a gesture of resignation and glanced at her reflection in the rearview mirror.

Shrugging her shoulders and squaring them, she opened the car door and slid out, giving the back of her cotton skirt a shake and smoothing the fullness of it over her hips.

Deep breaths, now, from 'way down, 'way down in the diaphragm. Deep breaths.

Standing on the blistering brick platform, Sally watched the conductor hand Lark down. She was pert like her mother, with quick, eager movements. And she looked like Mrs. Erhardt, only shorter. Standing beside her, Sally felt custodial.

They covered their strangeness with empty observation, searching for a firm spot of familiarity on which to stand.

"You're even prettier than your mother," Lark told Sally, while privately noting that Sally was gaunt and unhealthy looking.

"Thanks." Sally grabbed Lark's suitcase. "The train was on time."

"Yes."

"Over here. I've got dad's car."

"The weather's warm, isn't it?"

"It's been a warm summer. Blue Lake?" Sally tossed the bag in the trunk of the car.

"There too."

Hand on the car door, Lark suddenly swung around, crossing to a depot window, cupping her hands around her eyes, and peering in. Here was where her mother had carved out a little apartment years ago. This was where the bedroom had been and the crib she'd slept in right up to the day they left.

"I guess I half expected to see my crib," she said without turning away. "No one lives here now. Does the agent still live upstairs?"

"I think so. It's a different agent." They stepped back to peer up at the second-story windows. "There are curtains, so I guess someone's living up there."

As she started the engine, Sally asked, "Would you like to stop at Eggers' and say hello to Beverly?"

"Godsakes, yes."

Laurence Lundeen sat at the far end of the counter, riffling through an *Atlantic Monthly*. Beverly was replenishing the domed glass doughnut display, her back to the entrance.

"Sally," Lundeen called.

This was the first time Sally had seen Mr. Lundeen since Drew Davis's death. She wanted to turn and run. "This is Lark Erhardt," she told him. "From Blue Lake."

Beverly whirled and came flying around the counter. "Godsakes, I don't believe it!" She grabbed Lark, hugging her,

387

then holding her away. "It's really you." Legging it back behind the counter, she asked, "You hungry? Thirsty?"

"Lemonade."

Beverly glanced at Sally. "You?"

"Me too."

"I remember Lark, and her mother too," Lundeen said. "How is your mother?"

"Fine. She's fine. She lives in California."

They discussed California, how much Mrs. Erhardt liked it, how little Lark did. "So I've been living with my grandma," she explained, eyes on the paper napkin she was folding and refolding.

"And you've just graduated," Lundeen remarked.

The drugstore was busy on Saturday afternoon, and the counter began filling up, so Beverly said, "I'll see you later. What're you doing tonight?"

Lark looked at Sally.

"Do you want to come over?" Sally asked.

"Sylvia and I're going to the Dakota," Beverly told her. "Wanta meet us there?"

"We'll see," Sally said.

Sally and Lark left soon after. Laurence Lundeen held the screen door and asked, "Any chance you'd have lunch with me tomorrow? The garden is nice right now. I have several new roses this year."

They stood beside the Wheeler car, Lundeen holding the furled *Atlantic Monthly* and tapping the palm of one hand with it. "They're ones Drew Davis suggested last winter when the nursery catalogs were arriving thick and fast." Staring down the street at the Majestic marquee, he smiled crookedly, tipped his panama, and said, "Call me if you can make it."

Lark did not protest when Sally suggested they see *Harvey* at the Majestic instead of driving over to Red Berry to the Dakota Ballroom. When the movie let out, the sky was still pale, and Sally asked, "Want to walk around town?"

They bought ice-cream cones at Anderson's and continued north on Main Street, around the schoolhouse, and into the park behind it where they sat on benches near the sandbox.

Noting the dark hulk of the band shell, Lark said, "It's too bad the Majestic put in air-conditioning. Think of all the little kids who'll never see Bessie Love outdoors in *Broadway Melody* or Douglas Fairbanks in *The Private Life of Don Juan*."

"Remember Grandpa Hapgood's popcorn wagon?"

"For six cents you could see a movie and eat a big bag of popcorn." Lark sighed.

"You've actually missed Harvester."

"Won't you miss it?"

Months had passed since Sally had thought about leaving, but she realized that she wanted to go. "I don't think so."

Lark let this pass. "Where will you go?"

"New York, I think."

"I want to see places like New York, but I want to live here."

"You don't know what you're saying."

"Yes, I do." As if she'd given it a good deal of consideration, she said, "Everybody has a Magnetic Home, a place that pulls them. This is mine."

"MotherofGod, what would you *do* if you lived here?"

Lark shrugged. "Teach school? Write books. Buy a little farm outside of town and write books."

"That's what you want to do . . . write books?"

"I believe it is. What about you?"

"I'm . . . not sure." After a moment she said, "I remember when you were moving away, you said you were going to come back."

"And you and Beverly said you were going to come visit me."

With cruel suddenness, Sally asked, "What happened in California?"

At the corner, a red convertible turned and drove slowly past the park, windows rolled down, Stan Kenton's "Laura" playing on the radio.

After a couple of minutes Lark said, "We'll talk about that when you and Beverly come back to visit me."

"Will we? Will we really talk about it? Because I want to know. And I'll still love your mother, no matter what."

In the dense twilight Lark was nodding. "And will you talk about Cole Barnstable?"

"Come in," Laurence told them. "I called Beverly. She's in the back. Go on through, and I'll be out in a minute."

"You never showed up at the Dakota," Beverly said, looking up at Sally from a canvas chair on Lundeen's terrace.

"We went to *Harvey*," Lark told her, "and then we got to talking and the first thing we knew it was midnight."

Beverly looked dubious.

Carrying a tray of cold drinks, Lundeen inquired, "Would you like the Cook's tour?"

Pointing out first the kitchen garden, abutting the terrace on the south, he drew them east toward the rear of the lot, through a cutting garden, then across lawn that ran down to a screened gazebo, girdled by low evergreens and furnished with electricity.

"Summer afternoons I spend hours out here," he said, indicating the gazebo, "reading or writing letters. Sometimes I paint. And at night my friends and I play bridge here. Pegeen Bailey and the Whites were here last night." The girls were not to worry about him.

"Weather permitting, I garden all morning, beginning at seven." He led on. "Sometimes I garden in the rain."

A tall picket fence, supported by substantial Georgian-style posts and blanketed on the south and east with climbing roses, held the world outside. The rampant roses, cascading and hurling themselves in a torrent of flora, were white, pink, yellow, and red, as were the many tea roses and shrub roses arranged in the opposite back corner around a giant gazing ball atop a marble pedestal. Lundeen reeled off the names of roses as though they were favorite pupils, letter-perfect in their lessons.

As the three girls followed him out of the rose garden, he pointed out the larger perennials and bushes along the north fence—lilacs and hydrangeas, mock orange, forsythia and viburnum. In front of these in a great long row were peony bushes, squat and plump and looking as if they could roll across the lawn like giant medicine balls.

"Next to roses, my favorites," he said.

Back on the terrace, lunch began with generous slices of muskmelon, followed by homemade Parker House rolls and chicken salad served on beds of homegrown lettuce. For dessert, Lundeen brought out little individual meringues filled with strawberries and whipped cream.

"Those were the sweetest strawberries I ever ate," Sally told him.

"My zipper's gonna bust," Beverly moaned as they sat over coffee, feeling as sophisticated as the Duchess of Windsor.

Pouring second cups of coffee, Lundeen asked Beverly, "How's the painting?"

"About the only thing I'm painting this summer is fragmentary flats for the Motleys."

"For Harvester Days?"

"Sally wrote a one-act called 'The Kingdom of Making Sense,' dedicated to Mr. Davis."

Sally held her breath, not daring to look at Mr. Lundeen.

"That is . . . brave," he said.

Sally flushed.

"Have you thought about studying acting?" he asked, laying his napkin beside his plate and glancing at Sally. "Drew rather hoped you would." He reached for the cream, pouring some into his cup, then returning the pitcher to the center of the table. "If you should head east, let me know. I still have one or two New York connections."

They sat in silence for several moments until Sally asked, "Which roses are the ones Mr. Davis wanted you to order?"

Carrying his cup, Lundeen crossed the terrace and stepped onto the flagstone path. The girls followed, carrying their cups, since this somehow seemed a worldly thing to do.

At the edge of the rose garden, he paused, pointing to a lemony tea rose. "That one," he said. Continuing toward the back fence, he indicated a blowzy pink climber only just taking hold. "And that. That is going to be a fine performer and a great beauty." While his voice did not break, the silkiness of it thickened, and he ran his free hand along the side of his perfectly barbered head in a gesture more of sudden emotion than of preening.

He turned, heading back toward the front of the rose garden. "I've ordered a bronze memorial plaque for this garden with Drew's name and one of his favorite quotations."

"What's it gonna say?" Beverly asked.

"It's Wordsworth. 'Intimations of Immortality': 'To me the meanest flower that blows can give / Thoughts that do often lie too deep for tears.'"

"Do you remember me, Mrs. Stillman?"

"Oh, dear. Oh, dear, dear, dear! It's Lark. Come in. Let me look at you."

She took Lark's hands. "I have to tell you," she said, leading the girls to the sofa, "I had a strange and wonderful feeling when I woke up this morning. I said to myself, 'Helen, be on the lookout for joy.'"

From the kitchen, she called, "I'm going to fetch us iced tea, and then we'll have a good jaw."

When Mrs. Stillman returned, Lark said, "You're reading *The Wayward Bus.*"

The old woman handed glasses of tea to Lark and Sally, saying, "John Steinbeck knows something about joy."

She passed the usual plate of vanilla wafers, then set it on the side table next to the sofa. "Now, then, Lark, you're still living with your grandmother?"

For an hour they chatted. At length Mrs. Stillman asked Lark, "What would you do if you could do what you wanted?"

"I'd write books."

"Fiction?"

"Yes."

"Well, I'm not surprised to hear it. Remember, Sally, when Lark came up with the story for the Christmas Program? We might have guessed that she'd end up writing books."

Lark had decided some time back that when people asked her what she wanted to do, she'd tell them, because it put her on her mettle: what you vaunt, you must perform. But telling people that you were going to write books had a self-important sound.

"Maybe I won't be any good and nobody'll want to publish them," she suggested.

"Better to fail at what you love then succeed at what you hate. People have strange ideas about success . . . too much to do with money, not enough to do with joy." She bit into a vanilla wafer and chewed thoughtfully. "What do you want to write?"

"I want to write about Harvester. Well, I'll have to call it something else, so I don't get in dutch."

"Oh, my," Helen said, genuinely surpised. She sipped iced tea and considered. "Promise to get us right, wearing our soiled apron, and with our niceness slipping."

"I'll try."

"Think of it, Sally. It's a little frightening, isn't it? If everyone thought they'd end up in a novel, they might live very differently."

Out-of-pocket, with birthday money from Edna, Sally paid for playbills printed up at the *Standard Ledger,* listing cast and crews for "The Kingdom of Making Sense," as well as the high-school band, the Donaldson sisters, and the girls from Martha Beaverton's Tap and Toe.

Leaving Helen Stillman's, Sally and Lark picked the programs up from the *Ledger* office. "I suppose it looks as if I'm Trying to Be Somebody," said Sally, handing one of the playbills to Lark. "My name's here twice: author and cast member."

Lark read.

"I had them printed for Mr. Davis," Sally explained. "See where it says, 'The Kingdom of Making Sense: dedicated to the late Drew Davis.'"

At the corner, Sally glanced up before stepping off the curb.

Catty-corner across the intersection, halted at the stop sign, sat a poppy red convertible, top down, Cole Barnstable at the wheel.

The girls crossed, heading up Third Avenue toward the Wheeler house.

The red car waited at the sign until a pickup truck pulled up behind, tooting its horn.

Thursday afternoon, Main Street was blocked off between Second Avenue on the south and Fourth Avenue on the north as carnival roustabouts assembled the Ferris wheel, merry-go-round, and other rides.

Members of the American Legion, Knights of Columbus, and Chamber of Commerce hammered and sawed, erecting booths from which they would later sell food and drink. Donald hoisted a board into place on the KC booth while Sonny Steen toenailed it to an upright.

Scratching mosquito bites, small boys and girls hung about, absorbed, impatient for the wheeze of the calliope. They dreamed of that intersection in life where Desire, Money, and Opportunity transect at a junction called Enough, and one has the dimes to ride all day.

While Sally paced and sighed and muttered her lines again and again, Lark wandered downtown to watch the carnival come together. The door of Anderson's Candy and Ice Cream was closed tight to keep the new air-conditioning in. At the Majestic, the marquee announced that *The Asphalt Jungle* was now playing, and out through the screen door of Mather's Five and Dime drifted strains of "If I Knew You Were Comin', I'd 'Ave Baked a Cake."

She stood watching the last seat being bolted to the Ferris wheel, imagining the chapters of a novel set in the pinkish brick buildings lining either side of Main Street.

"The Kingdom of Making Sense" was last on the program. Out front, twenty feet up in a box elder, Ronald Oster manned an ersatz follow spot he'd rigged up earlier in the day and prayed that no one on the ground would accidentally unplug it. Backstage, Duane Steiner ran the sound and light switches, adding to Ronald's misgivings, since Duane was, until this afternoon's rehearsal, untrained in these matters. Didn't know a follow spot from a Fresnel. Hadn't an aesthetic bone in his body.

Ronald shifted his bony bottom, brushed away box-elder bugs, and tried to avoid the small branches stabbing him in all his tender parts. Crossing himself, he gripped the handles of the spot in sweaty anticipation of the first light cue.

Beside the small bank of wall switches, Duane Steiner looked up at the pages of script taped to the wall and read his cues for the hundred and first time. If he got out of this alive, never again would he mix in with theatrical doings. He'd thought he knew these people. But they were crazy when they got near a stage, yelling at him for the least little hesitation, much less a mistake.

"For God's sake, Steiner, the third music cue has *got* to come up the *moment* Peregrina moves away from the King of Law. Now, let's do it again!" And so on.

Sally fretted about Duane Steiner running lights and sound. No one with experience had been available, but Duane was not acute. The only way to have everything the way she wanted was to do it herself.

Although she did not entertain any traditional notion of heaven, she believed that Mr. Davis would be watching from his connect-the-dots vantage.

Worrying her lower lip, Sally waited for Neddy to give Duane Steiner the nod to begin pre-"curtain" music. No stage curtains existed in the band shell, of course, so the only cover for actors waiting to go on, and for Duane and the tape recorder, was a pair of folding screens, one at either side of the proscenium, which Mr. Lundeen had constructed the past week, covering them with artist's canvas on which he'd painted generic landscapes, rolling hills, and groves of trees.

The band shell's one redeeming feature as a stage was that it magnified the actors' voices and projected them out toward the audience sprawled on blankets and park benches, fanning damp faces with the programs Lark had distributed.

Wearing clown face, Neddy waited behind the screen on the side of the stage opposite Sally. He raised his hand to signal the music cue. Duane Steiner flipped the switch of the tape recorder, and soft strains of "Gaité Parisienne" quieted the crowd. Gradually, Duane increased the volume as here and there people began clapping in rhythm with the cancan music.

So this was how it felt to make an audience quiet down, Duane thought, to get their attention and make them wonder what's going to happen. From where he stood, behind the screen, he could see them clapping—reticent Norwegians; stoic Germans (including his parents); and not-so-shy Bohemians, like the Steiners' neighbors, the Vargos. He could not see the grin softening the planes of his own face, flat and square as his father's farm.

As the Offenbach drew to a close, Neddy signaled again. Duane brought the volume slowly down and flicked on the switch controlling the follow spot rigged in the box elder. Although a mosquito was biting the back of his neck, he didn't take time to swat it. "Gaité Parisienne" died away, and a Mozart horn concerto, lighter than the evening air, floated out from the recorder, with Duane adjusting the volume.

Sally, barefoot and wearing a full, gored skirt in a dull, dusty blue and a short, loose cotton tunic in a deeper blue, danced out onto the stage in the circle of the follow spot. From the opposite side of the stage, Neddy as the Clown emerged to stand in the shadows observing Peregrina.

From behind one of the fragmentary flats on which Beverly had painted part of a Doric column and a garden, Sue Ann Meyers as the King of Science swept out in robes and crown. Peregrina's search was underway.

From the King of Science to the King of Law and, after that, the King of Philosophy, Peregrina fled, finding each of them pompous and contradictory. All the while, the Clown followed, trying vainly to gain her notice with somersaults and handstands.

Finally Peregrina gave up hope and sank down weeping. With handsprings and back flips the Clown courted her attention.

Taking her hand, he conducted her back through all the kingdoms she had rejected. With the follow spot lighting the way, he led her through a proscenium arch barely four feet high, painted with cherubs and velvet curtains. Ducking his head as he passed through, onto the "stage," the Clown emerged wearing a crown.

"Welcome to the Kingdom of Making Sense," he told Peregrina, "where everything is possible. Sunshine?" He clapped his hands and light flooded the band shell. "Summer?" The taped sound of twittering birds surrounded them, and Charlie and Babe Ridza, hidden behind huge cardboard flowers, appeared on stage. "Love?" From one side of the band shell, Louis Flegel emerged, carrying a three-foot cardboard heart, from the other, Sylvia Donaldson, bearing another. In front of the "flowers," they met, embraced, exchanged hearts, and disappeared once more offstage behind the screen.

"Happiness can be found in the Kingdom of Making Sense," the Clown continued. "It's in the script. And when the play calls for sadness," (he took down a tragic mask from the proscenium, holding it in front of his face), "it rarely lasts beyond an hour."

Removing the mask and hanging it on its peg, he pointed out, "In the Kingdom of Making Sense, all things can be understood, and if they can't, we call it *avant-garde*." He did a tumbling "walk-over" and asked, "Doesn't that make sense?"

Turning to the audience, the Clown threw open his arms. "Welcome to my kingdom!"

Beneath these final words, the barely audible music of "Gaité Parisienne" had begun to play again, and as the Clown concluded, the music came up. When he took Peregrina's hand, the rest of the cast joined them, and all linked arms to form a cancan line. With the high kicks of the cancan, they danced off the stage, and the lights were extinguished, although the music continued.

The audience clapped and whistled. The lights came up, and the cast danced raggedly back onstage for the curtain call, laughing and blowing kisses.

August 11, 1950

Although the carnival began Friday noon, Sally and Lark waited until evening to knock at Mrs. Stillman's screen door. Inside, an electric fan purred, and they could hear Helen Stillman in the kitchen, washing the few supper dishes.

"Mrs. Stillman?" Sally called through the door.

A moment later the old woman appeared in a cotton house-dress and bib apron, wiping her hands on the apron as she came. Her face was pink with heat, and the humidity had crimped her white hair.

"We've come to take you to the carnival," Lark told her, opening the door.

"Oh, but I couldn't. I'm not dressed. You're dear to ask, but I couldn't."

"You can change your clothes if you want," Lark said. "We'll wait."

Lark sat down on the sofa, and Sally joined her.

"Well, if you don't mind waiting . . . It would be such a treat."

When she emerged, Sally exclaimed, "Mrs. Stillman! Slacks!"

"Is it all right, do you think?"

"It's fine. I didn't know you owned a pair of slacks, is all."

"Well, I only just bought them this week at Lundeen's to wear to the performance last night. I always get so eaten by the mosquitoes, I said to myself, 'Why not slacks?'" She giggled. "So here I am. Is this shirtwaist all right?"

On the Ferris wheel she said, "Do you know, I haven't been on a carnival ride since Hillyard was in high school."

After the Ferris wheel, the three climbed on the merry-go-round, and Sally caught the brass ring. The man who operated the ride gave her tickets for the three of them to ride twice more.

"Did you ever catch the brass ring before?" Mrs. Stillman asked when they'd dismounted their horses.

"I should have. I'm so tall. But I never did."

"It's a sign," Helen Stillman told her as they strolled along the street toward the tilt-a-whirl.

"What's a sign?" Sally asked.

"Catching the brass ring. Why, it's the surest sign of luck I know. Better than a four leaf clover or finding a penny." She linked an arm through Sally's. "When I was a girl, I had a friend who caught the brass ring. Her name was Alice. Two or three days afterward she saved her two younger brothers from drowning. Over in Lake Okabena, that was. Somehow, word of this reached Washington, and Alice received a handwritten note from President McKinley and the offer of a scholarship to a college in Ohio. President McKinley was from Ohio, you see. Well, Alice ended up a professor at a women's college somewhere back east and an authority on . . . I forget . . . something in the literature area." She stopped and turned to Sally. "And it all began with the brass ring."

Sally laughed scornfully, but she felt gay as they walked up the ramp to find a seat on the tilt-a-whirl.

When the ride spun to a stop, Mrs. Stillman said, "I've had one of the best evenings I can remember, but it's time I got home." They would not let her go without a cone of cotton candy.

Parting from Helen Stillman, Lark noted, "It's time to meet Beverly."

Beverly was pulling down the shade on the front door of Eggers' Drug Store. "Just a minute," she said, "while I get my purse."

They meandered down one side of Main Street, then the other, stopping to buy Eskimo Pies and to talk to Mr. Hardesty who took their picture.

"Mr. and Mrs. Navarin!" Lark called, running ahead to way-lay them. Mr. Navarin stood with his arm around his wife's shoulder.

Sally calculated that Danny Navarin had been dead, what, five years? Desiree was her old self. No, not her old self. You were never your old self after someone died. You were a new, sort of scarred-over self. Mrs. Navarin tended to her clothes and hair and makeup, and at the library, her work absorbed her. Still, a profound quietness overtook her at times and a hint of resolve that had not found its purpose yet, as if one day she might lead a crusade or revolt.

Grasping Sally's hand, she held it firmly, kneading the fingers slightly. In the pressure and in the hooded eyes was the sugges-tion, neither a plea nor a demand, "Let us be friends."

Sally nodded.

"Would you tell your father that the new John C. Calhoun biography has come in?"

"Yes."

"The play you wrote. It would have meant a good deal to Drew Davis." She held Sally's hand in both of hers now and seemed to study it, although in truth their hands were a conduit through which they telegraphed one another.

"I have this notion that you'll be a kind of testimony to him." She tossed her head, impatient with the way she was expressing herself.

'Round and 'round, swooping up and down, the individual planes on the ride called "The Barnstormer" revolved. Sally gazed out at the crowded street where people's faces in the im-pending night were illuminated by a sweet, tawdry light that painted them to glow like cheap icons. Was that Angela Bussey in the candy pink dress by the souvenir stand? Across the way, Ronald Oster rode the tilt-a-whirl with Sylvia Donaldson.

And on the Ferris wheel — Cole. Cole with his arm around a pretty girl Sally'd never seen before.

As the airplane swooped, Sally twisted to stare behind her, looking and looking again.

Up and up he went, rocking the gondola and laughing. And the girl, too, was rocking and laughing, her head thrown against his shoulder.

"Aannh," Sally cried out, one of those cries that is lost amongst the many other cries and the music. The grief was not for herself, at least not mainly, but for Cole and the girl beside him.

Climbing down from the plane ride, Beverly said, "Let's buy ice cream and root beer and go home and make floats."

Earlier, Sally and Lark had hauled the old rollaway up from the basement and made it up beside Sally's bed so that the three of them could sleep together. Now they sat cross-legged on the beds, or Lark and Beverly did, spooning vanilla ice cream from tall glasses of root beer. Sally was not hungry, she had said, and she sat with her back against the headboard, listening to chatter as soothing as birdsong.

"It's too bad you're gonna miss Katherine Albers," Beverly told Lark. "She's coming back next week." Turning to Sally, she observed, "They were gone a long time, weren't they?"

"The whole family?" Lark asked.

"Just Katherine and her mother."

"Must be nice."

"I wouldn't want Reggie Albers for my dad if he gave me the entire British Isles," Beverly told her.

"Why?"

Beverly wriggled. "Makes my skin crawl."

"Katherine always had everything," Lark recalled. "That playhouse in her backyard was enough to make me hate her."

"And she was the first to have white figure skates," Beverly added. "I didn't get figure skates 'til high school."

"And blonde curls and perfect pitch and straight teeth. It's a wonder she had a friend," Lark laughed.

"She's okay, though."

"Well, she must be if Neddy Barnstable dates her. Unless she's fast."

"There's worse things than being fast," Beverly observed. "Anyway, I've got a private theory that Neddy likes her like a sister."

"Really?"

"He used to ask Sally out, and she'd never go."

"You think he likes Sally?"

Sally roused herself. "Don't," she said softly. "Please, don't." She climbed off the bed. "Come downstairs. I want to show you something."

Bemused, they followed. Sally led them through the house and out the back, the screen door creaking behind them. In the middle of the backyard, beside the clotheslines, she pointed up.

"Look. Up there."

They tried to follow her direction.

"Where I'm pointing. Do you see that big star? And the smaller ones that go up and sort of to the right?"

"I guess."

"Don't you see? Don't you see what it is?"

"I don't know."

"Lark, you wouldn't know because you never met him. But, Beverly, don't you recognize him?"

"Who?"

"Mr. Davis. Don't you see his profile? It's so clear."

"Mr. *Davis?*"

"Remember his short nose and how thick his hair was."

"I remember, but I don't see all that up there."

"They say that in New York you can't see the stars because of all the lights," Sally told them.

As they headed into the house, she turned back to look again at the sky. "I hope that isn't true."

Faith Sullivan was born and raised in southern Minnesota. Married to drama critic Dan Sullivan, she lived twenty-some years in New York and Los Angeles, returning to Minnesota three and four times a year to keep her roots planted in the prairie. Since 1989 the author and her husband have lived in Minneapolis where their grown daughters Maggie and Kate reside as well. Son Ben is a journalist in Budapest, Hungary.

Interior design by Will Powers
Typeset in Cochin by Stanton Publication Services, Inc.
Printed on acid-free Liberty paper
by Quebecor Printing

WINNERS OF THE MILKWEED
NATIONAL FICTION PRIZE

Confidence of the Heart
David Schweidel
1995

Montana 1948
Larry Watson
1993

Larabi's Ox
Tony Ardizzone
1992

Aquaboogie
Susan Straight
1990

Blue Taxis
Eileen Drew
1989

Ganado Red
Susan Lowell
1988